Teaching Intensive and Accelerated Courses

Instruction That Motivates Learning

Raymond J. Wlodkowski and Margery B. Ginsberg

JOSSEY-BASS
A Wiley Imprint
www.josseybass.com

Library of Congress Cataloging-in-Publication Data
   Wlodkowski, Raymond J.
      Teaching intensive and accelerated courses : instruction that motivates learning /
   Raymond J. Wlodkowski, Margery B. Ginsberg.
         p. cm. – (The Jossey-Bass higher and adult education series)
      Includes bibliographical references and index.
      ISBN 978-0-7879-6893-9 (pbk.)
      1. Educational acceleration.   2. Motivation in education.   I. Ginsberg, Margery B., 1954-   II. Title.
      LB1029.A22W63 2010
      370.15′4–dc22

                                                                              2010013826

Printed in the United States of America

FIRST EDITION
PB Printing   10 9 8 7 6 5 4 3 2 1

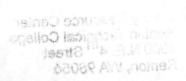

The Jossey-Bass Higher and
Adult Education Series

Contents

Preface vii

About the Authors xiii

1 Understanding Accelerated and Intensive Courses as Excellent
Learning Experiences 1

2 Using a Motivational Framework to Enhance Learning in
Accelerated and Intensive Courses 14

3 Being a Motivating Instructor 31

4 Establishing Inclusion in a Learning Environment 50

5 Developing Positive Attitudes Toward Learning 79

6 Enhancing Meaning in Learning 100

7 Engendering Competence Among Learners 136

8 Designing Instruction for Intensive and Accelerated Courses 164

9 Strengthening Instruction and Retention 189

References 203

Index 217

Preface

AS AN INNOVATIVE format, only online learning has exceeded accelerated and intensive learning programs in providing working adults with access to postsecondary education. For over a half century, most colleges have offered their students intensive learning formats to accommodate summer schedules, shortening their sixteen-week semester courses to eight weeks or less. However, in the last thirty years, the number of colleges and universities offering accelerated courses—shortened not only in terms of duration (eight weeks or fewer) but also in terms of contact hours with an instructor (thirty-two hours or fewer)—has grown to over 360 institutions (Commission for Accelerated Programs, 2008). In addition, many, if not most, colleges offer intensive courses and programs throughout the entire academic year.

Adults are increasingly enrolling in accelerated and intensive college programs because they offer flexibility; sensitivity to the demands of their lives; and, most important, a shorter time to earn a coveted degree. Generally, these adults are twenty-one years of age or older; hold a job part-time or full-time; and want to complete courses as quickly as possible. Often such other obligations as family and work require the most efficient means of acquiring a college diploma.

These are pragmatic students. Rather than seeking scholarly professors for teachers, they prefer realistic experts who live professional lives in which there are accountability standards, frequent deadlines, economic restraints, and far-from-perfect circumstances. Although friendly, they are not looking for friends. Their social calendars tend to be full, and spending a Friday night at a party on campus with unfamiliar college students would likely require these adults to sacrifice time away from more valued activities.

Estimates are that about 13 percent of adult students are enrolled in accelerated courses, with at least as many in intensive courses. That's roughly one in four adult students (Wlodkowski, 2003). These courses usually take from four to eights weeks to complete. These courses also tend to be taught by part-time or adjunct faculty (we use these terms interchangeably throughout the book).

Most of the time, these adjunct faculty are professional people who are teaching a subject directly connected to their own work: accountants teaching accounting courses, nurses teaching nursing courses, teachers teaching education courses, and executives teaching administration courses. For these faculty, teaching is often an avocation done for enjoyment, feeling connected to students, and for being in the midst of learning about fundamental aspects of their own careers (June, 2009). From a financial perspective, the rewards for this kind of teaching are relatively poor—most adjuncts make only a few thousand dollars for each course they teach. But from a motivational perspective, the rewards can be relatively rich. It is the work itself: modeling a new skill, telling a captivating story, collaborating to solve a problem, guiding a good discussion, seeing insight move across a room of people, dissolving conflict into dialogue before class time runs out, and feeling a sense of community with people who were strangers a few weeks ago. This book provides special attention to the needs of such faculty.

This text is a guide for providing excellent instruction for nontraditional learners, most of whom are part- or full-time working adults, in accelerated and intensive courses. Almost all of our professional experience is in urban universities and colleges. For over twenty years, we've been teaching adults in accelerated and intensive programs in Denver and Seattle. Both of us have been able to study firsthand the various ways educators effectively teach accelerated and intensive courses: one of us is founding executive director of the Commission for Accelerated Programs, and one leads an intensive alternative doctoral program for working adults at the University of Washington-Seattle. However, the most important voice in this book is that of the students themselves. Through their relationships, reactions, participation, feedback, and evaluations, they continue to help us improve and teach more thoughtfully.

Teaching Intensive and Accelerated Courses is written in the style of a handbook—an easily readable and concise reference for teaching adults for you to literally carry with you as a practical resource. Like a good travel guide, it should orient you and put you at ease in a teaching format that is often long (three to eight hours), occurring in the late evening or on weekends, and quite challenging for instructors and students alike. Most teachers of evening courses for adults have heard some version of this refrain from earnest students: "No matter what the teacher does, after eight o'clock I just don't seem to have any energy left." That's why this book gives you a basic framework and the best motivational strategies we know for teaching in longer blocks of time.

Yet we do not want our pragmatism to be simply expedient. As Robert Bellah (1991, p. 61) has written, "Education can never be merely for the sake of individual self-enhancement. It pulls us into the common world or it fails altogether." As in our previous books, our goal is to support instructors in constructing learning experiences that respect the integrity of every learner while allowing each person to attain relevant educational success and mobility. We embrace this goal because we believe that a primary purpose of higher education is the intellectual and moral empowerment of learners to achieve personal goals that matter, not only for them but also for a pluralistic and just society. To accomplish this, the teaching methods in this book draw from our personal experience and research that spans academic disciplines, offering a culturally relevant and inclusive approach to instruction.

We have been careful to avoid educational jargon and esoteric research. The references we cite are either important studies to validate what has been stated or reliable resources to expand your teaching capabilities. We offer a culturally responsive and well-tested motivational model for planning courses that are short but offered in long blocks of time.

Many of the fifty motivational strategies for instruction in accelerated and intensive courses included in this book have been excerpted and adapted from the third edition of *Enhancing Adult Motivation to Learn: A Comprehensive Guide for Teaching All Adults* (Wlodkowski, 2008), which was written for the field of adult education. This discipline has a rich literature focused on instructional methods for adults. It provides a foundation for developing teaching practices that can be adapted to accelerated and intensive courses and that are relevant to nontraditional adult learners.

This book offers an *intrinsically motivational* approach to teaching working adults—illustrating how to vitally engage these students and how to create conditions that evoke their innate desires both to learn and to use what they have learned in daily life. Although the techniques in this book can be applied to online learning, they mainly address face-to-face learning. What follows are the most important ideas we have found for making learning an optimal experience for *all* adults in accelerated and intensive courses.

Overview of Contents

Chapter One addresses the need for intensive and accelerated courses. It discusses evidence for the high quality of these formats, which are often questioned because of their brevity and their employment of adjunct faculty. We detail and discuss research studies that examine such criteria as accreditation, student learning and attitudes, alumni attitudes, and persistence and success. This chapter comprehensively describes how intensive and accelerated courses differ from conventional courses, with their focus on working adults, large blocks of instructional time, preparation for student absenteeism, guidance for independent study, active engagement of students, cohort organization, and use of instructional modules and standardized syllabi. In order to be more precise about the applied research discussed in this chapter, we use the terms *accelerated* and *intensive* to distinguish the two formats. However, in the rest of the chapters, with the exception of the last chapter, Chapter Nine, we use the term *intensive* to represent both accelerated and intensive formats in order to simplify expression and to avoid redundancy.

Chapter Two begins with a discussion of why motivation is essential to learning and how it is inseparable from culture. After establishing why intrinsic motivation is so effective as the core for instruction of nontraditional learners, the chapter introduces the four conditions that enhance students' intrinsic motivation to learn—inclusion, attitude, meaning, and competence. These conditions are woven into the Motivational Framework for Culturally Responsive Teaching, a model for designing instruction and teaching. The chapter ends with an example of planning and carrying out a lesson in an intensive course based on the motivational framework.

Chapter Three begins with a discussion of the professional status, financial compensation, and employment benefits of adjunct faculty who most often teach intensive and accelerated courses. It outlines norms and procedures that can contribute to the support and morale of these faculty. The chapter then discusses the essential characteristics of a motivating instructor in intensive courses—expertise, empathy, enthusiasm, clarity, and cultural responsiveness. We offer performance criteria for each characteristic, so the reader can personally learn as well as assess each characteristic. The chapter concludes with a discussion of *critical consciousness* as a guide to constructing a learning environment in which the way students learn encourages their contribution to the common good of society.

Chapters Four through Seven make up the principal content of this text. Each chapter offers an in-depth treatment of one of the motivational conditions: inclusion is covered in Chapter Four, attitude in Chapter Five, meaning in Chapter Six, and competence in Chapter Seven. Each of these chapters describes and exemplifies specific motivational strategies for engendering a particular motivational condition in a culturally relevant way. We have selected fifty motivational strategies based on their usefulness in evoking intrinsic motivation among nontraditional students in intensive educational formats, in which blocks of instructional time may be longer but the overall length of the course or program is significantly shorter than that of its conventional counterpart.

Chapter Eight summarizes all the motivational strategies and their main purposes. It explains the two main ways to use the motivational framework and its strategies for designing instruction in intensive courses: the *superimposed* method for enhancing previously used instructional plans and the *source* method for developing new instructional plans. This chapter also discusses three real-life examples of instructional planning from intensive courses in general education, business leadership, and clinical nursing. The chapter concludes with a detailed overview and survey for assessing student motivation to learn.

Chapter Nine offers specific ideas for the instructor's role in strengthening teaching and retention—supporting the continuing enrollment and success of working adults in accelerated and intensive courses. It closely examines how the instructor is central to the engagement of nontraditional learners with their peers, faculty, and school. Given today's economic challenges, we discuss continuing professional development as an important self-directed process for instructors. We conclude this chapter with our perspective on how intensive and accelerated formats appear to be evolving in this decade and suggest what is needed for these programs to expand access and success for underserved nontraditional learners.

Acknowledgments

Teaching relies on a certain amount of trial and error, especially if the instructor wants to remain innovative. In many ways, this book is the filtered accumulation of what worked and what didn't work in our more than twenty years of teaching accelerated and intensive courses. Much of our understanding is the result of students' suggestions, and we are grateful for their partnership. We also owe a special thank you to David Brightman, senior editor of the Higher and Adult Education Series at Jossey-Bass, and Aneesa Davenport, editorial program coordinator, for their unflagging patience and support.

In particular, Raymond would like to thank the staff and members of the Commission for Accelerated Programs (CAP), especially from those early years when we learned so much together. Margery would like to offer her appreciation to the faculty and staff of the Leadership for Learning Program at the University of Washington-Seattle College of Education for their ongoing collaboration and wisdom.

Finally, we thank Daniel Mark Ginsberg-Jaeckle and Matthew Aaron Ginsberg-Jaeckle for their inspiration and love.

Raymond J. Wlodkowski
Seattle, Washington
Margery B. Ginsberg
Seattle, Washington

April 2010

About the Authors

RAYMOND J. WLODKOWSKI is a professor emeritus at the College of Professional Studies, Regis University, Denver. He is a psychologist who specializes in adult motivation and learning. He is the founding executive director of the Commission for Accelerated Programs (CAP) and the former director of the Center for the Study of Accelerated Learning at Regis University.

Wlodkowski received his Ph.D. in educational psychology from Wayne State University and is the author of numerous articles, chapters, and books. Among them are *Enhancing Adult Motivation to Learn: A Comprehensive Guide for Teaching All Adults* (2008), now in its third edition, and twice the recipient of the Phillip E. Frandson Award for Literature. Four of his books have been translated into Spanish, Japanese, and Chinese. He is also the coauthor with Margery B. Ginsberg of *Diversity and Motivation: Culturally Responsive Teaching in College*, 2nd edition (2009). He has received the Award for Outstanding Research from the Adult Higher Education Alliance, the Award for Teaching Excellence from the University of Wisconsin-Milwaukee, and the Faculty Merit Award for Excellence from Antioch University, Seattle. He currently lives in Seattle.

Margery B. Ginsberg is an associate professor in educational leadership and policy studies at the University of Washington-Seattle, College of Education. Having taught on two Indian reservations and served as a Texas Title I technical assistance contact for the U.S. Department of Education, her primary interest is innovative instruction and professional learning to create schools that are increasingly responsive to diverse learners.

Ginsberg's publications include *Diversity and Motivation: Culturally Responsive Teaching in College*, 2nd edition (2009, coauthored with Raymond J. Wlodkowski), *Creating Highly Motivating Classrooms: A Schoolwide*

Approach to Powerful Teaching with Diverse Learners (2000), and *Motivation Matters: A Workbook for School Change* (2004). In addition, her work provides the foundational material for two video series, *Encouraging Motivation Among All Students* (1996) and *Motivation: The Key to Success in Teaching and Learning* (2003). She has a Ph.D. in bilingual/multicultural/social foundations of education from the University of Colorado-Boulder.

Teaching Intensive and Accelerated Courses

Chapter 1

Understanding Accelerated and Intensive Courses as Excellent Learning Experiences

"The biggest obstacle to innovation is thinking it can be done the old way."

JIM WETHERBE (2001, p. 3)

BECAUSE ACCELERATED AND intensive learning formats reduce the amount of time to earn a credential or degree, working adults prefer these compressed formats for their efficiency in reaching such important goals (Aslanian, 2001). Today, we know that four out of five of high school graduates will be attending college within eight years of graduation (Attewell, Lavin, Domina, and Levey, 2007). Most of these college students will be nontraditional learners, working adults who commute to school and often are married with children. Accelerated and intensive programs offer these adults a flexible and advantageous means to a postsecondary education and a greater opportunity for satisfying work and economic security.

Before 1980, if you were a working adult—especially a working-class adult—a college education seemed impossible in terms of accessibility. At that time, with courses only available in a sixteen-week time frame, adults could usually only schedule one course a semester. Even with summer school, it would take roughly ten years to complete a degree. Now, taking an accelerated or intensive course every five to eight weeks, a working adult can expect to complete a degree in four to five years (Wilson, 2010).

This is a significant benefit for the individual and for society. Higher education has learned that it can serve many more people, often without the added expenses of huge residential halls, large bodies of full-time faculty, and restrictive selection criteria.

Quality of Accelerated and Intensive Courses

Because of their shortened duration, both accelerated and intensive courses can be reasonably critiqued as being overly compressed; sacrificing reflection, breadth, and depth; and resulting in crammed and poorly developed learning (Wolfe, 1998). However, as with conventional academic courses and programs, we cannot make a general assessment that fits all the accelerated and intensive courses and programs in postsecondary education. Quality in higher education is a conundrum, a perplexing question rife with the conflicting values, standards, and criteria of scholars and the general public alike.

Of the two formats, accelerated learning is the more unconventional because it requires fewer contact hours with an instructor than do conventional and intensive courses. Instead of completing forty to forty-five contact hours, an adult can finish a three-credit course with as few as twenty contact hours in a term of five weeks. Given this shortened interaction between the learner and the instructor, it is prudent to ask, what do standard barometers of quality in higher education indicate about these courses and programs? We have applied five criteria to answer this question: accreditation, learning, student attitudes, alumni attitudes, and student persistence and success.

Accreditation

Regional accrediting bodies, such as the North Central Association of Colleges and Schools, assess accelerated learning programs as part of their accreditation process for colleges and universities. These accreditation reviews generally suggest to the public that an accredited institution has met acceptable academic standards and has the resources to provide a satisfactory college education. Colleges offering accelerated programs generally receive accreditation in accordance with the applied norms of conventional college standards (Commission for Accelerated Programs, 2009).

Learning

Herbert Walberg's synthesis (1988) of the research investigating student time spent on learning concluded that time is a necessary but insufficient condition for learning. Time, in and of itself, is only a modest predictor of achievement. Other factors that influence learning as much as or more than time spent on learning are learner capability, the quality of instruction, and students' personal motivation (Wlodkowski, 2008). Further, there is evidence that the neural networks that make up long-term memory, the part of learning that lasts, fade unless the learning is used in relevant future work or life situations (Ratey, 2001).

Studies of accelerated courses have generally found that adult student learning meets a college standard of satisfactory to excellent (Wlodkowski, 2003). Pass rates of students from accelerated programs on the national registered nursing exam, for example, indicate that these students do as well as or slightly better than students from conventional nursing programs (Korvick, Wisener, Loftis, and Williamson, 2008). The evidence thus far suggests that adults in accelerated courses and programs learn satisfactorily and in a manner that meets the challenge of conventional college course work. Characteristics of adults, including personal motivation, desire for career advancement, work experience, and a history of self-directed responsibilities, fit readily with such aspects of accelerated formats as pragmatic courses, efficient academic progress, and experiential teaching methods. This symmetry and interaction may catalyze overall learning. Studies of accelerated courses commonly require adult learners to demonstrate writing skills, critical thinking, content mastery, and application of a knowledge base. Most of this research has been directed toward the disciplines of business management, nursing, teaching, and computer science. Investigations of the effectiveness of accelerated and intensive formats need to be expanded to the physical and natural sciences, medicine, and engineering to understand how widely applicable these approaches to learning are.

Student Attitudes

Historically, college student evaluations of conventional courses have been positive (Astin, 1993). This trend also holds true for adult student perceptions of accelerated and intensive courses and programs: adult students appreciate their effectiveness and the strong interest they cultivate (Scott, 1996; Wlodkowski, 2003).

Alumni Attitudes

Because alumni have hindsight and have been in the workforce after completing their accelerated programs, their perceptions are tested by time and actual work experience. Evidence to date is from business management programs, whose alumni found their courses to be well taught, effective, and motivating (Wlodkowski, 2003).

Student Persistence and Success

We know that persistence and success as measured by graduation rates vary widely among universities and colleges. We also know that today's adult learners are intermittent students who stop out, often leaving for more than a semester to take care of family, work, and financial obligations, but eventually returning to obtain their certificates or degrees. For example, 28 percent of bachelor's degree recipients earn their diplomas more than six years after enrolling in college (Attewell, Lavin, Domina, and Levey, 2007). Today's adult students are people whose education has fit into the rest of their lives. With this context in mind, researchers have found that in accelerated programs the undergraduate degree completion rate for adult students averages close to 40 percent within six years (Wlodkowski, Mauldin, and Gahn, 2001). Nationally, the six-year graduation rate is 38 percent for undergraduate students, regardless of age, in large urban state colleges and universities (American Association of State Colleges and Universities, 1997).

As reported as early as 1996 (Scott), and with respect to the more recent standards of quality in postsecondary education, accelerated and intensive programs continue to effectively educate and accommodate nontraditional students. Yet these programs are confronted by the same issues that face their conventional counterparts: how to provide a high-quality education for *all* students, and how to be agents of equitable social and economic improvement in a global society. In the pages ahead, we will focus on how instruction can contribute to meeting these challenges.

How Intensive and Accelerated Courses Differ from Conventional Courses

Adult participation in postsecondary education has reached unprecedented levels within the last decade. Due to online learning and flexible educational programming, colleges are more accessible to working adults. Working in tandem with this transformation is the fact that most adults are now aware that advancing their education is the vehicle to career enhancement (Ginsberg and Wlodkowski, 2010).

Working Adults

When you teach accelerated or intensive courses, you will likely teach working adults who are going to school part time, unlike eighteen- to twenty-one-year-old, full-time residential students. Looking beyond this distinction, our experience indicates that community colleges and universities are significantly affected by their regional placement, with urban institutions varying dramatically from residential colleges in smaller towns away from large cities. One of us is a tutor at an urban community college, at which the students tend to be younger adults (twenty to thirty-five years of age); working-class or low-income; first-generation college students; and representing a racial and ethnic mix that includes at least fifty different nationalities, mostly students of color. Also, one of us teaches graduate courses in a large urban university, at which most students are white, over thirty-five years old, work full-time in professional roles, and earn in excess of sixty thousand dollars per year. We do not believe that using a description of "the average adult student" or any stereotypical label—such as the "millennial student"—will adequately serve the vast majority of readers of this book (Hoover, 2009). Regional differences are too particular. But we do know that the cultural experiences and life responsibilities of working adults affect them motivationally, and make them likely to have the following characteristics in formal learning settings (Wlodkowski, 2008):

- *Working adults want their experience, perspectives, and opinions to matter to their teachers.* For example, they may have a very different opinion about the results of a research study because people like themselves were not part of the sample investigated. Although their opinions may vary from the findings, adult students want their teachers to appreciate their perspectives.

- *Working adults use relevance as the ultimate criterion for sustaining their interest.* They may become bored with a topic because it does not concern them or relate to their experience, and, just as easily, they may become energized because a topic does concern them or relate to their experience.

- *Working adults are critical and self-assured about their judgment of the value of what they are learning.* They are living lives with real responsibilities, and they know what is important or useful to them. Such pragmatism influences their acceptance or rejection of course assignments and requirements.

- *Working adults respond to respect from their teachers as a condition for learning.* Learner opinions and perspectives need to be authentically acknowledged and integrated in course discussions, because they offer insights and opportunities for further learning. If learner opinions and perspectives are ignored or diminished by the instructor, adult learners are likely to feel offended or patronized.

- *Working adults want to actively test what they are learning in real work and life settings.* For example, adults appreciate assignments that offer them opportunities to apply what they are learning in their jobs or communities.

- *Working adults want to use their experience and prior knowledge as consciously and directly as possible while learning.* For example, an instructor might introduce a topic with a discussion focusing on what learners in the course already know, and might publicly list their perceptions, skills, history, and wisdom regarding the topic at hand.

Because these motivational characteristics of working adults are so essential, we suggest that you take a few moments now to reflect on them and to consider this question: How do your experiences as an instructor (or an adult learner) relate to the previous list of characteristics? In the chapters ahead, we will build upon these characteristics and use them to develop a motivational framework for guiding instruction.

Large Instructional Blocks of Time

When you teach accelerated or intensive courses, you will likely teach classes in blocks of time ranging from two to eight hours rather than from fifty to ninety minutes as in conventional courses. The advantages of longer classes are more opportunities for immersion, enrichment, and gaining in-depth experience in a topic or subject area; a more relaxed learning atmosphere; greater chances for developing inclusion, rapport, and collaboration with and among students; and the opportunity to include interactive and student-directed learning. Although there are significant benefits of longer classes, there are also necessary adjustments that instructors must make. Combining our experience with findings from studies that have explored intensive learning formats, we suggest the following critical modifications for instruction scheduled in large blocks of time (Scott, 2003).

Careful Preparation for Student Absenteeism

This planning includes both creating needed rules and offering empathetic and professional assistance to students. Students will inevitably be absent from class. In a five-week course that meets for four hours once a week, two absences equal 40 percent of the contact hours for that course. Most postsecondary schools have policies for dealing with student absences, and being familiar with these regulations will facilitate making any additional rules or choosing which ones to emphasize. We have found that only allowing for absences that have been excused either prior to or after the student misses a class prevents miscommunication and sustains respectful relationships with adult students. We have also found it helpful to be clear and consistent, and to publish any rules we have about absenteeism in the course syllabus. Because individual student circumstances and course content vary markedly, it is often informative to talk with colleagues about how they handle this issue.

Assisting students who are absent is definitely a part of effective instruction for accelerated and intensive courses. We like to create partnerships or cooperative learning groups in our courses. If a member has to be absent, these structures allow students to share notes and information. In addition, these groupings provide a means for practicing any skills that may have been learned in the class from which the student was absent. We also encourage you as an instructor to make yourself available by e-mail, phone, or appointment in order to respond to the absent student's possible questions and requests. Sometimes adults feel self-conscious about being absent, and a warm welcome back goes a long way to dispel such feelings.

Guidance for Independent Study Outside of Class

With fewer class sessions, a shorter term for the course, and possibly fewer contact hours between students and the instructor, the instructor has greater reliance on students reading, studying, and practicing outside of class for their learning to occur. Although some adult educators have come up with a formula for student independent study, such as five hours of study outside of class for every contact hour in class, we have not found a comparable algorithm in our own work. However, there is no doubt that the quality of accelerated and intensive courses *depends* on student independent study, a process that is enriched by student collaboration outside of class. For example, when students are individually responsible for teaching different parts of an assigned reading to one another in a small cooperative group that meets prior to or after class (see the jigsaw method in Chapter Four), they can reduce their reading time and increase the depth of their learning. Such shared responsibility can lead to better learning and, just as significant, to enjoyment of learning. Clear, calendared outlines for readings and assignments with students being held accountable for this work in-class (see Chapter Five) and, just as importantly, receiving instructor or peer feedback on it as well (see Chapter Seven) can stimulate and sustain student work outside of class. In general, for every outside assignment, there needs to be a clear path for the student that makes this work worthwhile, either through a connection to a classroom activity, such as a discussion or simulation, or through some form of assessment, such as a project or test.

Planning and Organization for In-Class Learning

In her research, Patricia Scott (2003) found that students regarded organization as one of the most important factors influencing a successful intensive course: "Because intensive courses progress so quickly, instructors need to be organized and present the material in an easy-to-follow manner. Without organization, intensive courses quickly become overwhelming and chaotic. Moreover, students recommended that instructors organize intensive courses to emphasize depth over breadth of learning. Too often, students said, intensive course instructors try to cover too much material, which creates information overload. Students preferred to delve into fewer areas in more depth and concentrate on major concepts rather than learning large amounts of seemingly inconsequential information" (pp. 32–33). On all counts, we heartily agree with Scott. We need to be selective, focusing on the powerful, central ideas and skills of a given topic or discipline (Donovan, Bransford, and Pellegrino, 1999). This approach helps adults both to develop understanding of a given subject and to create networks of meaning for future use and long-term memory. For example, the idea of *patriarchal power* in the study of history also has meaning for psychology and the social sciences, as well as for political theory and cultural studies. Discussing and exemplifying this concept in depth through relevant learning activities is far more important than asking students to remember the date when a particular monarch used his patriarchal power.

We acknowledge that there are many instructors who are intimidated by the need to cover everything in the course text. That is how many of us were taught or trained, recalling facts and demonstrating knowledge through multiple choice tests. However, such an approach keeps learning at the surface, a level at which it is easily forgotten and seldom applied. Intensive courses are an ideal format for applying what we have learned in cognitive science: take more time for students to deeply learn principles that cross disciplines and provide relevant knowledge for future learning (Wlodkowski, 2008). Chapter Eight offers methods and examples for designing lessons that can accomplish this goal.

Creation of Learning Activities to Engage Students During Longer Instructional Periods

Patricia Scott (2003) found that students preferred activities and assignments that allowed them to synthesize learning, and to apply or experience the subject matter personally as they might with in-class collaborative assignments. This finding dovetails with a major purpose of this book: *To provide instructors of intensive and accelerated courses with a motivational framework and related teaching strategies that engage adult learners for extended periods of time to deeply learn relevant knowledge and skills.* Chapter Two introduces the Motivational Framework for Culturally Responsive Teaching and Chapters Four through Seven comprehensively describe and exemplify specific motivational strategies to engage adults in continuous learning. An important advantage of this motivational framework is that because it is organized according to four motivational conditions—inclusion, attitude, meaning, and competence—you can use it to effectively pace a variety of learning activities across a longer block of instructional time.

Reading and Writing Assignments Prior to the First Class Session

The requirement that students read textual materials before their first class session is probably more important for accelerated than intensive courses, but it is relevant to both. When students have a background and familiarity with the subject matter through prior reading, they will find the first meeting's activities more relevant, useful, and memorable, leading to a productive initial session and worthwhile learning experience. Many instructors accomplish this goal by sending welcoming letters and e-mails as soon as students register for the course. (Please see Exhibit 4.2 in Chapter Four for an example of such a letter.)

It may also be necessary to require students to complete writing assignments prior to the first class session. Having an early chance to assess how well a student can respond to the writing expectations for a course allows for prompt feedback (see Chapter Seven, Strategy 39). Students generally appreciate being given as much of a chance as possible in the beginning of a course to understand what they need to do to plan for or revise their written work. This also gives the instructor an opportunity to suggest—where necessary—possible tutoring or other forms of assistance for the learner.

In our own work, we have found that early writing assignments need to be relevant and immediately applicable—not some form of test or standard assessment that may convey low expectations or mistrust. For example, we have asked students to write responses to case studies to be discussed at the first class meeting. We have also used students' essays on their personal theories of motivation as preassessments, which we then ask students to compare to their theories of motivation written at the conclusion of the course.

A Modular or Standard Syllabus for Course Instruction

For most accelerated courses and for many intensive courses, colleges have teams of faculty create a standard course syllabus to be used by all faculty who teach the course. This centralized version of the course syllabus or learning module has common elements, which usually include the course description; appropriate learning outcomes; prior-knowledge requirements; goals and objectives; required learning resources, such as texts and readings; designated assignments; evaluation forms and procedures; and a guide for each class session with suggested activities. Choosing which suggested evaluation procedures and class activities to use is often left to the discretion of the individual instructor. A major goal of this book is to increase the options for instructors regarding possible assessments and activities, which may also include assignments, giving both the teacher and students an approach that elicits students' intrinsic motivation.

For the prewritten modular activities for each class session in any course we teach, we can choose alternative activities to those modular activities based on the motivational framework and strategies discussed in this book. In general, planning or substituting with strategies from the motivational framework allows instructors to be more creative and feel less constricted by the activities in a standard module whose design may be limiting, given their particular students and their prior knowledge, diversity, and experience. The *superimposed method* of instructional planning found in Chapter Eight provides a means for selecting motivational strategies and activities from this book that may be preferable to what is provided in a course module for deepening student motivation and learning.

Because many of the instructors for accelerated and intensive courses are adjunct faculty, a centralized course syllabus offers consistency of purpose, content, and outcomes among different instructors that might not otherwise be present (Husson and Kennedy, 2003). The modular design can enhance quality control while allowing for faculty members' own creativity. In addition, with a standardized syllabus, students can review the learning module before they take the course and can identify the necessary books and materials for study prior to the first day of class, making the most efficient use of their valuable time. In Exhibit 4.2 in Chapter Four, we offer an example of a syllabus for an eight-week, accelerated Introduction to Research course conceived, developed, and taught using the Motivational Framework for Culturally Responsive Teaching and its related strategies.

Cohorts and Collaborative Learning

A characteristic of many intensive and accelerated programs is that they feature *cohorts* of students who enroll at the same time in a program and proceed through their courses as a cohesive group, beginning and ending their required courses together. This structure provides for stronger social connections among students, increased student interaction inside and outside of class, and greater collaboration for learning. In addition, when students can integrate their social and academic activities and feel a greater sense of belonging to an on-campus community, this often positively affects their capacity to persist in their courses and in their programs overall (Tinto, 1987).

Collaborative learning is an effective and motivating strategy for working adults (Barkley, Cross, and Major, 2005). Adult students can learn from the diversity in their groups, benefiting from one another's different cultural perspectives on matters ranging from economics to history. Their work and their life goals require cooperation. More broadly, whether in regard to something as personal as raising one's children or as global as safeguarding the environment, we need to learn how to foster mutual goodwill. The way we learn in groups in college can profoundly develop these skills. This book provides instructional methods to effectively implement collaborative and cooperative learning, which we describe in detail in Chapter Four.

Course Quality and the Instructor

Whether a course is conventional, intensive, or accelerated, although its quality relies on the institution that sponsors it, it only truly exists through the instructor who teaches it. Institutions provide regulations, standards, resources, monitoring, and instructors—and it is the instructor, online or in the classroom, who makes this entire enterprise come alive. The essence of quality is in the relationships, interactions, and learning that take place among a teacher and students over the period of a course. The possibilities are many. A course can be a charade with little offered, less expected, and a guaranteed acceptable grade. Or it can be a form of oppression with irrelevant subject matter that is taught as absolute truth, for which students are tested on their retention of little other than trivia. Or, possibly, it can be what this book is written to support: an experience in which all students feel respected, the subject is relevant, and students are engaged in and competently learning what they consider authentic and valuable in their real world.

Because intensive and accelerated courses require less time to complete than conventional courses, a necessary criterion by which to judge them is by how well they generate learning. Today, probably more than ever before, we rely on postsecondary education to produce student learning. Politically and socially, this goal is primary, with how we teach students being appraised by how well they learn (Tagg, 2003). Yet in this process, students are integral and communal beings, not simply recipients of instruction. We see the focus on academic learning as a necessary—but not the only—needed emphasis. The fundamental criteria for assessing the quality of a college experience are both the growth of students' knowledge and the broadening of their humanity. Ultimately to what kind of world does a college education contribute? As instructors, the values we encourage and reflect permeate every learning experience we foster and, therefore, are a fundamental component of anything students learn with us.

We propose careful assessment of the students' mastery of the learning objectives for any course, a process we discuss in depth in Chapter Seven. Measures of academic learning tend to be straightforward. When it comes to the values of a course, the degree to which it contributes to the moral empowerment of learners, and how their learning matters for a more just world, most measures of academic learning are insufficient. We have yet to discover a valid assessment for how much a learner cares or how that person will contribute, as a consequence of a particular course, to a more equitable social order. In fact, there is considerable debate within adult education about how much this field of study has actually contributed to transforming individuals or society (Wilson, 2009).

Our approach is to offer instructors a way to make the value of diversity a pervasive part of any course, a characteristic of quality that can be planned and implemented throughout a course. To accomplish this, we provide the Motivational Framework for Culturally Responsive Teaching to consistently create learning experiences that allow learner differences to be mutually understandable, safely communicated, and avenues for building trust and collaboration (Ginsberg and Wlodkowski, 2009). The essentials of this motivational framework are that it (1) respects diversity; (2) engages the motivation of a broad range of students; (3) creates a safe, inclusive, and respectful learning environment; (4) derives teaching practices from across disciplines and cultures; and (5) promotes equitable learning. We offer this framework as an instructional compass and at the same time realize its limitations: the complexity of our human family eludes a single set of educational principles. This realization requires us as instructors to appreciate how a healthy amount of humility and doubt can guide our teaching, arousing our empathy in order to understand the truth that views unlike our own also bear. With this understanding in mind, the next chapter explores what motivates adults to learn and how the motivational framework can guide the teaching of intensive and accelerated courses in ways that apply this knowledge.

Chapter 2

Using a Motivational Framework to Enhance Learning in Accelerated and Intensive Courses

"I remember a very important lesson that my father gave me when I was twelve or thirteen. He said, 'You know, today I welded a perfect seam and I signed my name to it.' And I said, 'But Daddy no one's going to see it!' And he said, 'Yeah, but I know it's there.' So when I was working in the kitchens, I did good work."

TONI MORRISON (1994, p. 73)

MOTIVATION IS A concept with a romantic charisma. Like the stars, motivation offers inspiration as well as direction. But what motivates adults to learn—younger as well as older, ethnically as well as racially diverse, and those who are immigrants or first-generation college students? Just as important, what can we, as instructors, do to help students succeed? Those students filing in for a four-hour class session will leave after nightfall. Most have worked a full day. Many are fatigued. And we may be weary as well. Yet we have to be prepared and supportive. We know we have to get off to a good start. Doing so means knowing something about human motivation, and doing so for four hours for any number of weeks means using that knowledge well.

Motivation Is an Essential Part of Learning

Motivation is always situation specific. Being motivated to play a game can be quite different from being motivated to read a book. We might not know how to predict even our own behavior in these situations, unless we at least knew what the game or book will be. This is just one of a few things that can make motivation puzzling. Change the person, or the goal, or the context, and motivation can shift dramatically.

What makes motivation compelling is our common understanding that without it, most performance—whether in play, work, or learning—is diminished. Throughout our lives we have seen the motivated person surpass the less motivated person, though both may have the same opportunities and very similar capabilities. We also know that when people are not motivated to do what they are required to do, their behavior is often accompanied by boredom, frustration, distraction, and hostility. Four hours for a teacher with a group of unmotivated adult learners? As a colleague once said, "That's like trying to feed hamburger to a humming bird."

Realizing how challenging and unstable motivation, including our own, can be, makes most instructors aware of the need to consider it as an important part of the instructional process. In a biological sense, motivation is a process that "determines how much energy and attention the brain and body assign to a given stimulus—whether it's a thought coming in or a situation that confronts one" (Ratey, 2001, p. 247). Simply put, it is the natural human process for directing energy to accomplish a goal (Wlodkowski, 2008). Being motivated means being purposeful. We use attention, concentration, imagination, effort, and passion to pursue such goals as learning a subject or completing a degree. But because motivation is a process that occurs within a person, and we cannot see or touch it, we have to infer it from what people say or do. We look for signs of interest, perseverance, and completion, or for such words as, "I want to … ," "I will … ," and so forth. Motivation is why people do what they do—a compelling mystery that has provoked human beings for thousands of years.

There is substantial evidence that motivation is consistently and positively related to educational achievement (Uguroglu and Walberg, 1979). People motivated to learn are more likely to do things they believe will help them learn (Pintrich, 1991). They pay attention more carefully to instruction. They rehearse material in order to remember it. They take notes to improve their studying. They are more likely to ask for help when they are uncertain. Motivation improves learning because it is a part of learning, the energy within the learning process. When we want to learn—to change what we know or can do through studying, practicing, or reflecting—it is motivation that gets us to pick up a book, surf the Internet, and so forth. Motivation also mediates learning, focusing our attention, deepening our concentration, and providing the effort necessary to learn. Finally, motivation is a consequence of learning. When we have a wonderful experience reading a particular book, we are often likely to be more interested in other books on a similar topic or books written by the same author. Similarly, we know from our own history as students that similar motivational outcomes often happen for us in courses in which we are successful learners gaining knowledge and skills we value.

Motivation and Culture Are Inseparable

Culture, the deeply learned mix of language, beliefs, values, and behaviors that pervade every aspect of our lives, greatly influences our motivation. What we learn in our cultural groups shapes the biological systems throughout our brains to make us unique individuals and culturally diverse people. Social scientists regard the cognitive processes such as what we pay attention to and what information we regard as important to be inherently cultural (Rogoff and Chavajay, 1995). The language we use to think and communicate cannot be separated from cultural practices and the context in which it was learned and used. When we feel certain emotions, such as joy, frustration, or jealousy, they have most likely been conceptually learned in the cultural context of our families and peers as we developed through childhood and adolescence (Barret, 2005). The emotion of frustration offers a useful example. Think of what is likely to frustrate you. Can you think of someone else for whom the same thing is not frustrating? What do you do when you become frustrated? Are you likely to be still? Angry? Withdrawn? Aggressive? Anxious? When some people become frustrated while learning, they stop what they are doing and come back to it later; others stop only momentarily and renew their behavior with greater determination; and others stop altogether. The list of possibilities goes further than these three behaviors, because what frustrates people is likely to have been learned in different families with different reactions modeled within those families.

Motivation is largely governed by emotion. When the thought of something—whether a person, place, or thing—makes us feel interested, attracted, or enthusiastic, we are more likely to approach it or become involved with it. When the thought of something makes us feel bored, repulsed, or indifferent, we are less likely to become involved. Because the socialization of emotions is so culturally influenced, the motivational response a student has to a learning activity reflects the strength and complexity of this influence. Each learner represents his or her own reality, especially in terms of what that person finds motivating. Students can only interpret an academic situation based on their unique history of experiences and their beliefs about them.

Such goals as "success" or "achievement" not only have different meanings to different people but for some may actually be questionable when considered in conflict with being generous; sharing talents for the benefit of the common good; or other values related to one's family, peers, or religion. The internal logic regarding why a student does something may not correspond to our own set of assumptions, but is present nonetheless. Being an effective instructor requires a willingness to understand that student's differing perspective and to construct *with* that student a motivating educational experience.

Our best strategy is to strengthen the shared meaning we have with students and to actively use culturally responsive teaching. With this orientation, we are less likely to intervene or to try to use gimmicks to "motivate" students. Instead, we can elicit or encourage their own capacity to make meaning from experience by being responsive to their language, values, and personal history. This stance is essential in an instructional approach that evokes and enhances students' intrinsic motivation to learn.

Intrinsic Motivation Is Powerful

The brain has an inherent propensity for knowing what it wants. Relevance guides our inclinations (Ahissar and others, 1992). We have to pay attention to things that matter to us. What matters to us is understood through our cultural perspectives, which carry language, values, norms, and frameworks to interpret the world we live in. As a concept, intrinsic motivation fits very well with a neuroscientific understanding of motivation.

Intrinsic motivation occurs when people act or respond for the satisfaction inherent in the behavior itself (Ryan and Deci, 2000). For example, we read a novel for the interest it generates while we read it. We solve a problem because we enjoy encountering the puzzle itself. We conduct an experiment because of how each step engages our curiosity. When people see that what they are learning makes sense and is important according to their own perspectives, their motivation emerges as a physical energy, an emotional state to support learning. What is culturally relevant to adult learners evokes their intrinsic motivation—they want to be effective at what they value.

When we are intrinsically motivated to learn, we usually care about what we are learning and we feel such emotions as interest, concentration, and satisfaction. We flow with the learning, often without self-consciousness (Csikszentmihalyi, 1997). Time goes by quickly, and we are immersed in what we are studying. Emotions influence engagement, which is the visible outcome of learner motivation. As an ongoing process, engagement—fully participating in learning activities, such as actively attempting to solve a problem—is a strong sign that people are motivated to learn and are learning.

We are also much more likely to remember things that engage us emotionally. It appears that the more powerful the feeling that accompanies an experience, the more lasting the memory. Strong feelings release hormones, including adrenaline and cortisol, which heighten alertness and enhance the memory of an experience (Abercrombie and others, 2003). These hormones are likely to be present while some of our strongest memories, like those of deep joy and romance, are being made. The biological process of how emotions affect memory is complex, and our understanding at this time is incomplete. However, scientists are reasonably certain that moderate stress and positive emotions, such as satisfaction, confidence, and creativity, help us retain what we are learning (Zull, 2002).

One of the most popular metaphors for motivation is the "carrot and the stick," an expression used by the media, by political pundits, and often by parents. This expression is an extrinsic orientation to motivation, in which rewards or punishment are used to increase or decrease the behavior they follow. For example, we complete an assignment for a higher grade (reward), or we stop making a calculation mistake because our grades are lowered (punishment). There is no doubt that people respond to rewards and punishment. Yet this is a complex relationship affecting outcomes and future attitudes toward the extrinsically reinforced behavior.

There are numerous studies illustrating that using extrinsic rewards to motivate someone to do something that he or she would have done for the sake of interest in the activity itself undermines that person's subsequent performance quality and attitude toward the activity (Ryan and Deci, 2000). There are studies in which people are paid to solve interesting problems while others solve the same problems without payment. Those who are paid rate the activity as less enjoyable, are less likely to do it again, and do not solve the problems as well as those who received no payment. Because our experience as teachers of adults validates these research findings, we advocate for the use of an intrinsically motivational approach to instruction.

A conservative estimate is that extrinsic rewards, such as grades, promotion, and money, do not work for at least a third of the students in our schools. Teachers have been threatening children and adults with poor grades, lower test scores, and ultimate failure for over a century, and students are still flunking, dropping out, and withdrawing from school with gusto. Using only extrinsic incentives is a form of educational engineering, enhancing an instructional perspective that views students as inferior, inert, and in need of motivation. Such an orientation dims our awareness of the learners' own determination and promotes their dependency.

The general principles of the American Psychological Association's Task Force on Psychology in Education support an intrinsic approach to motivation in teaching and learning (Lambert and McCombs, 1998). The goal of the task force was to synthesize knowledge from research throughout the twentieth century that could improve student learning and enhance the design of educational systems. The task force concluded that it is part of human nature to be curious, to be active, to initiate thought and behavior, to make meaning from experience, and to be effective at what one values. These primary sources of motivation reside in people across all cultures. This is a *macrocultural* understanding of motivation to learn. When people can see, from their points of view, that what they are learning is important, their motivation emerges.

The most favorable conditions for learning vary among people. Involving learners requires us to be aware of the various ways they make sense of the world and interpret their learning environment. People who find reading, writing, calculating, and expanding their stores of knowledge interesting and satisfying are likely to be lifelong learners (Merriam, Caffarella, and Baumgartner, 2007). The tendency to find such processes worthwhile is considered to be the trait of a motivation to learn: a propensity for learning that develops over time (Brophy, 2004). As instructors, we have the responsibility and opportunity to increase students' access to a life in which learning is the compelling means to a better future.

What Motivates Learning?

When we ask the question, "What motivates learning?" we know that the answer "intrinsic motivation" most benefits learners as well as ourselves as instructors. It is necessary, however, to translate the abstract concept of intrinsic motivation into concrete action that will permeate not just a class lasting up to eight hours but also an entire course. We approach this goal by attempting to understand and put into action four motivational conditions that are fundamental to developing intrinsic motivation for learning: inclusion, attitude, meaning, and competence. Let us take a look at how each condition evokes motivation to learn within and across diverse student groups.

Each condition has two criteria so that instructors and learners can assess whether the condition exists in the learning environment. These criteria help us to know when the condition is present. If the condition is not present, the same criteria help us to understand how to create the condition with the appropriate teaching strategies and learning activities.

Inclusion

The criteria for establishing inclusion are *respect* and *connectedness*. People generally believe they are included in a group when they feel respected by and connected to the group. Respectful environments welcome each person's form of self-expression without threat or blame. People generally feel safe and accepted under these circumstances. They feel respected because they know their perspectives matter. In a climate of respect, intrinsic motivation emerges because people are able to be authentic and accept responsibility for their actions. Fear and alienation do not prevent them from voicing their opinions.

Connectedness is a person's sense of belonging in a learning group—of knowing that he or she is cared for by at least some of the group and cares for others in turn. When connectedness is present, students feel a shared purpose to support one another's well being. Learners experience trust and community, which allow for a measure of uncertainty and dissent. Feeling connected elicits intrinsic motivation because learners can meet their basic social needs and speak to what matters to them. Conversely, when people feel excluded, they tend to protect themselves through withdrawal or aggression, guarding their resources and weaknesses. For learners, inclusion and community are at the core of their empowerment and intrinsic motivation because such factors help them feel free enough to indicate and work toward learning goals they value.

Attitude

An attitude is a combination of information, beliefs, values, and emotions that results in a learned tendency to respond favorably or unfavorably toward particular people, groups, ideas, events, or objects (Samovar, Porter, and McDaniel, 2005). Attitudes powerfully affect behavior and learning because they help us make sense of our world and give cues as to what behavior will be most helpful in dealing with that world. *Relevance* and *volition* are the two criteria for developing a positive attitude toward learning among adults.

A course's personal relevance to students is understood by the degree to which they can identify their own perspectives and values in the course content, discussions, and methods of learning. The presence of instructional relevance means the learning processes are connected to who the students are, what they care about, and how they perceive and know. For example, if you were learning about the economy, which of the following topics would be most relevant to you: home mortgages for low-income borrowers, credit card interest for community college students, or employment opportunities for African American college graduates? If you chose one of these topics, what would be the most relevant way for you to pursue learning about it? Would you rather read about it in a newspaper or magazine, view a television special, surf the Internet for information, or interview local bank representatives? As we hope these questions show, relevance is present when learning is contextualized within the personal and cultural meanings and learning orientations of the student. Relevance is intrinsically motivating because it stimulates natural curiosity (Hodgins and Knee, 2002). We want to make sense of things that matter to us, and we are prone to seek out challenges to further our understanding. We usually experience this feeling as interest, the emotional nutrient for a positive attitude toward learning.

Interest usually leads to volition, the second criteria for developing a positive attitude. Depending on one's cultural orientation, volition can range from choice or self-determination to personally valued compliance. In the latter situation, some learners will follow suggestions or directives because they adhere to their culturally approved norms. For example, research by Chirkov, Kim, Ryan, and Kaplan (2003) indicates that in some East Asian societies, people willingly comply with choices that significant societal figures make for them. These significant individuals may be familial, religious, or educational leaders. Another source for compliance may be the learner's own beliefs about collective values. In any case, for learning to be intrinsically motivating, learners have to see themselves as able to *personally endorse* their own learning. Psychological research and global history merge to support the fact that people consistently strive to shape their lives as expressions of their beliefs and values (Ryan and Deci, 2002).

Translating this knowledge into an instructional question means asking, how can we provide adults with relevant learning options that respect their perspectives, values, strengths, and needs? As we will see in Chapter Four, part of the answer lies in collaboration and coauthorship with learners to construct these options.

Meaning

According to the adult learning theorist Jack Mezirow (1997, p. 5), a "defining condition of being human is that we have to understand the meaning of our experience." Although making, understanding, and changing meaning is imperative for adults and a vital condition for evoking intrinsic motivation, meaning is a difficult concept to define. Here are three perspectives of meaning, each of which provides its own insight. Together, these perspectives broaden our understanding of meaning and of how to make instruction enhance meaning and thus more motivating for students.

According to a neurological perspective, when the brain receives new information it searches existing neural networks for a place for the information to "fit." If there is a connection, the new information makes sense. Prior knowledge—what we already know—allows us to understand the new information. However, in order to have meaning, the new information has to be connected to something that matters to us (Sousa, 2006). For example, an adolescent watching television and seeing a commercial about early retirement planning might make sense of it, but the advertisement would likely not matter to her. To a working older adult, the same information would likely make sense and also hold meaning.

We can also see meaning as an increase in the complexity of an experience, as it relates to our values and purposes. For example, when we have experiences that relate to strong cultural, spiritual, or philosophical beliefs, those experiences take on a deeper meaning because of the relevance of these beliefs to how we live our lives. Topics ranging from morality to friendship to environmentalism can have great significance for us. Sometimes the meaning may be beyond articulation but of extraordinary importance, as in the case of art and spirituality, elements that are essential to human existence (Tisdell, 2003).

Meaning may also be understood as an interpreting of information that gives greater clarity, such as when we say that the word "shadow" means "the dark figure cast upon a surface by a body intercepting the rays from a source of light," or when we recognize our address in a listing. This kind of meaning involves facts, procedures, and behaviors. It contributes to an understanding of how things relate, operate, or are defined, but it doesn't deeply touch us. As instructors, we know that to make information and skills meaningful or significant for learning we have to recast them within a context of goals, problems, or interests that are relevant to students, so that they in turn can infuse them with deeper meaning. To illustrate, the previous definition of the word *shadow*, if presented to learners with the following example, might initially seem clear but technical or dull. "While standing in sunlight we cast a shadow." So we might ask the learners if this word has ever had significance for them. Maybe someone has seen an image of a shadow that was frightening or memorable. Maybe someone has shadowed someone or has been shadowed by someone for an important reason. We could ask, "What significant associations do you have with the word shadow?" For learners to imbue any form of information with deeper meaning, we want to be mindful to give them an opportunity to relate that information to their own cultural or personal contexts.

The criteria for enhancing meaning for learning are *engagement* and *challenge*. When engaged with learning, the learner is active and involved. He or she might be searching, evaluating, constructing, creating, or organizing some kind of learning material into new or better ideas, memories, skills, values, feelings, understandings, solutions, or decisions. Usually the learner creates a project or reaches a goal. The student often has transformed concepts and exerted mental, emotional, or physical energy (Nakamura and Csikszentmihalyi, 2003).

We are challenged when we have to apply current knowledge or skills to situations that require further development or extension of them (Wlodkowski, 2008). A challenge could include a range of behaviors, from talking with an instructor about a vague idea to conducting a complex experiment. For clarification, it helps to think of a challenge as the available learning opportunity and engagement as the kind of action a person has to take to meet the challenge. Successful engagement requires that the learner possess some capability, knowledge, or skill. For example, reading a challenging book with understanding requires a certain vocabulary and level of comprehension. A challenging learning experience in an engaging format about a relevant topic is intrinsically motivating because it develops conscious understanding for reaching an important goal. Acting purposefully to reach relevant goals is essential to human existence (Csikszentmihalyi, 1997).

Competence

People naturally strive for effective interactions with their world (White, 1959). We are genetically programmed to explore, reflect, and change things in order to have a more influential interaction with our environment. The desire to be competent extends across all cultures. Mastering such tasks as moving a hanging mobile or playing with building blocks evokes positive emotions among infants everywhere (Watson and Ramey, 1972). All adults need to be competent, to be effective at what they value: competence is part of our human will to matter and to have dreams that we may reach.

The criteria for engendering competence are *effectiveness* and *authenticity*. Socialization and culture largely determine what we think is worth accomplishing, what we value and want to do effectively (Plaut and Markus, 2005). When we have evidence, usually through feedback, that we are learning, we make such internal statements as, "I understand" or "I can do this." We experience intrinsic motivation because we are competently performing an activity that leads to a valued goal. Biologically, our prediction of the expected outcome of our learning is confirmed, activating pleasure structures in the brain as we proceed (Schultz and Dickinson, 2000).

Authenticity is present when learning is connected to an adult's actual life circumstances, frames of reference, and values. For example, an authentic assessment of learning would ask students to solve problems that have a parallel in the real world or their future work: a graduate student in education designs a lesson plan for the grade level he is teaching and for students likely to be in his class, or a student in a construction course practices safety routines with high-voltage batteries she might actually use on the job. Authenticity evokes intrinsic motivation because adults can see their learning as the grasp of important knowledge that is applied in a realistic context that they actually may face. They know that the problems they solve and the projects they develop are relevant to their families, jobs, and communities.

The Motivational Framework for Culturally Responsive Teaching

Now that we have discussed the four conditions that evoke intrinsic motivation to learn across and within cultural groups, we need to place them in a framework that you can use for planning lessons and for instructing students in large blocks of time. We offer the Motivational Framework for Culturally Responsive Teaching in Figure 2.1 as a heuristic, a functional model for problem solving and meeting the challenge of teaching intensive and accelerated courses (Wlodkowski and Ginsberg, 1995). (From now on

FIGURE 2.1

The Motivational Framework for Culturally Responsive Teaching

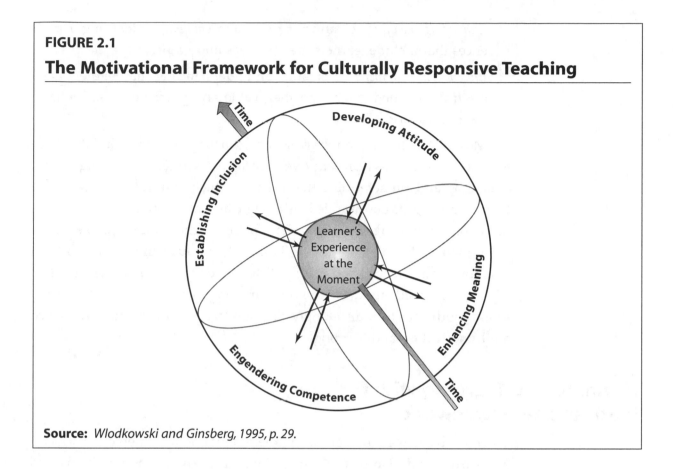

Source: *Wlodkowski and Ginsberg, 1995, p. 29.*

we will refer to the Motivational Framework for Culturally Responsive Teaching as the *motivational framework* and intensive and accelerated courses as simply *intensive courses*.) This motivational framework has been field tested and used nationally and internationally (Wlodkowski, 2008). It is respectful of different cultures and capable of creating a common culture within the learning environment that all learners can accept. The motivational framework systematically represents the four motivational conditions of inclusion, attitude, meaning, and competence, which act individually and in concert to enhance intrinsic motivation to learn.

When applying the motivational framework, we define each condition dynamically and briefly, using the two criteria that indicate, from the learners' perspective, that the condition is present in the learning environment.

1. *Establishing inclusion:* creating a learning atmosphere in which learners and instructors feel *respected* by and *connected* to one another.

2. *Developing attitude:* creating a favorable disposition toward learning through personal *relevance* and learner *volition.*

3. *Enhancing meaning:* creating *engaging* and *challenging* learning experiences that include learners' perspectives and values.

4. *Engendering competence:* creating an understanding that learners have *effectively* learned something they value and perceive as *authentic* to their real world.

Most instructional plans have specific learning objectives and therefore tend to be linear and prescriptive. Instructors sequence learning events over time and predetermine the order in which concepts and skills are taught, practiced, and applied. Although human motivation sometimes does not follow a logical or an orderly path, we can plan ways to evoke it throughout a learning sequence. However, because motivation is both emotionally influenced and readily distractible, it has a natural instability. With these considerations in mind for teaching intensive courses, we have found it judicious to painstakingly plan most academic activities to enhance adult motivation and learning.

Planning and Teaching with the Motivational Framework

The most basic way to begin using the motivational framework to devise an instructional plan is to transpose its four motivational conditions into questions to guide selecting motivational strategies and learning activities (Wlodkowski, 2008). *In the following list, items in parentheses indicate the point in the lesson at which the motivational condition is most applicable:*

1. *Establishing inclusion:* How do we create or affirm a learning atmosphere in which we feel respected by and connected to one another? (Best to plan for the *beginning* of the lesson.)

2. *Developing attitude:* How do we create or affirm a favorable disposition toward learning through personal relevance and learner volition? (Best to plan for the *beginning* of the lesson.)

3. *Enhancing meaning:* How do we create engaging and challenging learning experiences that include learners' perspectives and values? (Best to plan *throughout* the lesson.)

4. *Engendering competence:* How do we create or affirm an understanding that learners have effectively learned something they value and perceive as authentic to their real world? (Best to plan for, when possible, *throughout* the lesson and, in general, at the *ending* of the lesson.)

Let us look at an actual episode of teaching in which the instructor uses the motivational framework and these questions to compose an instructional plan. In this example, the instructor is conducting the first three-hour session of an introductory course in research. Please note how each question prompts a motivational strategy and its corresponding learning activity to optimally influence learners' motivation. We define, describe, and exemplify strategies for each motivational condition in Chapters Four, Five, Six, and Seven.

> The class takes place on Saturday morning. There are twenty adult learners ranging in age from twenty-five to fifty-five. Most hold full-time jobs. Most are women. Most are first-generation college students. A few are students of color. The instructor knows from previous experience that many of these students view research as abstract and irrelevant learning. Her instructional objective is as follows: The students will devise an in-class investigation and develop their own positive perspectives toward action research. Using the four motivational conditions and their related questions, the instructor creates the sequence of learning activities found in Table 2.1.
>
> Here's the narrative for this teaching episode. The instructor explains that much research is conducted collaboratively, an approach this course will model. For a beginning activity, she randomly assigns learners to small groups and encourages them to discuss any previous experiences they may have had doing research, as well as their expectations and concerns for the course (*motivational strategy: collaborative learning*). Each group then shares its experiences, expectations, and concerns, as the instructor records them on a whiteboard. She is thus able to understand her students' perspectives and increase their connection to one another and to her (*motivational condition: establishing inclusion*).
>
> The instructor explains that most people are researchers much of the time. She asks the students what they would like to research among themselves (*strategy: relevant learning goal*). After a lively discussion, the class decides to investigate and predict the amount of sleep some members of the class had the previous night. By having students choose the research topic, this strategy engages adult volition, increases the relevance of the activity and contributes to the emergence of a favorable disposition toward the

course (*motivational condition: developing attitude*). The students are learning in a way that includes their experiences and perspectives.

Five students volunteer to serve as subjects, and the other students form research teams. Each team develops a set of observations and a set of questions to ask the volunteers, but no one may ask them how many hours of sleep they had the night before. After they ask their questions, team members confer, and each team ranks the five volunteers in order of the amount of sleep each had, from the most to the least (*strategy: critical questioning and predicting*). When the volunteers reveal the amount of time they slept, the students discover that no research team was correct in ranking more than three volunteers. The students discuss why this outcome may have occurred and consider questions that might have increased their accuracy, such as "How much coffee did you drink before you came to class?" or "What was the last television program you watched before you slept?" The questioning, testing of ideas, receiving feedback, and predicting heighten students' engagement, the level of academic challenge, and the complexity of this learning activity (*motivational condition: enhancing meaning*).

After the discussion, the instructor asks the students to write a series of statements about what this activity has taught them about research (*strategy: self-assessment*). Students then break into small groups to exchange their insights. Their comments include such statements as "Research is more a method than an answer" and "Thus far, I enjoy research more than I thought I would." Self-assessment helps the students extract from this experience a new understanding they value (*motivational condition: engendering competence*).

This snapshot of instruction illustrates how the four motivational conditions constantly influence and interact with one another. Without establishing inclusion (small groups discussing concerns and experiences) and developing attitude (students choosing a relevant research goal), the enhancement of meaning (research teams devising questions and predictions) might not occur with equal ease and energy, and the self-assessment to engender competence (what students learned from their perspectives) might have a dismal outcome. Overall, the total learning experience encourages equitable participation, provides the beginning of an inclusive history for the students, and enhances their learning about research.

TABLE 2.1

An Instructional Plan Based on the Four Conditions from the Motivational Framework for Culturally Responsive Teaching

Motivational Condition and Question	Motivational Strategy	Learning Activity
Establishing inclusion: How do we create or affirm a learning atmosphere in which we feel respected by and connected to one another? (Beginning)	Collaborative learning	Randomly form small groups in which learners exchange concerns, experiences, and expectations they have about research. List them.
Developing attitude: How do we create or affirm a favorable disposition toward learning through personal relevance and learner volition? (Beginning)	Relevant learning goal	Ask learners to choose something they want to research among themselves.
Enhancing meaning: How do we create engaging and challenging learning experiences that include learners' perspectives and values? (Throughout)	Critical questioning and predicting	Form research teams to devise a set of questions to ask in order to make predictions. Record questions and predictions.
Engendering competence: How do we create or affirm an understanding that learners have effectively learned something they value and perceive as authentic to their real world? (Ending)	Self-assessment	After the predictions have been verified, ask learners to create their own statements about what they learned about research from this activity.

Source: *Wlodkowski, 2008.*

Instruction is a systemic process. Removing any one of the four strategies in the example above, or the motivational condition each evokes, would likely affect the entire experience. For example, would the students' attitudes be as positive if the teacher arbitrarily gave them the task of researching sleep among themselves, rather than allowing them to choose the topic? Probably not, and this mistake would likely decrease the research teams' efforts to devise questions.

The motivational framework allows for as many strategies as the instructor believes are needed to complete an instructional plan. For a six-hour class, for instance, an instructor may need more than one motivational plan, each varying in the number of strategies and amount of time allotted to it. The instructor's knowledge of the learners' motivation and cultures, the subject matter, the setting, the technology available, and the time constraints will determine the nature and number of the motivational strategies and their related activities. This motivational framework provides a time orientation for planning and a culturally responsive approach to teaching to foster intrinsic motivation from the beginning to the end of an instructional unit. The purpose of the framework is to respectfully enhance the motivation to learn which all adults possess by virtue of their own humanity, while making the instructor a valuable resource and vital partner in their realization of a motivating learning experience. In the next chapter, we discuss the characteristics and skills that are essential to an instructor for effectively using this framework.

Chapter 3

Being a Motivating Instructor

"To love something is to find it inexhaustible."

ANONYMOUS

MOTIVATING INSTRUCTORS ARE not cool, at least not in the withdrawn, above-it-all sense. They care—about their subject; about arousing their students' interest in this subject; and, above all, about taking learning seriously. Think about a teacher who evoked your enthusiasm for learning. Regardless of the topic of study, we could safely wager that this instructor was not indifferent toward it or you. Yet, as we will see, the qualities of a motivating instructor go well beyond enthusiasm and caring.

From the outset, we also want to acknowledge that the working conditions of postsecondary instructors can either support or challenge the development of the instructor's own motivation to teach. Let's begin by looking at the role of part-time and adjunct faculty in postsecondary education. (We realize that in some colleges and universities part-time faculty may be distinguished from adjunct faculty for reasons such as voting privileges, pay scales, teaching responsibilities, and so forth. Currently these are very fluid faculty designations. However, we use these terms synonymously because the majority of part-time and adjunct faculty are discriminated against as described below.)

Part-Time (Adjunct) Faculty

We have both been adjunct faculty and regular faculty, and one of us is currently an adjunct faculty member. As part-time faculty, we have taught at ten colleges and universities in four different U.S. states and Canada. Most people outside of postsecondary education do not realize that there are approximately 800,000 adjunct faculty in the United States (June, 2009). In general, compared to regular faculty, adjunct faculty receive proportionately less pay and professional development, have no health benefits, have lower status, and have no guarantee of continued employment. In our opinion, these systemic differences between types of academic employment are a form of discrimination (Hoeller, 2009; June, 2009). They make adjunct faculty continuously vulnerable to such influences as economic hardship, employment instability, and lower professional esteem. Colleges and universities often keep this system in place by capping their number of full-time faculty members and increasing their number of lower paid, lower benefit, part-time faculty. This may be an uncomfortable realization, but it is also unfair treatment that can diminish the motivation of any professional. We have, therefore, four suggestions for further reflection and action for those who govern and administer postsecondary institutions:

1. Legislate policies leading to equal pay for equal work that remunerate adjunct faculty based on a salary prorated at 100 percent of a full-time teaching load.

2. Offer annual contracts to adjunct faculty who have taught half-time or better for three years.

3. Create institutional policies that allow adjunct faculty to have their own bargaining unit separate from the faculty or administrators who supervise them.

4. Study college systems, such as Vancouver Community College, where both full-time and part time-faculty are treated based on a standard of equality.

We know of numerous adjunct faculty members who are excellent teachers, many of whom are on a par with excellent full-time teachers. In fact, there are no general studies that demonstrate that full-time faculty teach more effectively than part-time faculty. Given their circumstances, that is an exceptional compliment to the motivation and professionalism of part-time faculty. Their craft appears to be sustained by the economics of their spirit rather than the economics of their institution.

We want to point out, however, that there are policies in current practice that do not eradicate the aforementioned unequal treatment, but that do enhance the status and dignity of adjunct faculty. In our own experience, we have found that certain college norms and procedures contribute to respect for and the morale of adjunct faculty. We acknowledge that the following list of such institutional practices is incomplete and not organized according to importance:

- A college mission statement in which the role and efforts of adjunct faculty are seen as essential to the quality of education at the institution.

- A welcoming attitude on the part of full-time faculty and administrators toward part-time faculty, with clear availability of mentors, advisors, and support systems for adjunct faculty.

- A responsible role for adjunct faculty in the governance, curriculum development, and assessment of teaching at the institution.

- A comprehensive orientation, no less than half a day, at which adjunct faculty meet the president of the institution, connect with full-time faculty, and get an authentic understanding of the institution and its most influential norms.

- Invitation of adjunct faculty to all important institutional events, professional development opportunities, and social celebrations.

- A selection and ongoing evaluation process indicating that professional standards of performance are being noted and applied (such as a teaching audition assessed by current faculty), a regular performance evaluation, and an internship for the first semester of teaching prior to further employment at the institution.

- A comprehensive handbook that includes administrative, instructional, and student-service policies and procedures.

- Complimentary subscription to the college's newsletter, with attention to the presence and needs of adjunct faculty within its text.

- Realization when approaching or hiring a prospective adjunct faculty member that any apologetic comment, such as, "We wish we could pay you more" or "This salary does not reflect your talent or worth" is cliché after forty-plus years of national repetition. It's far better to say, "We have recently increased the salaries and benefits of our adjunct faculty and are committed as an institution to equity among all faculty."

Although we do not address issues of equity for full-time faculty, we do not want the reader to assume by our silence that inequities do not exist. We know, for example, that funding postsecondary education is a national as well as global issue, with justice implications for both faculty and students (Schuetze, 2009). It is our opinion, however, that the need for greater equity for part-time faculty is an obvious discriminatory issue in many postsecondary schools in the United States. The economic disparity between part-time and full-time faculty is the greatest between any two groups occupying the same professional role in postsecondary education. It is an example, we suggest, of executive political will (including full-time faculty and administration) lagging behind financial feasibility. An institution does not have to completely resolve this issue to increase equitability. In our opinion a valid set of questions to begin addressing this problem are: Has there been progress within the institution to effect such change? How long ago? And what needs to be done next?

Essential Characteristics of a Motivating Instructor: The Five Pillars

We believe instruction is a pragmatic art, a technical skill under the command of artistic expression. As teachers, we imagine, compose, plan, and perform for the benefit of learning. Professional artists, such as musicians, have practice regimens with fundamental exercises to maintain the elements essential to their artistry. No matter how experienced they are, daily practice is a necessary ritual for outstanding musicians. The fine musculature and dexterity needed to play an instrument well only survive with focused engagement. There are also basic elements that make up the infrastructure for motivating instruction. These core characteristics—*expertise, empathy, enthusiasm, clarity, and cultural responsiveness*—are the five pillars that support what we as instructors have to offer learners. We know through research and common sense that they are not abstractions or personality traits. Instead, these characteristics are made up of skills and actions that can be learned and improved through effort and practice. Each is discussed here in terms of functional criteria to guide a personal assessment of how an instructor can express the characteristic.

Expertise: Knowledge and Preparation

As instructors, our expertise is our personal knowledge or skill about what we teach. Three criteria for understanding the depth of our expertise are (1) we know our subject well; (2) we know how to make our knowledge or skills beneficial for adults; and (3) we are prepared to construct this knowledge with adults through an instructional process.

Knowing Your Subject Well

Here are a few questions to explore how well you know your subject:

1. *Do I understand what I am going to teach?* I should at least be able to explain what I am teaching in my own words, offering multiple examples, which may include stories, facts, research, media, and

metaphors. Good examples demonstrate the depth and breadth of our understanding.

2. *If I am teaching a skill, can I demonstrate it?* A demonstration establishes our credibility with adult learners, who are keen to note its absence when we cannot. One of us remembers an education professor who wanted to teach how to write a lesson plan while obviously having no lesson plan to do so. If we cannot demonstrate a skill, which happens frequently when the appropriate technology is unavailable, we should determine whether there are guest speakers, visual models, films, or videos that could do the job.

3. *Do I know how to connect what I am teaching to the world of the learners, addressing their prior knowledge, experience, interests, and concerns?* We need to consider how we will guide learners to apply what they know to what we are teaching. Probably the easiest step in this direction is to focus on what is relevant to students. When both the instructor and the learners establish a deep understanding of a subject, students are often able to transform mere information into useable knowledge (Donovan, Bransford, and Pellegrino, 1999). For example, students can apply the math they master to the daily tasks of saving, budgeting, or spending.

Constructing Knowledge Beneficial for Adults

Adult learners are pragmatic learners. They want to apply what they learn to solve problems, build new skills, advance in their jobs, and make friends—in general to do, produce, or decide something that is of real value to them. Their primary question for any instructor is, can what you know really help me? In recent years, with the rising costs of postsecondary education, that seems a reasonable question.

Simply knowing a lot about a subject is not enough to teach it effectively. There are many knowledgeable college instructors who teach quite poorly. In some instances, they have not considered what students might know or be able to contribute. Often, they have not taken the step of connecting their knowledge to the daily needs and lives of their students—and have therefore failed to establish a bridge to common understanding or a means to construct knowledge collectively.

When we instruct a group for a lengthy period, we eventually become quite naked: our actions peel away the camouflage of our academic degrees to reveal to adult learners whether or not what we know really matters. Joining our expertise with their perspectives and prior knowledge builds everyone's confidence that we are learning something of value.

Being Prepared for the Instructional Process

We should have a well-designed lesson (Chapter Eight is an extensive treatment of this criterion) and be organized and prepared to deliver it to students. Being well prepared for instruction requires a relaxed familiarity with our materials, which will allow us to converse with and look at our students most of the time. We should be ready to have a conversation with them. This allows learners to be participants who can talk with us, rather than being a cardboard audience pinned to their seats by a poorly delivered lecture. If we are tied to our notes, if we cannot put our manuals down, if we are not sure what the next step is, our chances of being motivating instructors are nil.

Vital instruction flows. Both instructors and learners feel part of a single process. Knowing our material sufficiently well gives us the opportunity to read student cues; to change our tone of voice; and to respond to signs of interest, insight, and boredom. We will have the chance for an authentic give-and-take.

For an experienced instructor, this preparation may be only the minutes required to review, adjust, and organize a familiar and well-designed lesson. For the novice, it may entail hours of review, rehearsal, and organization. Notes, index cards, outlines, and media and technology are all appropriate, as long as they do not stultify our interactions with students. PowerPoint is a bit tricky. It can clarify, illustrate, and organize complex material, but if we become overly dependent or too casual in our use of this tool, it can reduce complicated ideas to simple bullet points and actually inhibit interaction with learners (Keller, 2003).

Any significant achievement requires readiness. Actors rehearse their roles, and athletes visualize their goals. We also need to mobilize our capabilities prior to instruction. This kind of preparation enhances our confidence, which carries over into how we feel when we enter the classroom, giving us better access to our expertise and to our skills for inviting our students' knowledge as well.

Empathy: Understanding and Compassion

Adults, for the most part, learn in accordance with their own goals and perceptions, not those of their instructors. Empathy is the skill that allows instructors to be aware of their students' perspectives and feelings. This characteristic is a requirement for motivating instruction. There seems to be universal agreement in the field of adult education concerning the importance of empathy in teaching adults (Rossiter, 2006). For centuries, religious and spiritual leaders have used words like "understanding" and "compassion" to describe how fundamental empathy is for life on earth (Goleman, 2007). We define empathy as an instructor's sensitive awareness of how a student feels while learning and being in the learning environment (Rogers, 1969). It is not about imagining *oneself* in someone else's situation; it is about imagining *that individual* in his or her situation. For example, a U.S.-born instructor who is challenged to define an unfamiliar English word is not like a Laotian English language learner struggling with the meaning of the same English word. That student has to reinterpret the word in her native language and context first, and then translate it again in English into her present world, one that is likely to be in some ways unfamiliar to her. The instructor demonstrates empathy when he imagines himself as her in this situation. When we are empathetic, (1) we continuously consider the learners' goals, perspectives, and feelings from their viewpoint, and (2) we adapt our instruction to the learners' levels of experience and skill development.

Consideration for Learners' Goals, Perspectives, and Feelings

Let's begin with how instructors can better understand the goals or expectations of adult learners. This is particularly important in an intensive course, in which there is less time to reach those goals. We may have to do prior work to know what those goals are likely to be, because we certainly want our syllabus to be in sync with the learners' expectations for our course or program. Some methods for gathering this information are as follows (Caffarella, 2002):

- Have conversations with colleagues who have taught the course and students who have taken the course. These informal discussions will reveal insights about how to design the course and its objectives.

- Survey students who will take the course. We have used print or online surveys to gather their opinions, needs, goals, strengths, preferences, and concerns.

- Pretest students who will take the course. For those courses requiring particular skill levels, for example, in writing and math, assess students' mastery of those skills in relation to learning goals so that you can both adjust instructional goals and convey to students what is expected of them.

- Spend time with learners in their communities by, for example, attending local farmers' markets, festivals, or political events. By doing this, we may gain some sensitivity to students' cultures, values, concerns, and goals.

Students also expect fair and manageable course requirements for intensive courses. In their eyes, how much we ask students to do is a measure of our fairness and humanity. Whether they involve reading, writing, practicing, or problem solving, meeting course requirements takes time. Numerous studies have found time constraints to be a serious obstacle to adult participation in education (Ginsberg and Wlodkowski, 2010). Our experience is that adults want to make sure they have enough time to meet requirements and have a chance to demonstrate their capabilities—to show they can be good at what they learn. Prior to teaching an intensive course and creating course goals and requirements, we should have some understanding of the learners' work and family responsibilities and the amount of time they can realistically afford. At that first meeting, remaining flexible, being open to learners' input, and, in some instances, creating or revising learning goals with them are ways to keep our course vital and culturally relevant. Rather than representing instructor uncertainty or weakness, this kind of discussion shows our respect for the learners and their needs.

We turn now to learners' perspectives and feelings. As with online learning, intensive courses demonstrate just how important it is for adult learners to know that we, their instructors, understand and care about them. Whereas the distance and technological interface inherent in online learning stir worries about teacher indifference, the brevity and speed of intensive courses raise similar concerns for students. ("This course will be over in no time. How could anyone really care?") This is why empathy needs to be as much an attitude as a skill: a constant effort to know what students are living and experiencing while learning with us.

Perhaps unsurprisingly, listening is the most important skill in demonstrating empathy. The way we listen conveys to adults more than anything else how much consideration we are giving them: Do we understand? Do we cut them off? Do we look over their shoulders for someone else? Do we change the subject? Do we actually have some idea of what they are feeling? When we *listen for understanding* we avoid judging people with our own conceptual frameworks, allowing us to become interested in how things look to them. In this way, we can be genuinely fascinated by how learners make meaning out of ideas and experiences, and such listening can elicit deeper conversations and mutual understanding. Empathy allows instructors and learners to express their thoughts and feelings to one another in ways that can benefit and—more important— extend their relationships.

Adapting Instruction to Learners' Experience and Skills

Have you ever lacked the skills or background to do what you were required to do, but could not excuse yourself from that situation? (Dancing in front of others comes to mind; so do a few unfortunate public presentations.) It's a special kind of misery—a mixture of fear, embarrassment, and infuriation. At times like these, our motivation is to escape or, at best, to endure.

Part of being an empathetic instructor is preventing learners from failure. This means assigning learners tasks that are within their reach. To fulfill this principle means striking a delicate balance: we don't want to construct assignments or activities that are too easy or with which learners have had too much experience, because they will be bored; however, we don't want to assign tasks that are too difficult and beyond their experience and skills. We need to make the learning process somewhat challenging while still matching learners' capabilities and experience.

Sometimes we may want to use formative evaluation procedures to better understand learner capabilities (see Chapter Seven). The purpose of such assessments is not to sort or categorize students, but to help us create optimal instructional procedures for enhancing their motivation and learning. Master coaches and teachers know from hard-learned experience that you cannot take anyone from anywhere unless you start somewhere near where they are. Scaffolding (see Strategy 12 in Chapter Five) is an excellent method for adapting instruction to learners' levels of knowledge, skill, and experience.

Enthusiasm: Commitment and Expressiveness

It's unavoidable: we are what we teach. And every learner knows it. Whenever adults are urged to believe something, they perform a keen intuitive scan of the advocate. Intuitively they ask themselves, what will believing in this do for me? If we as instructors cannot show by our presence, energy, and conviction that our subject matter has made a positive difference for us, learners are forewarned. They will literally want to stay away from what we have to offer. That is survival: No one wants to invest in something that has not done its own advocate any good.

In educational research, enthusiasm has long been linked to increased learner motivation and achievement (Cruickshank, 1980). Numerous studies have demonstrated that when we focus on other people, we tend to embody their emotions (Niedenthal, Barsalou, Ric, and Krauth-Gruber, 2005). For example, in one study, when a person was watched by another person describing the happiest or saddest event in her life, the observer felt similar feelings. Biologically, this identification probably occurs because our neurons "mirror" the neurons representing the emotions of other human beings, allowing us to improve both our communication with them and our chances of survival in a social world (Rizzolatti, Fogassi, and Gallese, 2008).

Because of enthusiastic instructors' energy and emotional appeal, learners are more likely to pay attention and understand what enthusiastic instructors are teaching. Since students become more alert to what is going on, they are likely to increase their learning, which makes paying attention in the future both more likely and more rewarding. And on it goes. An educational, self-perpetuating chain of events has been established. No wonder learners "can't wait" for the next class session with an inspiring instructor.

The two criteria for being an enthusiastic instructor are: (1) we value what we teach, for ourselves as well as for learners, and (2) we display our value for our subject with appropriate degrees of emotion and expressiveness. Focusing on these two criteria helps sustain our enthusiasm during instruction, a considerable challenge in an intensive course, in which energy can naturally wane after a couple of hours.

Valuing What We Teach

Actively maintaining our own interest in what we teach is probably the surest indicator that we value it. As instructors we have to ask ourselves, how do we devote time to understanding our subject better? Are we participating members of organizations that specialize in the discipline we teach? Do we read journals and magazines or take workshops in our subject area? How can each of us bring a singular insight or style to what we teach?

Keeping the effects of our lessons in mind may help us to appreciate our subject matter. For example, knowing what learners will experience as "firsts" with us as instructors can be a potent influence on our own—as well as their—enthusiasm. (The first time each of us, in a faculty workshop, learned to use a personal computer to send e-mail to colleagues was quite a kick.)

Through our own experience teaching adult educators the motivational framework (see the section Designing an Instructional Plan in Chapter Eight), we know that when students design and teach their first lessons using the framework, their appreciation for it will probably increase. Personally acknowledging such moments to ourselves helps us sustain our vitality, even for a topic we have been teaching for over a decade.

Showing Value for Your Subject with Emotion and Expressiveness

Openly demonstrating your commitment to your subject area is a primary means of conveying enthusiasm during instruction. As instructors we're a bit like cheerleaders: we root for what we believe in, and to allow ourselves to have feelings about what we teach is key. Some examples include getting excited about new concepts, skills, materials, research, and events related to our subject; showing wonder about insights and questions that emerge from learners; and sincerely expressing emotions about the learning process ("I feel frustrated by these problems myself" or "I'm happy to see the progress you're making"). We can tell interesting stories about what we teach; role-play our subject matter (by becoming historical figures, simulating characters in problems, enacting relevant scenarios, and so forth); and use the arts and media, such as music, videos, and film excerpts, to extend and further reveal the vibrancy of our subject.

In terms of behavior, when does instruction express enthusiasm? Research has commonly shown five indicators (Larkins, McKinney, Oldham-Buss, and Gilmore, 1985):

1. Speaking with some variation in tone, pitch, volume, and speed

2. Gesturing with arms and hands

3. Moving around the room to illustrate points and respond to questions

4. Making varied, emotive facial expressions where appropriate

5. Displaying energy and vitality

Although these indicators are worthy of serious consideration, they are not mandatory. How people express and perceive enthusiasm varies across cultures. There is no instrument to assess enthusiasm that is both precise and culturally relevant. A good exercise might be to reflect on these indicators as they apply to instructors whom you found to be excellent models, and who displayed sensitivity to their students as well as enthusiasm for their subject.

Let's end this section by answering a question we often are asked when discussing instructor enthusiasm: What if you are required to teach a course and you don't honestly have enthusiasm for the subject? This happens a lot, for reasons ranging from departmental expediency to actual emergency. Other instructors in such situations have cited this answer as having the most practical value for them: find another instructor who teaches this course and is genuinely enthusiastic about the subject. That person has found ways to appreciate the topic. Consult with that person. If possible, observe that person teaching the course and, where appropriate, allow that person to coach you. Enthusiasm is infectious—you might be pleasantly surprised.

Clarity: Language and Organization

We achieve instructional clarity when we teach something in a manner that is easy for learners to understand, and that is organized so that they can smoothly follow and participate in the intended lesson or program. Many studies confirm that instructional clarity is positively associated with learning (McKeachie, 1997). Berliner (1988) found that expert teachers, effective teachers who have developed fluid and often masterful solutions to common classroom problems, were extremely well organized and thoughtful about teaching procedures. Instructional designers have long focused on how instructors can organize knowledge so that students can readily integrate it with their prior knowledge (Morrison, Ross, and Kemp, 2006).

It is important to remember, however, that what may be easy for one person to understand may not be so for another. There is a dynamic between what the instructor does and what the learner brings to the instructional situation. This is the interaction between the instructor's language and teaching methods and the learner's language and experience. We as instructors have to construct a bridge from what we know to what the learner knows as that knowledge culturally exists for him.

For an illustration of how easily a breakdown in this interaction can occur, suppose that an instructor is teaching the concept of cooperation and uses an example with which some learners are unfamiliar. Perhaps she refers to a hockey game to exemplify fluid interdependence. On the face of it, everyone seems to understand, but one learner in the group has never seen a hockey game, and another is learning English and cannot translate the word "hockey." Rather than being enlightened, these learners are only confused by the example. Adult learners can become frustrated when they believe that they have the capability to learn but find the instructor's language or methods bewildering.

With respect to being instructionally clear, the two criteria are: (1) we plan and conduct instruction so that all learners can follow and understand, and (2) we provide a way for learners to comprehend what has been taught if it is not initially clear.

Planning and Conducting Instruction for Diverse Learners

This criterion emphasizes instructional organization and language. Organization comprises the logical connections and orderly relationships among the parts of the instructional process. Our instruction should be like a good map—one that enables students to follow us from one learning destination to the next. Further, instruction should properly emphasize the most important concepts and skills, just as a road map highlights the larger cities.

Beyond good outlining, planning for instructional clarity includes the following elements:

- Anticipating problems learners will have with the material and having relevant examples and activities ready to deepen their understanding.

- Creating the best possible examples, analogies, and stories to make ideas easier to understand. (More information about this idea is found in Strategy 29 in Chapter Six.)

- Knowing the learning objectives and preparing a clear introduction to the lesson so that students know what they will be learning.

- Using advance organizers and visual tools. These are questions, activities, graphics, and diagrams that support understanding of new information. They should direct learners' attention to what is important in the coming material, highlight the relationships among the ideas to be presented, and remind learners of relevant information or experience. (For further discussion and examples, see Strategy 25 in Chapter Six.)

- Rehearsing directions for such learning activities as simulations, case studies, and role playing so that learners are clear about how to do the activities and can experience their maximum benefits.

Providing Clarification for Initially Incomprehensible Material

The range of possibilities for meeting this criterion spans from reviewing difficult material with students to announcing office hours for those who want personal help. Two helpful methods within this range are checking in with questions or problems to make sure learners are able to understand and follow the lesson; or having learners compare notes near the end of class and to ask you any questions they could not answer among themselves.

These suggestions for clarity may have particular resonance for instructors with English language learners in their courses. Postsecondary learning is often abstract, with minimal contextualization, and frequently lacks visual images, concrete objects, and social clues like facial expressions. Kate Kinsella (1993) offers helpful suggestions for increasing clarity for English language learners during instruction:

- Pair less-proficient English users with sensitive peers who can clarify concepts, vocabulary, and instructions in their primary language.

- Increase wait time (by three to nine seconds) after posing a question to allow adequate time for the learner to process the question effectively and formulate a thoughtful response.

- Make corrections indirectly by mirroring in correct form what the learner has said. For example, suppose a student says, "Many immigrants Seattle from Southeast Asia." You can repeat, "Yes, many of the immigrants in Seattle come from Southeast Asia."

- Use these conversational features regularly in class discussions, lectures, and small-group work:

    Confirmation checks: "Is this what you are saying?"

    Clarification requests: "Will you explain your viewpoint so that I can be sure I understand?"

    Comprehension checks: "Is my use of language understandable to you?"

- Write as legibly as possible on the board or other media, keeping in mind that students educated abroad may be unfamiliar with cursive writing.

- Allow students to use a recorder for repeated listening to comprehend and retain information.

- Modify your normal conversational style to make your delivery as comprehensible as possible: speak more slowly, enunciate clearly, limit idiomatic expressions, and pause adequately at the end of statements to allow time for learners to clarify their thoughts and take notes.

- Relate information to assigned readings whenever possible, and give the precise page numbers in the text or selection so that learners can later find the information for study and review.

The Instructional Clarity Checklist in Exhibit 3.1 provides a way to survey these suggestions with learners and use their feedback to tell you how clearly they understand the lessons. Also, if you should videotape yourself during instruction, you can use this checklist to assess the clarity of your instruction while seeing and hearing yourself interact with learners. Statements relating to guideline one ("we plan and conduct instruction so that all learners can follow and understand") are preceded by an O. Statements that relate directly to criterion two ("we provide a way for learners to comprehend what has been taught if it is not initially clear") are preceded by an X.

EXHIBIT 3.1

Instructional Clarity Checklist

	As Our Instructor You ...	All of the Time	Most of the Time	Some of the Time	Never	Doesn't Apply
O	1. Explain things simply.					
O	2. Give explanations we understand.					
O	3. Teach at a pace that is not too fast and not too slow.					
O	4. Stay with the topic until we understand.					
X	5. Try to find out when we don't understand and then repeat things.					
O	6. Show graphics, diagrams, and examples to help us understand.					
O	7. Describe the work to be done and how to do it.					
X	8. Ask if we know what to do and how to do it.					
X	9. Repeat things when we don't understand.					
O	10. Explain something and then use an example to illustrate it.					
X	11. Explain something and then stop so we can ask questions.					
O	12. Prepare us for what we will be doing next.					
O	13. Use words and examples familiar to us.					
X	14. Repeat things that are hard to understand.					
O	15. Use examples and explain them until we understand.					
O	16. Explain something and then stop so we can think about it.					
O	17. Show us how to do the work.					
O	18. Explain the assignment and the materials we need to do it.					
O	19. Stress difficult points.					
O	20. Show examples of how to do course work and assignments.					
X	21. Give us enough time for practice.					
X	22. Answer our questions.					
X	23. Ask questions to find out if we understand.					
X	24. Go over difficult assignments until we understand how to do them.					

Source: *Adapted from Gephart, Strother, and Duckett, 1981.*

Cultural Responsiveness: Respect and Social Responsibility

As discussed in Chapter Two, cultural responsiveness is a complex set of beliefs and actions. A necessary characteristic of a motivating instructor, it is largely understood as a respect for diversity and an ongoing understanding that people are different as a result of history, socialization, experience, and biology. Learners naturally have different perspectives, and all of them have a right to instruction that accommodates this diversity. Growing evidence demonstrates that learning and engaging in diversity through knowledge acquisition and personal interaction enhances student learning (Denson and Chang, 2009).

Because people are, by nature, socially interdependent, the second quality of cultural responsiveness in an instructor is the ability to teach in a socially responsible manner. Human motivation does not occur in a vacuum—it is energy with a consequence. We are obliged, therefore, to see teaching as vitally related to social justice: individuals' motivation and persistence toward academic learning depend, in part, on their belief in a hopeful future (Tatum, 2003). Understanding this essential human need to see a promising future requires us to foster learning for *all* students, with attention paid to the collective good of society. How we do this may, however, at times conflict with the methods of others with the same intent, whether they are learners or colleagues. Therefore, the following guidelines for cultural responsiveness are needed: (1) we create a safe, inclusive, and respectful learning environment, and (2) we relate course content and learning to the social concerns of learners and the broader concerns of society.

Creating a Safe, Inclusive, and Respectful Learning Environment

In a safe learning environment, there is little risk of learners suffering any form of personal embarrassment because of self-disclosure, a lack of knowledge, a personal opinion, or a hostile or arrogant social atmosphere. We can go a long way toward developing this kind of security by assuming a nonblameful and realistically hopeful view of people and their capacity to change. Disregarding empathy and accusing and finding fault with people can create a cycle of mutually hostile attitudes that damages relationships, especially among culturally different people (Ginsberg and Wlodkowski, 2009).

Rather than placing blame when conflicting opinions emerge from or among students, instructors can model and support increased understanding and mutual problem solving and can exploit these opportunities for further learning. Beverly Daniel Tatum (1992) offered an excellent example of such supportive instruction in teaching her course, The Psychology of Racism. She explicitly taught with the assumption that because prejudice was inherent in her students' environments when they were children, they could not be blamed for what they were deliberately or unintentionally taught. Nonetheless, she recognized that they all had a responsibility to interrupt the cycle of oppression and needed to realize that understanding and unlearning prejudice may be a lifelong process. Removing blame from a learning environment does not mean that we as instructors give up our critical reasoning or avoid facing the truth as we understand it. It does, however, entail realizing that different views can give us information that leads to shared understanding and a clearer path for communication, and that a difference of opinion does not have to lead to mutual disrespect. Accordingly, we invite the ideas, feelings, and concerns of every learner in the community, placing exploration of differences at center stage rather than in the shadows.

This kind of instruction encourages all learners to understand their own construction of meaning (Rogoff and Chavajay, 1995), to realize that they reconstruct their knowledge and opinions, changing them with experience and learning. When learners know that the sharing of ideas is a sincerely respected norm in the learning environment, they will be more likely to expose their thinking. In fact, sharing opinions is one of the few ways students can come to realize that there are multiple viewpoints on any issue, and to appreciate how others construct their own learning and grasp of truth. Nevertheless, under the safest of circumstances, adults from dominant groups are more likely to feel safer than adults from marginalized groups. As instructors we still need to determine who is probably going to feel safer or less safe and what guidelines or processes we need to develop so that everyone has an opportunity to express themselves (see Strategy 8 in Chapter Four).

Relating Course Content to the Concerns of Learners and Society

Education contributes to the construction of the individual and society. We are, to a significant extent, what we learn to be. Ethics and politics are inherent in the instructor-learner relationship (authoritarian or democratic); in readings chosen for the syllabus (those left in and those left out); and in the process of learning (for example, which questions get asked and answered, and how deeply they are probed). The connection between our instruction and broader social concerns that affect how people live and work is inescapable. As instructors we have a responsibility to promote equity and justice.

In recent years, *cultural competence* has emerged as a set of processes to enable instructors to be more equitable and effective with students from a variety of cultures. Practitioners from disciplines as broad as medicine, counseling, and education suggest that cultural competence includes three critical elements (Chiu and Hong, 2005):

1. Self-understanding and awareness of one's own cultural values and biases

2. Specific knowledge and information of the history, perspectives, and values of the culturally different groups with which one works as a practitioner

3. Adapting one's own behaviors and skills to conduct appropriate and successful interactions with culturally different people

Although these competencies make sense and are desirable, cultures are so dynamically complex, and interactions are so nuanced, that being competent to teach adults from different cultures does not entail a static set of skills that one can master. Rather, while we remain aware of our own limitations, we strive to become more competent in an evolving set of skills that will change as the culture they represent also changes. Living authentic experiences with culturally different groups, participating in events that take us into the homes and neighborhoods of culturally diverse people, and being open to encounters that allow us to learn their values and practices promote our intercultural understanding and contribute to our cultural competence.

This book discusses the three elements of cultural competence in sections that are aligned with the motivational framework and its related strategies. Chapter Eight focuses on the first element of cultural competence, *self-understanding and self-awareness*, as part of an instructional analysis under the heading of Motivational Self-Awareness. The second element, *specific knowledge of the culturally different groups*, has been addressed earlier in this chapter within the context of the core characteristic empathy. Ideas for the third element, *adapting one's behavior and skills for successful interactions*, are found in this chapter as part of the earlier discussion of clarity (and in our discussions of inclusion throughout the book).

Paulo Freire's notion of a *critical consciousness* (1970) is a useful guide to creating a learning environment that will respect the social concerns of diverse adult learners and contribute to the common good of society. Instructors with a critical consciousness reflect the following qualities (Shor, 1993):

- *Power awareness:* approaching instruction and content with an understanding that society is constructed by organized groups; realizing who has power and how power is structured and used in society, especially as it influences learners in the course. Closely related is *positionality*—sensitivity to how qualities of identity, such as privilege, class, and gender, among both instructors and students can affect the learning process, and an awareness of whose worldviews dominate the learning environment.

- *Critical literacy:* using analytic habits of thinking, reading, writing, and discussing that go beneath surface impressions, conventional myths, and routine opinions; understanding the social contexts and consequences of any topic or subject; being willing to probe for the deeper meaning of an event, reading, image, or situation, and applying the meaning found to one's own as well as the learners' situations.

- *Desocialization:* recognizing and challenging prejudicial myths, values, behaviors, and language, especially those learned in mass culture, such as class bias and excessive consumerism.

- *Self-education:* using learning opportunities and projects to initiate constructive social change: for example, using action research in a course to inform a local paper, corporation, or community organization about discovered abuses or inequities.

In this chapter, we examined and discussed the five core characteristics of a motivating instructor—expertise, empathy, enthusiasm, clarity, and cultural responsiveness. They are five necessary, interdependent, and vital building blocks that form a strong foundation for culturally responsive teaching. We could not consider the material that follows in this book without first acknowledging these core characteristics. They are essential to strengthening the strategies outlined in the rest of this book, making them more likely to have a maximum influence on the motivation and learning of adults.

· · ·

Each of the next four chapters discusses and exemplifies particular strategies for enhancing each condition of the motivational framework—inclusion, attitude, meaning, and competence. Many of these strategies have been selected from a larger collection based on their usefulness for evoking intrinsic motivation among students in intensive educational formats (Wlodkowski, 2008).

Chapter 4

Establishing Inclusion in a Learning Environment

"There is no way of measuring the damage to a society when a whole texture of humanity is kept from realizing its own power."

ADRIENNE RICH (1984)

ENABLING ADULT LEARNERS to realize their own capabilities relates to our dual obligation to provide these students with excellent postsecondary education opportunities and an equal opportunity to be motivated to learn in our courses. The two responsibilities are inseparable. We have to be vigilant in monitoring the patterns we see in our courses by asking such questions as: Are some people left out? Do particular income groups or ethnic groups do less well than others? Who are the people whose motivation to learn is not emerging or seems diminished among the adults we teach? How might we as instructors be responsible for or contribute to these trends?

Feelings of cultural isolation can cause students' motivation to deteriorate. When learners don't feel safe, complex information is often blocked from passage to higher cortical functioning and memory storage, slowing learning and increasing students' frustration, aggression, or withdrawal. A sense of community with which all learners can identify establishes the foundation for inclusion in a course. Our challenge as instructors is to create a successful learning environment for all learners that (1) respects different cultures and (2) maintains a common culture that all learners can accept. We are fortunate in that adults are community-forming beings: our capacity to create social coherence is always there (Gardner, 1990). The more quickly a learning group arrives at a sense of mutual community—in which they feel connected and can identify with the particular course and instructor—the less students' energies will be diverted into resistance and self-protection, and the more easily their motivation to learn can emerge. It simply makes sense to set a tone in which learners can come together in friendly, caring, and respectful ways.

The strategies that follow contribute to establishing a *climate of respect*. Learners can begin to develop trust. We have set the table for a relaxed and alert social environment, in which relevant learning is possible. These strategies also enable learners to feel connected to one another, a fulfillment of students' social needs that draws forth their motivation. When people feel included, they are freer to risk making the mistakes that true learning involves, and to share their resources and strengths. Our experience suggests that establishing a sense of community within an intensive course should be a primary goal for the first class session. Learners should leave this session feeling that they know a few people (and their names) with whom they would be comfortable talking or learning outside of class, have a sense that they are generally accepted by their peers, believe that their perspectives will matter in the course, and look forward to the learning and group participation they anticipate for the next session. Accomplishing these goals with the strategies found below is worth the time and effort, especially in the first class meeting.

Motivational Strategies

Each *motivational strategy* is a deliberate action or process that an instructor can use to enhance adult motivation to learn. For example, when an instructor gives a learner accurate and positive feedback (a motivational strategy) about his performance, this action evokes feelings of competence in the learner that prompt and support his effort at the task. You can organize motivational strategies and their related activities throughout a lesson to produce the four motivational conditions of the motivational framework—inclusion, attitude, meaning, and competence—evoking intrinsic motivation among adult learners on a continual basis. The strategies that follow are organized according to the motivational condition to which each most directly relates. These strategies are well documented by research and practice as being effective with adult learners (Wlodkowski, 2008). We have numbered the strategies throughout this book for organizational purposes, not to indicate an order of preference or a particular sequence to follow. The selection of each strategy you use will depend on your teaching philosophy, situation, and goals. In order to establish inclusion, we begin with those strategies that can engender a feeling of connection among learners.

Engendering Connection

Strategy 1: Allow for Introductions

This strategy is definitely meant for the first meeting of the group. Say a few things about who you are, where you're from, why you're conducting the course, and welcome the group. We find it particularly beneficial when we can mention something we sincerely appreciate—about the group, its history or locale, our purpose, or other unique factors that make the situation distinct or special. Five to ten minutes seems like an appropriate amount of time for your personal introduction.

Give the learners a chance to introduce themselves as well. This emphasizes their importance and your interest in them as people. It also helps the students start to learn one another's names (name tents are a valuable supplement to this strategy) and significantly reduces the tension so often present at the beginning of most courses. Scores of books describe different exercises for helping people get acquainted in new social situations (Johnson and Johnson, 2006). Among such methods is multidimensional sharing, the next strategy we discuss.

Strategy 2: Provide an Opportunity for Multidimensional Sharing

Multidimensional sharing activities differ from most icebreakers in that they tend to be less gamelike and intrusive. For adults from backgrounds that value modesty, introductory activities requiring self-disclosure or the sharing of deeper emotions may seem contrived and psychologically invasive. Multidimensional sharing activities also provide insight or new learning relevant to the subject of the course. For example, we ourselves have used "Decades and Diversity," an activity found later in this section, to demonstrate the influence of age and popular culture on adult norms and perspectives.

Opportunities for multidimensional sharing, ranging from introductory exercises to personal anecdotes to celebrations of course achievements, are those occasions when people have a better chance to see one another as complete, evolving human beings with mutual needs, emotions, and experiences (Ginsberg and Wlodkowski, 2009). These opportunities give a human face to a course, break down biases and stereotypes, and provide experiences in which we may see ourselves in another person's world.

As an example of multidimensional sharing, "Decades and Diversity," an activity which we use in a course on adult development, offers learners a chance to realize mutual experiences as well as relevant information about cultural influences on different generations. Students divide themselves into smaller groups according to the decade in which they would have graduated or did graduate from high school (the sixties, seventies, eighties, and so on). Each smaller group brainstorms a list of items in three to five categories for that decade: popular music, clothing styles, major historical events, weekend social opportunities (What did you usually do on a Saturday night?), and moral standards (What was considered immoral behavior for you as an adolescent—something forbidden by your family?). Each group then reads its list to the whole class. The activity concludes with a discussion by the members of the entire group about their insights, the possible meanings of the lists, and their brainstorming processes. These discussions illuminate the powerful influences of the time period of adolescent socialization on future adult norms and values.

Multidimensional sharing activities are most inclusive and motivating when they validate the experiences of the adults involved and establish feelings of affiliation with the instructor and other learners. The more natural and appropriate such opportunities feel, the more likely it is that a genuine sense of community can evolve.

Strategy 3: Concretely Indicate Your Cooperative Intentions to Help Adults Learn

Because of the short duration of intensive courses, adults are more vulnerable to a nagging fear—what if I really try, and I can't learn it? If students fall behind or cannot immediately learn something, they don't have as much time to recover or catch up. Letting learners know at the outset that you are there to assist them will help learners reduce their fears and save face. Whether we as instructors are announcing our availability during office hours or at breaks, arranging online tutorial assistance, or creating a procedure whereby learners who are having difficulty can use special materials or aids, our message is, "As instructor and learner, we are partners in solving your learning problems. I want to help you, and it's okay to seek help." We are telling the learners that we will safeguard their vulnerability and that they will receive a nonjudgmental and interested response to their requests for assistance (Hill, 2004). By employing this strategy, we offer early evidence that we do care about the people who learn with us.

Strategy 4: Use Collaborative and Cooperative Learning

Most collaborative learning methods emphasize the value of the learners' interpretation of course material as much as they do the instructor's explanation. Having everyone participate, working as partners or in small groups, and generating questions and facing challenges together, energizes group activity and learning. Instructors who use collaborative procedures tend to think of themselves less as singular transmitters of knowledge than as co-learners and co-constructers of knowledge. Because we are highly evolved and social human beings, we naturally want to know what other people are thinking and feeling (Brothers, 2000). These tendencies enhance our emotional involvement in learning.

Barkley, Cross, and Major (2005) have found abundant evidence that nontraditional students—those from underrepresented racial and ethnic groups, working adult students, commuters, and reentry students—tend to find collaborative learning an effective and motivating educational format. They argue, "The evidence…is so strong that collaborative learning has multiple advantages if done well, that it would be folly not to learn how to operate collaborative learning groups productively" (p. 24). Among the many collaborative learning possibilities, cooperative learning represents the most carefully organized and researched approach (Johnson and Johnson, 2009). When adults learn cooperatively, they tend to develop supportive relationships across multiple sociocultural and linguistic groups. Cooperative learning groups create a setting in which learners can do the following (Johnson, 2003):

- Construct and extend their understanding of what is being learned through explanation and discussion of multiple perspectives

- Receive interpersonal feedback as to how well they are performing

- Receive social support and encouragement to take risks in increasing their competencies

- Establish a shared identity with other group members

- Develop a "voice" to validate their learning

As Johnson and Johnson (2006) emphasize, cooperative learning is a rigorous procedure whose fundamental components are: (1) positive interdependence, (2) individual accountability, (3) promotive interaction, (4) social skills, and (5) group processing. Organizing lessons so learners can work cooperatively requires a conscientious implementation of these five basic elements. A significant proportion of cooperative learning also needs to take place within the learning environment, so that instructors can monitor students and offer groups support as they initially establish themselves.

1. *Positive interdependence* occurs when learners perceive themselves as linked with group members such that they cannot succeed unless their

group members do (and vice versa), or when learners must coordinate their efforts with those of their partners to complete a task (Johnson and Johnson, 2006). They sink or swim together. Each group member has a unique contribution to make to the group because of his or her resources, role, or responsibilities. Positive interdependence works best when all group members understand that each person has a part to do, that all members are counting on one another, and that all members want to help one another do better. The following are ways to create positive interdependence:

- With p*ositive goal interdependence*, the group is united around a common goal, a concrete reason for being. It could be to create a single product, report, or answer, or it could be to improve on a task so that all members do better this week than they did last week.

- With *positive resource interdependence*, each group member has only a portion of the resources, information, or materials necessary for the task to be accomplished, and the members have to combine resources in order for the group to achieve its goals. The metaphor for this approach is a puzzle, with each group member possessing a unique and necessary piece to contribute to the puzzle's solution. For example, for an upcoming exam, each member of a group might be responsible for a different study question; when the group convenes, members share their knowledge of the question and check to make sure all group mates have satisfactorily comprehended this information.

- With *positive role interdependence*, each member of the group selects a particular role that is complementary, interconnected, and essential to the roles of the other group members. Suppose, for example, that the learning goal is the development of some skill, such as interviewing. One group member is the person practicing the skill (the interviewer), another person is the recipient of the skill (the interviewee), and a third person is the observer-evaluator. In this manner, each person has an essential contribution to make in terms of either skill practice or feedback.

2. *Individual accountability* occurs when the learning of each individual in the group is assessed, the results are shared with the learner and the group, and each learner is responsible to the other group members for contributing a fair share to the group's success (Johnson and Johnson, 2006). One of the main purposes of cooperative learning is to support each member as a vital, competent individual.

Individual accountability also prevents *hitchhiking*, or contributing little to the group's success but reaping large benefits from the contributions of other group members. Our experience is that this seldom occurs when cooperative norms are well in place. Specific ways to enhance individual accountability are:

- Keep the size of the groups small. A typical size is two to four members.
- Assess learners individually as well as collectively.
- Observe groups while they are working.
- Request periodic self-assessments and outlines of responsibilities from individual group members.
- If grading, assess and assign a grade for individual contributions to the group's performance or product.

A simple and positive way to support individual accountability and prevent related conflict among group members is to brainstorm answers to the question, how would we like to find out or be told if someone in our cooperative learning group thought we were not doing enough to contribute to the benefit of the total group? Then write the possible actions or communications for all to see and discuss them. Such a procedure can go a long way to avoid unnecessary suspicion or shame.

3. *Promotive interaction* occurs when group members encourage and assist one another to reach the group's goals (Johnson and Johnson, 2006). This includes sharing information, resources, and emotional support to achieve the relevant goals. Mutual care should permeate this interaction, as it does, for example, when someone in a cooperative writing group reads something she has written and a fellow group member offers sincere and helpful suggestions to improve the manuscript.

4. *Social skills* facilitate communication that enables group members to reach goals, get to know and trust one another, communicate accurately, accept and support one another, and resolve conflicts constructively (Johnson and Johnson, 2006). Even though adults want to cooperate, they may not be able to do so effectively if they lack conventional social skills.

Our experience with diverse adults is that when the course participation guidelines (Strategy 8) are discussed and made explicit, they create a learning climate that significantly reduces aggressive conflict. There is then less need for direct training in conventional interpersonal skills, such as *active listening*, which can seem contrived and strange to people who do not identify with the dominant culture.

It is appropriate for an instructor to intervene in a group, when necessary, to suggest more effective procedures for working together. Sometimes, simply asking group members to set aside their task, describe the problem as they see it, and come up with a few solutions and decide which one to try first is enough to get things moving along satisfactorily.

5. *Group processing* occurs when members reflect on their group experience, describe actions that were helpful and unhelpful, and make decisions about what actions to continue or change (Johnson and Johnson, 2006). When groups with the same members continue for more than a few hours or for the duration of an intensive course, discussing group functioning is essential. Adults need time to have a dialogue about the quality of their cooperation, to reflect on their interactions, and to learn from how they work together. This processing time gives them a chance to receive feedback on their participation and understand how their actions can be more effective for the next group session. As instructors, we need to allow enough time in the learning environment for this activity to take place and to provide some basic structure for it—for example, by suggesting that the group discuss a few things it is doing well and one thing it could improve. Such early group processing significantly reduces the likelihood that aggressive conflict will emerge.

• • •

In general, heterogeneous groups tend to work well together. Where possible, regularly remixing groups at the beginning of new activities often has a revitalizing effect and makes working with different people a course norm. However, practical reasons may sometimes override the benefits of heterogeneity. For example, students' interest in a specific topic, student availability for meetings outside of class, very limited academic skills, or language acquisition issues might require more homogeneous groups. For projects or activities with significant assessment consequences (for example, if they represent a large proportion of a course grade), we usually accept individual completion as an option. We do this to respect the more individualistic students as well as other possible cultural orientations that may exist among class members. In addition, for some activities (usually informal), we find that having students form their own groups, ranging from two to four members, can be quite beneficial and a pleasant change of pace. Exhibit 4.1 is an outline for planning cooperative learning activities.

EXHIBIT 4.1

Cooperative Lesson Planning Guide

Step 1: Select an activity and desired outcome(s).

Step 2: Make decisions.

  a. Group size:

  b. Assignment to groups:

  c. Room arrangement:

  d. Materials needed for each group:

  e. Roles:

Step 3: State the activity in language your students understand.

  a. Task:

  b. Positive interdependence:

  c. Individual accountability:

  d. Criteria for success:

  e. Specific behaviors to encourage:

Step 4: Monitor group activity.

  a. Evidence of cooperative and encouraged behaviors:

  b. Task assistance needed:

Step 5: Evaluate outcomes.

  a. Task achievement:

  b. Group functioning:

  c. Notes on individuals:

  d. Feedback to give:

  e. Suggestions for next time:

Source: *Adapted from Johnson, Johnson, and Smith, 1991.*

Related to cooperative learning are *learning communities*. These planned structures enable learners to take more than one course together, giving them an opportunity to work as a team for a semester or longer. Forming these groups often involves integration of curricula (such as combining psychology and English literature or math and economics) and team teaching on the part of faculty. Research on learning communities has indicated they have positive effects on the persistence and graduation rates of college students, including working adults (Kuh and Associates, 2005).

Another group structure is the *cohort*. Generally, cohorts are composed of between twelve and thirty students who are placed together in classes with the expectation that they will proceed through their college programs taking most of their courses together. This form of scheduling is designed to give them ample time to become acquainted, to collaborate, and to be mutually supportive in their academic work. Although cohorts are widely used in intensive programs, we could find no studies at this time that offer evidence to confirm or disprove their effectiveness.

With our obvious emphasis on collaboration, cooperation, and community, one might ask, is there a role for competition? We think there is, if learners can freely choose whether or not to participate. Good competition is about choosing to elevate others and oneself to a higher level of performance, whether it is in dancing, basketball, debate, or making wine, and about knowing you need one another because achieving your very best vitally depends on others' accomplishing their very best. Also, for less consequential learning, for drill practice, and for enjoyment—when the stakes are not very high and the most you can win is a round of applause—individual and intergroup competition can be quite effective as a method for learning.

For any learning task in which students' individual differences and capabilities are significant, as in math or writing, an individualized approach may be more helpful to some learners that a cooperative one. Also, there are occasions when cooperative learning can take too much time to organize. What matters most is that cooperation is the norm for learning, that students form a community of learners who genuinely care about the learning of their peers. The more intellectually and socially connected adult learners feel—to one another and to their instructors—the more they will persist in their education (Tinto, 1998). A good resource for collaborative and cooperative learning with specific, subject-related examples is *Collaborative Learning Techniques: A Handbook for College Faculty* (Barkley, Cross, and Major, 2005).

Strategy 5: Clearly Identify the Learning Objectives and Goals for Instruction

Alerting students to the objectives of a course or instructional unit allows them to know more clearly the learning, choices, and competencies necessary for accomplishing those goals. In an intensive course, such information is probably more urgent because there is less time to complete the objectives. For adults, with their pragmatism and responsibilities, clarity about these matters is essential. Objectives also have a unifying force: they show learners why they are there and, at the very least, what they presently hold in common, regardless of their backgrounds. Objectives can provide students with a mutual stake in learning and show why cooperation makes sense. For English language learners, *clear* objectives are particularly critical. They help these learners to understand and discuss what is expected of them in a course. In postsecondary education, the two types of most frequently used objectives are (1) clearly defined goals and (2) problem-solving goals.

1. *Clearly defined goals.* When specific objectives, skills, or competencies are appropriate and meaningful, clearly defined goals let learners know what skills and knowledge they need to acquire and inform them about what may be necessary to achieve those skills and knowledge. For instructors, these goals provide a focus for designing instruction, guide decisions about lesson content, and give an understanding of what assessment is needed. The three essential elements for constructing a learning objective are *who* (the learners), *how* (the action verb), and *what* (the contents) (Caffarella, 2002). For example, "As a result of this class, students (the learners) will create (the action verb) a résumé containing their professional achievements (the contents)." (These three elements are also exemplified in the syllabus found in Exhibit 4.2.) Learning goals are clearer when authentic examples accompany them, such as a former student's completed and graded research paper—whatever it takes so that confusion does not detract from learners' expectation to succeed.

Sometimes two more elements—beyond the who, why, and what—are used for clearly defined goals (Dick, Carey, and Carey, 2004). The first of these comprises the conditions under which students will demonstrate learning, such as "using this software" or "given this case study." The second element is made up of the standards or criteria for acceptable performance, such as "with three or fewer errors" or "as supported by two documented studies." The examples of learning objectives in Table 4.1 illustrate all five elements. They are arranged according to the cognitive complexity required of student thinking, based on Benjamin Bloom's revised taxonomy (Anderson and Krathwohl, 2001). In this categorization, the highest complex cognitive processes begin with the capacity to *create*, followed by the capacities to *evaluate*; to *analyze*; to *apply*; to *understand*; and, finally, to *remember*. In Table 4.1, each of the examples includes action words that represent some form of the cognitive process aligned with them, such as "imagine" or "pretend" for "create." The examples pertain to a course in adult development. Each objective addresses the learner.

TABLE 4.1

Action Words and Learning Objective Examples

Process	Action Words	Objective
Create	Imagine, pretend, design, invent, envision	With consideration of the characteristics of older adults, design an urban park in which they could be physically or artistically engaged.
Evaluate	Judge, critique, assess, recommend, appraise	Given this case study of a working adult, recommend, in order of priority and with accompanying rationales, four actions he might take to improve his chances of attaining his bachelor's degree within three years.
Analyze	Distinguish, compare, organize, modify, refine	Using your own timeline of significant life events, compare the insights provided by Perry's Scheme of Cognitive and Ethical Development with those from Belenky, Clinchy, Goldberger, and Tarule's *Women's Ways of Knowing* for three events that altered your life profoundly.
Apply	Practice, use, demonstrate, employ, complete	After reading a relevant biography of your choice, use at least four central concepts from our course to demonstrate your own adult developmental understanding of this person's life.
Understand	Explain, discuss, outline, summarize, teach	Choose an economic or political problem facing low-income adults in your community and outline a research study that could provide findings or data to more effectively address this problem.
Remember	Recognize, recall, define, describe, identify	Using your text, describe Paulo Freire's emancipatory philosophy and one study in which it has been effectively applied.

Source: *Adapted from Wlodkowski, 2008.*

2. *Problem-solving goals.* Much of what we know as human beings escapes a uniform and specific description. How, for example, could one convincingly define integrity or describe how water tastes? As Eisner (1985, p. 115) has indicated, many of the qualities of things we value are not "verbally describable or measurable."

In working on a problem-solving goal, the learners formulate or are given a problem to solve. Although the goal—to solve the problem—is clear, the learning is not definite or known beforehand. For example, in a social science course, learners might be asked how to reduce crime in a particular area. There is a range of possible solutions and learning outcomes. Problem-solving goals place a premium on intellectual exploration and the higher mental processes, while supporting different cultural perspectives and values. Because they allow students to construct rather than apply knowledge, they are an excellent means of initiating transformative learning (see the section Transformative Learning near the end of Chapter Six). Students' alternative solutions to a given problem offer explicit evidence of the benefits of diverse talents and viewpoints. Relevant and genuine problems are the most likely to elicit learner motivation. Because authentic problem solving encourages deep and lengthy engagement as well as the combining of various skills and content knowledge, they are a valuable staple in intensive learning courses (Center for Adult Learning in Louisiana, 2009).

Strategy 6: Emphasize the Human Purpose of What Is Being Learned and Its Relationship to the Learners' Personal Lives and Contemporary Situations

This strategy is based on the assumption that *anything* worth teaching matters to adults and relates to human need, feelings, or interest. For us as instructors, the question then is, what are the human ramifications of what we are helping learners know or do? Once we have an answer to this question, the relevance of what we instruct will be clearer, and we can think of ways to make this meaning part of the learning process. Whether we are teaching people how to wire a circuit, how to speak another language, or how to write a complete sentence, these skills and knowledge serve human purposes. If we can understand these qualities, especially as they may relate to the daily lives of our learners, we will have some guidance in selecting what social aspects of the learning experience to emphasize.

When the topic falls within the realm of the physical and natural sciences, such as biology, chemistry, physics, or geology, demonstrating to students how this knowledge relates to understanding challenges faced by humanity, or how it can make life saner and more peaceful, bonds them together in a common cause. In the technological fields, such as computer programming or systems engineering, accentuating the contributions these processes make to human endeavors can diffuse their mechanistic isolation and humanize the learning process. Consider a basic education instructor teaching the difference between a circle and a square. This may seem a highly abstract concept, but if, as a point of discussion, the instructor asks the learners to think of important circles and squares in their own lives, something abstract instantly becomes concretely relevant. The closer we bring our topics and skills to the personal lives of our learners in the here and now, the more their emotional involvement and sense of common purpose will become apparent.

Creating a Climate of Respect

In most cultures, if you are respected in a group, you have at minimum the freedom to express yourself with integrity without fear of threat or blame—and you know your opinion matters. When mutual respect is present in a learning environment, adults normally feel safe, accepted, and able to influence the situation when necessary. Misunderstanding can undermine feelings of safety and respect. The first strategy in this section is meant to help all members of a learning group avoid misapprehending their situation at probably the most vulnerable time in an intensive course—the beginning.

Strategy 7: Assess Learners' Current Expectations, Needs, Goals, and Previous Experience as They Relate to Your Course or Lesson

We confirm or alter student expectations with information we give during the opening segment of a course or lesson. Using this strategy as part of the introductions, we might say, "When you are introducing yourself, please include your expectations for the course." We might also ask learners to fill out a short questionnaire, or give learners the chance to describe areas of worry or concern about the course. These methods also provide insight into their perspectives.

It is just as important to *check in* frequently with learners during an intensive course. We have found that the more diverse the group, the more important this process is in determining how well the course is meeting students' expectations (Adams, Jones, and Tatum, 2007). For example, we will check in at the end of every intensive course session, no matter how well things seem to be going. When we work with diverse learners, it is often easy to inadvertently leave people out in terms of their goals and experience without realizing it. Frequent checking in helps us adjust our instruction with minimum difficulty, and we find that most adults see checking in as a caring and respectful thing to do.

Checking in can be as simple as having students answer a few scaled questions, such as "On a scale from 1 to 5, with 5 being high and 1 being low, rate (1) how effectively you could participate, (2) how relevant the topic was to you, and (3) how much today's lesson challenged your thinking." Or specific questions, such as, "In your opinion, what aspects of this topic still need to be addressed?," "What is the most relevant idea you will take away from tonight's discussion?," and "Are there any ways you would like to suggest to improve this course?" Student comments are welcome, and learners should remain anonymous. Strategy 45 in Chapter Seven offers a number of more comprehensive self-assessment methods for this process.

Strategy 8: Explicitly Introduce Important Participation Guidelines

When course content is challenging and the learning process is interactive, adults often appreciate *participation guidelines.* By clearly identifying the kinds of interactions and discussions that will be encouraged and discouraged, instructors and learners create a climate of safety, ensuring that everyone will be respected.

The first meeting is an appropriate time to establish these guidelines and to request cooperation in implementing them. We have found the following rules to be generally acceptable as well as extremely beneficial for establishing inclusion (Ginsberg and Wlodkowski, 2009):

- Listen carefully, especially to different perspectives.

- Keep personal information shared in the group confidential.

- Speak from your own experience, saying, for example, "I think..." or "In my experience I have found... ," rather than extending your experience to others by saying, for example, "People say..." or "We believe..."

- Express perspectives without blaming or scapegoating.

- Avoid generalizing about groups of people.

- Share airtime.

- Focus on your own learning.

Instructors who use participation guidelines usually have a few that are nonnegotiable (Tatum, 1992). This makes sense because everyone is safer when we know what our professional limits are. Although the list is sometimes longer or shorter, most adults accept and construct these guidelines because these rules reduce feelings of fear, awkwardness, embarrassment, and shame. They also provide a safety net for critical discourse.

We can establish some participation guidelines through consensus. Learners might suggest which guidelines are needed and which need editing or specific discussion. At this time other guidelines may be added.

After this discussion, we want to gain the group's consent to accept the guidelines that have been negotiated. Johnson and Johnson (2006) offer a useful consensus decision-making model for facilitating this process. Leaving participation guidelines open to further additions and referring to them when necessary keeps the boundaries of the learning environment both clear and dynamic.

When instructors have a discussion with adult students that directly addresses their tensions and fears, learners have a chance to more completely engage thoughts and emotions in their learning. We also must keep in mind that these discussions contain dilemmas that may remain unresolved, possibly providing information and insight, but not a neatly packaged ending. When we anticipate this outcome in our own instruction, we alert students that the content or experience we have planned may make some of them uncomfortable, and indicate a few reasons why this might occur. In general, this signaling usually relieves some anxiety and allows the class, including us, to be more patient with and open to learning that challenges personal beliefs.

Strategy 9: Acknowledge Different Ways of Knowing and Different Levels of Knowledge or Skill to Engender a Respectful Learning Environment

To relieve tension as well as to support equity in a course, we can tell students we would appreciate knowing when they understand something differently from the way it is taught, or when they might use similar language but it significantly differs from ours in meaning. It is sometimes necessary to acknowledge that for those adults who are English language learners, the language they most readily speak may define certain aspects of reality differently from the conventions of standard English (Fong, 2006). For example, in Chinese Cantonese, the words for *heat* and *cool* usually do not refer to the *temperature* of food and drink but to the *nature* of food that produces a cool or warm effect on your body.

For many courses, from child psychology to computer science, adult learners may differ greatly from one another in their experience, skill, and knowledge: some will be novices and others will have more experience than the instructor. After assessing to understand these disparities and acknowledging that they are reasonable to have in the learning environment, it is necessary to find a way to move forward together. We often do this using such instructional methods as project work (see Strategy 34 in Chapter Six), peer tutoring, or cooperative learning, having students work at different paces with varied learning options, based on their readiness and prerequisite skills—whatever allows students to learn most effectively and develop as a mutually respectful community.

Strategy 10: Create a Clear, Inviting, and Inclusive Course Syllabus

Creating a clear, inviting, and inclusive course syllabus is critical to the initial motivation of adult learners in an intensive course. Given the course's shorter duration, working adults will want to know as soon as possible what to expect and what is required of them. In our experience, students regularly contact us a month or more before our courses begin in order to prepare in advance.

Composing a course syllabus is similar to making a map for a particular terrain. It creates definite directions, expectations, and boundaries. It also conveys what is essential to you as the instructor, sets a tone for the course, and delivers a direct communication about what students can expect in terms of support and evaluation (O'Brien, Millis, and Cohen, 2008).

Many postsecondary institutions have their own requirements and formats for how a syllabus is to be constructed. Wiggins and McTighe (2005) wisely suggest that faculty begin to design a syllabus with the end in mind while considering three questions:

1. What is important and worthwhile to understand? (Focus on those "essential understandings," to deepen comprehension and promote application of relevant knowledge.)

2. How can evidence of this understanding be observed or assessed? (This evidence might be gathered through informal and formal evaluation practices.)

3. What learning activities and instructional practices support motivation, understanding, and excellent performance? (In this book, these are the learning activities constructed from the strategies of the motivational framework as it is used to design instruction for a course. This process is detailed in Chapter 8)

We offer a composite model of a syllabus, in Exhibit 4.2, which one of us created for an introductory research course. We begin with brief descriptions of critical syllabus components, adapted from the exemplary outline in *The Course Syllabus* (O'Brien, Millis, and Cohen, 2008). These are followed by Exhibit 4.2, which has the actual examples from the syllabus constructed for the research course. Although we describe their necessary content, we do not specifically illustrate those components that need to be current, such as instructor information, course readings and resources, and course calendar dates.

Syllabus Components

Instructor Information

Because instructor accessibility is so important, students want to know how and when to reach their teachers. Basic information on a syllabus should include the course meeting room; days when the course meets; inclusive times for class sessions; and the instructor's full name, e-mail address, office hours, and office and phone numbers.

Introduction and Teaching Philosophy

This syllabus section offers students an opportunity to become acquainted with the values and approach to learning the course will offer. It also affords the instructor a more personal connection with students and sets the tone for the course. It is a place where the instructor can identify course norms, such as cooperation and cultural relevance. For intensive courses, we often send the introduction in a letter to students at least two weeks before the course begins to welcome them and give them an opportunity for an early start on course requirements.

Course Purpose

This section offers the main rationale for the course, explaining why it is relevant for the student and the program of study. This component is an opportunity to appeal to the pragmatism as well as the ideals of adult learners.

Course Description

This section provides an overview of the course and its content. It gives the instructor a platform to emphasize the specific value of the course's subject matter. (Exhibit 4.2 does not contain an example of a course description because this section is covered in the Introduction.)

Learning Goals or Objectives

This section indicates to students what they will actually learn, do, or perform, and what they can expect as outcomes of the course. These goals explicitly address students' responsibilities. They are the focus of the course and bear a direct relationship to the forms of assessment and evaluation that are used in the course. See examples discussed in Strategy 5.

Readings

This section identifies the texts and readings for the course. Because books are costly and time is at a premium for working adults, it is important to identify which materials are required and which are supplemental. The availability and ease of acquiring these reading materials are also considerations for discussion in this section.

Resources

This section identifies the course resources. It may contain such items as media and Web site references, outlines, published materials, graphics, and examples of previous students' work and assessments. Students are usually appreciative when these materials are compiled and distributed along with the syllabus.

Course Outline or Calendar

This section is the "guts" of the course syllabus. It tells students what will be happening in terms of topics, activities, assignments, readings, assessments, exams, projects, and their dates for occurrence, completion, or collection. This schedule gives adult learners a way to manage their time and the clearest notion of what is expected of them for the course and at the first class meeting. Instructor questions for shaping this outline include:

- What are the most important learning objectives to emphasize in this course?

- What can students be expected to cover in this intensive course?

- What do I omit? (All topics and parts of the texts and readings are not equally important and need to be prioritized based on their relevance. For further discussion of this, see Chapter Eight (pp. 164–165) in this book and Donovan, Bransford, and Pellegrino [1999]).

- How do I organize and integrate what is learned so that the objectives are connected with clear relationships to acquired knowledge and skill?

- Which assignments and assessments deepen understanding and encourage students' application of the most important learning objectives?

- How does this outline support transfer of learning to the students' daily lives or future work?

The course calendar should help students to organize their time and to plan the steps to complete assignments and prepare for assessments. Notice that in the course calendar in Exhibit 4.2, there is an assignment due at the first session to encourage advanced study and to allow the instructor to assess students' writing and comprehension of the topic as soon as possible. An early assignment gives the instructor a chance to intervene and advise students at the beginning, when such feedback is most beneficial in an intensive course.

In the course outlined in Exhibit 4.2, feedback, a powerful motivational strategy (see Strategy 39 in Chapter Seven), is a designated activity in four out of eight class sessions. We also encourage designing a course calendar with some flexibility in mind, so that learning that takes longer, or more student input, or revisions based on the needs of the class can be integrated into the flow of the course. This calendar emphasizes what we have found working adults appreciate—an intensive course dense with relevant applied activities and substantive collaborative learning. Nonetheless, what to leave in and what to leave out is usually an ongoing source of personal tension for the instructor.

Course Requirements

Students reasonably expect a clear explanation of course requirements, which determine what they must do to receive course credit and a grade. Under this heading we discuss attendance, participation, assignments, and assessment and grading procedures. Some syllabi include these topics separately or as part of Course Policies and Evaluation. Even though we have both taught for more than twenty years, we continue to be challenged by this syllabus section more than any other. To be fair to students as well as responsive to evidence of learning remains a work in progress for us. In general, check to be sure your course requirements coincide with those in the institutional or departmental catalogue.

Attendance

Because of the short duration and applied nature of intensive courses, attendance is extremely important. As policy, most intensive programs do not allow more than one absence from a course without loss of credit, and discourage the enrollment of any students who expect to be absent. In the case of an absence, make-up procedures tend to be very rigorous.

Participation

Student participation is essential to deeper learning (Donovan, Bransford, and Pellegrino, 1999; Zull, 2002). However, student participation is not limited to speaking in front of a class, and can include small-group participation, active note-taking, reflective journaling, written feedback, and individual questioning. If collaborative and experiential learning activities are already integral to a course, participation is usually not a problem. As instructors, we encourage participation but do not grade for it. If you are using participation guidelines, this part of the syllabus is the place to define these (see Strategy 8).

Assignments

In an intensive course, assignments are like attendance: they are mandatory for learning to occur, even more so when the course is highly experiential and collaborative. Some instructors go so far as to require a valid medical excuse for acceptance of a late assignment such as a project or research paper. Our course norm is to only allow teacher-excused late assignments.

Assessment and Grading Procedures

The range for assessing and grading learning is extensive and complex. Chapter Seven addresses many of the possibilities to consider. As instructors, we tend to use learning contracts and rubrics. Learning contracts, which we describe in Strategy 19 in Chapter Five, involve the instructor and the student in a collaborative process and concretely enhance student self-direction, self-assessment, and expectancy for success. Rubrics offer clear, reliable standards that students can use to direct and improve their learning (see Strategy 44 in Chapter Seven). When implementing learning contracts or rubrics, we can employ models of previous student work to serve as exemplars of specific grades or evaluation criteria. We use rubrics in Exhibit 4.2 because the course is a research course with a linear progression of requisite knowledge and has limited possibilities for negotiating a grade.

In the course outline shown in Exhibit 4.2 there are four opportunities for students to receive feedback on their work. Each graded assignment allows for at least one revision to improve learning and raise one's grade. We have found that students in intensive courses immensely appreciate a chance for what happens in real life—first performance, feedback, improved performance, feedback, further improved performance, and so forth. Adults know this cycle from their participation in work, sports, and family matters.

Chapter Seven discusses feedback and its powerful, positive impact on student motivation and learning. Intensive courses require extensive feedback and frequent opportunities for student revision in order for deeper learning to occur—learning that is the equivalent of or greater than that in conventional courses (Wlodkowski and Stiller, 2005). In general, being as clear and specific as possible in the syllabus about how grades are determined will relieve students' anxiety, reduce their most common cause of complaints, and allow grades to be what they were meant to be: accurate representations of the quality of learning (O'Brien, Millis, and Cohen, 2008).

Course Policies

This section generally focuses on departmental and institutional rules and regulations, which may address attendance, academic honesty, professional standards, disability accommodations, safety procedures, and how Incompletes are officially transcribed. This is a very important part of the syllabus because it invokes the legal authority of the college and the regulatory systems that set the standards for particular faculty and student responsibilities.

Course Suggestions for Learning

This section is as important for encouraging students as it is for offering specific guidance. In order to respect cultural differences as well as the varied needs and experiences of adult learners, we tend to paint this section with a broad brushstroke, applying common sense but avoiding being too controlling or patronizing. The latter reason is why we avoid the common subtitle, "How to Succeed in This Course." We do not think there is only one way to effectively learn, and do not wish to imply that "success" is everyone's primary goal. Adults are sometimes selective in their achievements. Gaining a particular skill or relevant understanding may override general success in a course. Indeed, from a values perspective, generosity and the common good may be preferred to individual success in course performance. It may help to take the experiences of past students into account when you are filling out some of the content of this section. Also, some instructors do not include this section because they may have covered it in the course introduction, outline, or other section of the syllabus.

EXHIBIT 4.2

Syllabus Example: Introduction to Research

Introduction

Welcome to Introduction to Research. The type of thinking and requirements for a course of this nature may appear formidable. Research has a jargon and set of symbols that can seem strange, difficult, and rigid. Yet it is a way of knowing that can be helpful and very creative.

As a student I came to research with a sense of inadequacy and genuine trepidation, and after having worked twenty-five years as a psychologist and educator, using and conducting research on a regular basis, I still feel those two emotions about research. They are more tempered now, however, because I am also more familiar with research as a discipline and as a way to understand the world and our experience in it.

Research as a means of knowing dominates our society. It influences every aspect of our lives, from the purity of the water we drink to the size of the federal budget. It has an authoritative influence on educational and social policy. To understand research and to know how to critique it are valuable assets in the pursuit of personal and social goals. Therefore, this course aims to increase conversational and critical skills in the use of research. As the syllabus indicates, we are going to use research for purposes we value.

Please access the texts as soon as possible and do the required reading. Most of the course activities are guided practice in the application of knowledge about research. No one has to be an expert, but if you have not done the necessary reading, this experience will be confusing. In addition, you will not be able to participate in discussions, which are essential to our shared learning. The first few classes will be much like a clinic. We will find out what we know and what we need and want to know about research.

Course Purpose

The purpose of this course is to develop an understanding of the primary assumptions, perspectives, and methods that guide research in the social sciences. This course also provides a framework and literacy for understanding and evaluating research studies found in professional journals and reports. Because of the nature of education, action research is offered as a research method to be learned at a level of useful proficiency.

Learning Goals

1. With cultural diversity as part of the context and with collaborative learning as a frequent teaching process, the instructor and students will discuss and explain the usefulness, limitations, advantages, and assumptions of research represented by the following topics:

   a. The nature of human inquiry and the ethics of research

   b. Inductive and deductive theory

   c. Correlation and causality

   d. Research design and operationalization

   e. Reliability and validity

   f. Questionnaire formats

   g. Sampling design

   h. Experimental designs

   i. Survey research

   j. Qualitative research

   k. Unobtrusive research

   l. Evaluative research

 m. Action research

    2. Students will interpret and critique two personally relevant research articles published in such education and social science periodicals as the *Journal of Teacher Education, Equity and Excellence,* and *Anthropology and Education Quarterly.*

    3. Students will construct an action research proposal for a problem of practice in order to know how to design a personal study that examines the outcomes of specific educational interventions and changes.

Course Outline and Calendar for Introduction to Research (eight four-hour sessions)

Date/Session: 1

Topics:	Human inquiry and science; ethics of social research; privilege, politics, and discrimination in research
Activities:	Introductions; review of the syllabus; conducting research among ourselves
Readings:	Chapters 1 and 3 (Babbie)
Assignment Due:	Reaction paper describing a research study that changed your behavior (Directions were e-mailed to you prior to this session.)

Date/Session: 2

Topics:	Research design; conceptualization and operationalization
Activities:	Feedback on 1st paper; reaction panels to controversial research articles; critiques and discussion; practicing operationalization
Readings:	Chapters 4 and 5 (Babbie)
Assignment Due:	Read and bring self-selected controversial research article

Date/Session: 3

Topics:	Indexes, scales, measurement, and sampling
Activities:	Small and whole group practice in evaluating research studies
Readings:	Chapters 6 and 7 (Babbie)
Assignment Due:	Read and bring self-selected research article addressing a personal concern

Date/Session: 4

Topics:	Survey and qualitative research
Activities:	Collaboratively designing research studies; discussion of exemplary research article critiques
Readings:	Chapters 9 and 10 (Babbie)
Assignment Due:	Description of a problem that needs to be researched (posted for class)

(Continued)

Date/Session: 5

Topics:	Evaluation research and quantitative data analysis
Activities:	Practice with elementary statistics, tests of statistical significance and chi square; formative assessment on research vocabulary and social statistics
Readings:	Chapters 12 and 14 (Babbie)
Assignment Due:	First research article critique

Date/Session: 6

Topics:	Qualitative data analysis and action research
Activities:	Feedback on formative assessment and first critique; practice with field research and data processing; discussion of problems of practice and exemplars of action research
Readings:	Chapter 13 (Babbie); Chapters 1 and 2 (Herr and Anderson)
Assignment Due:	Second research article critique

Date/Session: 7

Topics:	Reporting, revising, and writing research
Activities:	Feedback and discussion of second critique; in-class lab to complete first draft of action research proposal
Readings:	Chapter 17 (Babbie); Chapters 3 and 4 (Herr and Anderson)
Assignment Due:	Revised first critiques; First draft of action research proposal

Date/Session: 8

Topics:	Action research, educational change, and professional learning
Activities:	Feedback and discussion of first draft of action research proposal; brief presentations of action research proposals; course assessment; course closure
Readings:	Chapter 5 (Herr and Anderson)
Assignment Due:	Revised second critiques; Final draft of action research proposal is due at this time or no later than three days from this session.

Course Requirements

Attendance

For this eight-week course, only one excused absence is allowed. The course experience deepens engagement with the written material and the research process, provides practice with and demonstrations of relevant applications, and allows for critique and nuanced understanding. Nevertheless, surprises and unexpected challenges are a part of adult life. If something serious requires your absence from class, kindly let me hear from you.

    Students who miss a class are responsible for the complete lesson scheduled for that date, including all work and assignments. If an absence is foreseeable, the student is required to submit all required work and assignments in advance or on the date they are due.

Participation

Please participate on a regular basis. In the whole group as well as in smaller groups, class participation includes offering ideas, opinions, and questions as well as listening carefully, sharing notes, and giving feedback. There are numerous ways in which we have been socialized to participate in groups. In a culturally diverse learning community such as ours, being sensitive to different ways to share information, make connections, and comment is necessary for social comfort as well as deeper learning.

Assignments

Because we are very interdependent in this course, and apply and practice our learning in class, written assignments are required on their due dates. Late assignments require a written excuse from the student with a due date that has been approved by the instructor. If assignments remain incomplete beyond the agreed-upon date, course credit will not be given. Due dates are specified in the course calendar.

Assessment and Grading Procedures

Your grade for this course is determined by an evaluation of three assignments according to the percentage values found below. Each assignment is assessed with a rubric. The rubrics are designed to facilitate your planning and self-direction. Models of excellent (A) and satisfactory (C) assignments by past students from this course will be provided to offer examples for discussion of the rubric criteria.

Please note that you will receive nongraded feedback on your first reaction paper (due the first class session) and on a formative assessment given in the fifth class session. I will use these evaluations to communicate assessments of the quality of your writing, research vocabulary, and understanding of commonly used social statistics. This feedback is information concerning both the quality of your knowledge about research and those areas in which you may need further study and practice.

Although this course is only eight weeks long, there is opportunity to revise each research article critique once, as well as the first draft of the action research proposal. Unless you prefer the grade on your first drafts of assignments, grades will be calculated only from your revised work. Feedback on the first draft of the action research proposal will be available online within two days after the seventh class session. Because learning how to do and evaluate research is cumulative and represents your overall integration of knowledge and skills, the percentage of a grade's value for later assignments is higher than for earlier assignments.

	Example 1	**Example 2**
First research article critique (20 percent)	B (3.0) × .2 = .6	C (2.0) × .2 = .4
Second research article critique (30 percent)	B (3.0) × .3 = .9	B (3.0) × .3 = .9
Action research proposal (50 percent)	A (4.0) × .5 = 2.0	A (4.0) × .5 = 2.0
	Grade = A– or 3.5	Grade = B+ or 3.3

A = 3.7 to 4.0
A– = 3.4 to 3.6
B+ = 3.2 to 3.3
B = 3.0 to 3.1
B– = 2.7 to 2.9
C+ = 2.3 to 2.6
C = 2.0 to 2.2
C– = 1.7 to 1.9
D+ = 1.3 to 1.6
D = 1.0 to 1.2
F = .9 and below

(Continued)

Rubric for Research Article Critique

Excellent (A): Critique contains an organized rationale that assesses the validity, reliability, sampling, and research design of the study. Strengths and weaknesses of the study are clearly indicated. Alternative ways to strengthen the study are specifically noted. Conclusions drawn from the study's findings are critiqued for their relationship to the researcher's proposed theory and their application to real life. Writing is clear and grammatically correct.

Very Good (B): Critique contains an organized rationale that assesses the validity, reliability, sampling, and research design of the study. Strengths and weaknesses of the study are indicated but their rationale is, at times, too diffuse or unconvincing. Alternative ways to strengthen the study are noted. Conclusions drawn from the study's findings are critiqued for their relationship to the researcher's proposed theory and their application to real life. Writing is clear and grammatically correct.

Satisfactory (C): Critique contains an organized rationale that assesses the validity, reliability, sampling, and research design of the study. Strengths and weaknesses of the study are indicated but their rationale is, at times, too diffuse or unconvincing. Also, alternative ways to strengthen the study are missing or inadequately addressed. Conclusions drawn from the study's findings are critiqued for their relationship to the researcher's proposed theory and their application to real life. Writing is clear and grammatically correct.

Marginally Acceptable (D): Critique contains an organized rationale that assesses the validity, reliability, sampling, and research design of the study. Strengths and weaknesses of the study are indicated but their rationale is too diffuse or unconvincing. Alternative ways to strengthen the study are missing or inadequately addressed. Conclusions drawn from the study's findings are critiqued but lack sufficient analysis regarding their relationship to the researcher's proposed theory and their application to real life. Writing is, at times, appreciably vague or obviously grammatically incorrect.

Fail (F): Critique contains a rationale that assesses three or fewer of the following qualities of the study: validity, reliability, sampling, and research design. Strengths and weaknesses of the study are indicated but their rationale is too diffuse or unconvincing. Alternative ways to strengthen the study are missing or inadequately addressed. Conclusions drawn from the study's findings are critiqued but lack sufficient analysis regarding their relationship to the researcher's proposed theory and their application to real life. Writing is frequently vague or obviously grammatically incorrect.

Rubric for Action Research Proposal

Excellent (A):

1. Connection to existing research and theory is clear and logical.
2. Relevance to the local setting is obvious and specifically applied to a problem of practice.
3. Research design is sound.
4. Sampling and means of data collection should result in relevant findings.
5. Writing is clear and grammatically correct.

Very Good (B):

1. Connection to existing research and theory is clear and logical.
2. Relevance to the local setting is obvious and specifically applied to a problem of practice.

3. Research design has no more than one obvious error.

4. Sampling or means of data collection may need revision to result in relevant findings.

5. Writing is clear and grammatically correct.

Satisfactory (C):

1. Connection to existing research and theory is clear and logical.

2. Relevance to the local setting is obvious and specifically applied to a problem of practice.

3. Research design has no more than two obvious errors.

4. Sampling or means of data collection will need revision to result in relevant findings.

5. Writing is clear and grammatically correct.

Marginally Acceptable (D):

1. Connection to existing research and theory is clear and logical.

2. Relevance to the local setting is not obvious or not specifically applied to a problem of practice.

3. Research design has no more than two obvious errors.

4. Sampling or means of data collection will need revision to result in relevant findings.

5. Writing is, at times, appreciably vague or obviously grammatically incorrect.

Fail (F):

1. Connection to existing research and theory is not clear and logical.

2. Relevance to the local setting is not obvious or not specifically applied to a problem of practice.

3. Research design has more than two obvious errors.

4. Sampling or means of data collection will need revision to result in relevant findings.

5. Writing is frequently vague or obviously grammatically incorrect.

Course Policies

Because most of these policies are legal codes that vary widely and are often the exclusive prerogative of the individual institution or state, we have chosen not to exemplify them here. Nevertheless, every instructor must include these formal statements where necessary and appropriate.

Suggestions for Learning in This Course

Because this is an intensive course, it is tightly organized and has less room than a conventional course (sixteen weeks) for catching up if you fall behind. Doing the required reading and assignments on time will contribute greatly to your understanding and application of research knowledge and skills. Please do take advantage of all the opportunities for feedback and revision of your work. Very few of us can do anything approaching excellence on the first attempt. Practice and revision are normal parts of everyone's learning.

There will be many opportunities for collaborative learning. As a community of learners we can help one another and deepen these essential skills for work as well. Staying on schedule, cooperating and supporting one another, and using feedback to practice and improve are the things that students report as being essential to completing this course and helping it become a special learning experience—and to use a simple distribution, that is 90 percent of past students! Thank you for the pleasure of working with you to join them.

• • •

Establishing inclusion is an ongoing challenge. It involves finding ways for adult learners to know they are respected and part of a community that genuinely engages their experience and perspectives for learning. As this chapter and its sample syllabus indicate, establishing inclusion is not just a few strategies. It is a cohesive set of instructional practices from the beginning to the end of every class throughout an entire course. Now let us take a look at how to further enhance adult motivation and learning through the next motivational condition, developing a positive attitude.

Chapter 5

Developing Positive Attitudes Toward Learning

"Everything can be taken ... but one thing, the last of the human freedoms—to choose one's attitude in any given set of circumstances."

VIKTOR FRANKL (2006, p. 66)

IT SEEMS A reasonable responsibility for us, as instructors, to influence student attitudes toward learning. However, our explanations and attempts at persuasion are not enough to shift student attitudes. Rather, the conditions and consequences involved in learning make the real difference—the *process* and *outcomes* are what make an impact on learners. Students are aware of these salient features of their learning environment, and therefore they—rather than we—control their attitudes.

In general, it is probably best not to try to talk adults into learning. There are far more powerful things we can do in the presentation of the subject matter and in our treatment of adults to help them build positive attitudes toward their learning and themselves as learners. This chapter will examine a number of strategies that encourage adults to look forward to learning and, perhaps more important, feel eager to learn more.

Four Important Attitudinal Directions

Adult attitudes usually focus on one or more of four directions: (1) toward the instructor, (2) toward the subject, (3) toward their self-efficacy for learning, and (4) toward the specific learning goal or performance. Together, these attitudes influence adult intentions to learn. They reflect the volitional (self-motivated) processes of *self-regulation theory*: self-efficacy, outcome expectations, task interest and value, and goal orientation

TABLE 5.1

Attitudinal Directions

Perception +	Judgment →	Emotion →	Behavior
I see my instructor (attitude toward the instructor).	He seems helpful.	I feel appreciative.	I cooperate.
The instructor announces the beginning of a new unit on family relations (attitude toward the subject).	I value learning more about being an effective parent.	I feel interested.	I pay attention.
It is my turn to present my project to the seminar (attitude toward self-efficacy for learning).	I am knowledgeable and well prepared for this task.	I feel confident.	I give a smooth and articulate presentation.
The instructor is giving a surprise quiz (attitude toward the learning goal or performance).	I haven't studied. I'm not prepared for this quiz.	I feel anxious and frustrated.	I can't think well. I do poorly on the quiz.

(Zimmerman and Kitsantas, 2005). We as instructors need to understand these attitudinal directions in the context of the cultural beliefs, values, and norms that adults bring to a learning situation.

Because of its usefulness for instruction, we have retained the basic interpretation of an *attitude* as a combination of a perception and a judgment that often results in an emotion that influences behavior (Ellis, 1989). The examples in Table 5.1 illustrate the possible influences that attitudes can have on behavior and performance in learning tasks.

Whenever we instruct, we want to establish a learning environment in which these four important attitudinal directions are positive and unified for the learner. We want adults to respect us, to find the subject appealing, and to feel confident that they can successfully learn from the specific task before them. If any one of these four attitudinal directions becomes seriously negative for adults, their motivation to learn can be impaired.

As instructors we should be aware of what can be done to influence learner attitudes positively at the beginning of any learning experience. Their attitudes will be there from the very start. Having learners' attitudes work for them offers the best chance for motivated learning. Although most of the following strategies can be implemented throughout the learning experience, the discussion here will stress their use at the beginning of learning activities.

Creating a Positive Attitude Toward the Instructor

Ask any adult learner—a negative attitude toward an instructor, whether the learning is online or face-to-face, makes that instructor a barrier between the material to be learned and the learner.

Instead of feeling at ease because a respected instructor is offering an appealing lesson, the learner may feel dissonance because a disliked instructor is offering such an engaging lesson. In such cases, the student will probably not give the instructor the benefit of the doubt and will find the lesson less appealing.

As discussed in Chapter Three, the core characteristics of expertise, empathy, and cultural responsiveness will be major influences in establishing students' positive attitudes toward an instructor. Because the learners' relationship to the instructor bears strongly on their feelings of inclusion, the strategies for creating positive student attitudes toward the instructor were presented in Chapter Four. The strategies in that chapter that are likely to enhance learners' attitudes toward the instructor are the following:

- Allow for introductions (Strategy 1).

- Concretely indicate your cooperative intentions to help adults learn (Strategy 3).

- Acknowledge different ways of knowing and different levels of knowledge or skill to engender a respectful learning environment (Strategy 9).

- Create a clear, inviting, and inclusive course syllabus (Strategy 10).

Building a Positive Attitude Toward the Subject

Consider the following subjects: English, math, and psychology. Which one evokes the strongest emotional response? Is it a positive or negative feeling? Every time we hear the name of a subject or a topic, especially one we have to study, it elicits an attitude. If we have had past difficulty with learning in a particular subject area, we may have feelings that range from apprehension to dismay, two emotions that can tilt our judgment more negatively and lead to resistant behavior. In addition, under many circumstances, new learning often asks us to become temporarily dependent, to open our minds to new ideas, to rethink certain beliefs, and to try different ways of doing things. This may be threatening for us, and our attitudes can easily lock in to support our resistance. Instructors as well as students are vulnerable to these patterns. In an intensive course, which may last only five weeks, diffusing a learner's negative attitude is challenging and requires early action. Whatever we can do to minimize negative attitudes and to foster positive attitudes toward the subject and its instructional process will improve the student's chances for learning. The following strategies are a means to this end.

Strategy 11: Eliminate or Minimize Any Negative Conditions That Surround the Subject

Robert Mager (1968) once wrote that people learn to avoid the things they are "hit with." It is a common fact of learning that when a person is presented with an item or subject, and is at the same time in the presence of negative and unpleasant conditions, that item or subject becomes a stimulus for avoidance behavior. Adults often associate things or subjects that frighten them with antagonists and situations that make them uncomfortable, tense, or scared. Therefore, it is best not to associate the subject with any of the following conditions, which tend to support negative learner attitudes and repel adult interest:

- *Pain:* acute physical and psychological discomfort, such as from continuous failure (when learner effort makes no difference), poorly fitting equipment, or uncomfortable room temperature

- *Fear and anxiety:* distress and tension resulting from anticipation of the unpleasant or dangerous, such as threat of failure or punishment, public exposure of ignorance, or unpredictability of potential negative consequences

- *Frustration:* an emotional reaction to the blockage or defeat of purposeful behavior, as occurs when information is presented too quickly or too slowly or when the learner receives unannounced tests (euphemistically called "surprise quizzes") or inadequate feedback on performance

- *Humiliation:* an emotional reaction to being shamed, disrespected, or degraded, as occurs when a person receives sarcasm, insults, sexist comments, or is publicly compared to another student because of inadequate learning

- *Boredom:* a cognitive and emotional reaction to a situation in which stimuli impinging on a learner are weak, repetitive, irrelevant, or infrequent, as occurs when learning situations lack variety, cover unimportant material, or contain excessively predictable discussion respondents (the same people talking over and over again)

This list is quite dismal. However, just as we have to wipe a slate clean before we can set down clear and lucid new writing, we must remove these negative conditions from the learning environment before positive conditions can take root. Otherwise, the mere presence of such oppressive elements can contaminate and diffuse the best efforts of motivating instructors.

Strategy 12: Scaffold Complex Learning

Scaffolding is giving clues, information, prompts, reminders, and encouragement at the appropriate time and in the appropriate amounts, and then gradually allowing learners to do more and more independently. Most of us naturally scaffold when we teach someone to drive a car or play a card game. The *zone of proximal development* (ZPD) is the phase in a learning task when a learner can benefit from assistance (Wertsch, 1991). The upper limit of the zone is the place at which the learner can perform the task independently; the lower limit is the place at which the learner can perform the task but needs assistance.

Most of us learned to drive a car with someone in the passenger seat who prompted and reminded us of what to do and when to do it as we navigated the road. In the beginning, this "coach" usually had to scaffold intensely: "Check your speedometer," "I think you might be speeding," "Watch out for that car," and so on. At this time, we were obviously in the lower limit of our ZPD for driving. But most of us eventually required less coaching; we reached the upper limit of our ZPD and began to drive independently.

Many other learning tasks can benefit from scaffolding. Whether adults are learning to solve math problems, conduct experiments, or use a personal computer, our assessing their zones of proximal development and structuring the appropriate scaffolds can lead to their success. Adults deeply appreciate the support such assisted learning offers because it tends to be concrete, immediate, and tailored to their obvious needs. The following are some of the methods to scaffold more complex learning (Tappan, 1998). The description of each method includes an example in which we model assisting students in learning to write a research report.

- *Modeling:* The instructor carries out the skill while the learners observe, or the instructor offers actual examples of learning outcomes, such as finished papers or solved problems. (We ask the learners to read two previously completed student reports. One is excellent, the other is satisfactory.)

- *Thinking out loud:* The instructor states actual thought processes in carrying out the learning task. (We talk about some of the goals and criteria we would consider before writing a report. We ask the learners why one report was considered excellent and the other only satisfactory. We supplement the learners' perceptions with our own.)

- *Anticipating difficulties:* As the learning proceeds, the instructor and learners discuss areas where support is needed and mistakes are more likely to occur. (Because the sections of the report that discuss findings and statistical analyses seem most challenging to learners, we discuss how these sections were completed in the two reports and arrange for prompt feedback on the learners' initial drafts of these sections in their own reports.)

- *Providing prompts and cues:* The instructor highlights, emphasizes, or structures procedural steps and important responses to help learners clearly recognize their place in and importance to the learning task. (We provide an outline for writing a research report with examples from previous reports.)

- *Using dialogue and discussion:* The instructor engages the learners in a conversation in which they can deepen and organize their understanding of concepts and procedures to write the report. The give-and-take of these mutual explorations and viewpoints also involves critique, but in a way that alternates between serious and playful discussion (Brookfield and Preskill, 2005). (We talk with the learners about the research they consider relevant and would like to know more about. We discuss what hypotheses and data their reports should include.)

- *Regulating the difficulty:* The instructor introduces a more complex task with simpler tasks and may offer some practice with these. (Using the previous discussion as a context, we give the learners a basic research scenario, a hypothesis, data, and an analysis scheme, and ask them to individually write a brief research report with this information.)

- *Using reciprocal teaching and practice:* The instructor and the learners rotate the role of instructor; in the instructor's role, each learner provides guidance and suggestions to others. (While we monitor, each learner presents his or her brief research report to a learning partner who acts as the instructor and gives supportive feedback. Then they reverse roles. The same process will be carried out with the first draft of their actual research reports.)

- *Providing a checklist:* Learners use self-checking procedures to monitor the quality of their learning (Gawande, 2009). (We give the learners a checklist of questions and quality criteria to consider as they write their reports.)

Possible metaphors for the provider of assisted learning are "sensitive tutor" and "seasoned coach": people who tell us just enough, what we need to know when we need to know it, trusting us to chart the rest of our journeys to learning. This image is not one of the rugged individualist or the solitary explorer. Rather, assisted learning evokes a vision of possibility nurtured by a caring instructor and community.

Developing Self-Efficacy for Learning

Self-efficacy is a personal assessment of one's own capability to perform a specific task (Bandura, 1997). Self-efficacy beliefs are stronger predictors of adult behavior than are such perceptions as self-concept and self-esteem, which are more general and have less specific meaning (Bong and Skaalvik, 2003). Some learners may not have a negative attitude toward their instructor or the subject, but they may believe they lack the capability to successfully learn from the task at hand. Adults who hold such perceptions have low self-efficacy for that learning goal, and their motivation to learn is usually diminished for the activity or course.

As instructors, we need to remember that adult perceptions of self-efficacy are always situation specific. A person might feel quite physically adept but very incompetent in academic situations. This kind of variation exists within academic subjects as well: a learner might feel quite superior in English and very inferior in math. Adults constantly modify their self-efficacy beliefs in specific areas of learning, which means that instructors can use various strategies during classes to positively influence learners' self-estimation.

Strategy 13: Help Learners to Realize Their Personal Control of Learning

For students to build self-efficacy from learning experiences, they need to realize that they are the ones most responsible for their learning. In this regard, it is necessary that students feel a sense of personal causation in the process of learning—and that they perceive themselves to have control over how, what, and when they learn (Plaut and Markus, 2005). It is to our advantage as instructors that adults are inclined toward autonomy in many aspects of their daily lives. In the United States individual responsibility is a strongly valued norm for adults. Once motivated, most adults will personally bring energy and direction to their own learning. The following methods, when combined, can significantly increase their sense of personal causation while learning:

- *Learners plan and set goals for learning.* Planning validates the learners as guides of their learning process. The section Establishing Challenging and Attainable Learning Goals later in this chapter offers specific strategies for how to do this.

- *To the extent appropriate, learners make choices about what, how, with whom, where, and when to learn something.* Choice permits learners to feel greater ownership of the learning experience. They can choose topics, assignments, with whom to learn, when to be evaluated, how to be evaluated, and so forth.

- *Learners use self-assessment procedures.* When learners can appraise their own mistakes and successes while learning, they experience a concrete sense of participation in and responsibility for that learning. See Strategy 45 in Chapter Seven for an elaboration of this method.

- *Learners have access to prompt feedback.* Prompt feedback while learning leads to stronger feelings of personal control and self-efficacy. This is one of the main reasons some online instruction programs can be so powerful for increasing motivation: the computer program can give immediate feedback so that learners have moment-to-moment awareness of their progress in learning. This constant back-and-forth dialogue between the software program and the learners gives them a strong sense of control in the learning process. The computer will not respond until the learners make the first move, and the learners' personal control is undeniable. See Strategy 39 in Chapter Seven for numerous ways to make feedback available to learners.

Combining these methods emphasizes that the majority of responsibility for learning is under the learner's control. Personal control is one of the main ways that our brains know to survive (Zull, 2002). In a neurological sense, feeling in control while learning is very motivating.

Strategy 14: Help Learners Attribute Their Success to Their Capability, Effort, and Knowledge

When students have a successful learning experience, it will probably enhance their self-efficacy and their motivation when they believe that the major causes for that success are their own capability, effort, and knowledge. Because learners internally control these causes for successful learning, they can feel genuine pride.

Capability is a stable quality (it lasts), so learners who see themselves as capable can feel more confident when similar learning tasks arise. Effort and knowledge are less stable (sometimes it's difficult to persevere or to remember information), but it is probably these aspects of behavior over which learners feel the most control. When their learning progresses, it makes senses to them that they obviously have been exerting their own combination of capability, effort, and knowledge. The learners' inferred causes for successful learning, such as capability, effort, and knowledge, are called *attributions*. There is considerable research indicating that *to what* learners ascribe their success affects their motivation while learning (Weiner, 2000).

Success in a broad sense can mean passing a test, receiving an excellent grade, completing a fine project, satisfactorily demonstrating a new skill, finding an answer to a problem—any achievement that turns out well in the eyes of the learner. Knowing that study and practice can lead to successful learning and that such efforts are often a matter of will can reduce learners' feelings of helplessness.

When attributions are offered strategically, they can be very effective for helping students acquire a sense of self-efficacy. We want students to believe there are "ways" to learn or perform a task better, to apply their own capability and knowledge to improve learning something—such as outlining, reviewing, practicing, revising, and so on. If this is so, applying reasonable effort in such tasks will make sense to students as a means to improve their learning. Here are some ways to help learners attribute their success to capability, effort, and knowledge:

- Provide learners with learning tasks suitable to their current capabilities. "Just within reach" is a good rule of thumb. These kinds of tasks challenge learners' capabilities and require knowledge and moderate effort for success.

- Before initiating a learning task, stress the importance of learners' persistence and knowledge for success. This should be a reminder and not a threat: for example, "Considering the challenge of this task, we'll have to practice and become proficient before we apply what we know." With this kind of cue, learners are likely to attribute their success to effort and knowledge.

- Send verbal and written messages to accentuate learners' perceptions of capability, effort, and knowledge in relation to their success. To reinforce capability, you might say, "That's a talented performance," or "You seem to be a natural at doing this." To acknowledge effort, you could say, "Great to see your dedication to this work pay off," or "I know a lot of perseverance went into this project." To emphasize knowledge, you might say, "Your skills at problems solving made a real difference," or "Your experience with outlining is apparent in your writing." The great thing about such attributions is that they can be made all the time: before, during, and after a learning task.

Such subjects as math, writing, and art are often thought to be ability driven, when in reality they require learners' application of their own experience, effort, and strategies (Sternberg and others, 2000). For example, knowing there are five interesting ways to begin an essay (with a statistic, quotation, question, anecdote, or revelation) is a strategy that can make starting a new paper an enjoyable challenge rather than an oppressive frustration. Like a motivational explorer, we want to be on the lookout for that moment when we can build learners' self-efficacy through sensitively given attributions.

Strategy 15: Use Relevant Models to Demonstrate Expected Learning

When we began using relevant models, we saw the largest immediate increase in motivation among reluctant and unsure students than when using any other strategy in this chapter.

Many adults find new learning unfamiliar and honestly wonder if they can meet the academic challenges they face. Any time we can provide examples of people similar to the learners who have successfully performed the expected learning activity, we have taken a significant step toward enhancing their self-efficacy. This strategy is originally derived from the research of Bandura (1982, pp. 126–127): "Seeing similar others perform successfully can raise efficacy expectations in observers who then judge that they too possess the capabilities to master comparable activities. Competent models also teach observers effective strategies for dealing with challenging or threatening situations." As an example, for the first day of our intensive research course we have invited three to five past students who represent the demographics of the current students. All of the former students have been successful in the course, and we have duplicated their reports (graded and with written comments) and made them available for the current students. The former students compose a panel and discuss with current students what their beginning attitudes toward the course were (not always positive), how they worked and cooperated to learn, what challenges they faced and overcame, and so forth. If we do not have former students join us, we nevertheless make their selected videos, papers, and projects available for current students to examine and discuss.

If a skill, technique, or discussion can be learned and demonstrated, today's technology enables us to bring it to our students in a visible successful performance that will raise their expectations for success. Research-based studies pertaining to observational learning in academics and athletics offer strong evidence that people who learn vicariously and adapt their model's methods to their own learning are more successful and motivated than those who rely solely on their own individual perception and understanding for learning (Zimmerman and Kitsantas, 2005).

Strategy 16: Encourage Learners

Encouragement is any behavior on our part as an instructor with which we show the learner (1) that we respect the learner as a person, no matter what is learned, (2) that we trust and believe in the learner's effort to learn, and (3) that the learner *can* learn. The primary foundation for encouragement is our caring about and acceptance of the learner. We can encourage the learner in the following ways:

- *For each learning task, demonstrate a realistic expectancy that the learner will learn.* Essentially we are conveying the message, "You can do it," but without implying that the task is easy. Whenever we tell learners that something is easy, we have placed them in a lose-lose dilemma. If they successfully complete the task, they feel no pride because the task was easy in the first place. If they fail, they feel shame because the task was supposed to be simple.

- *Give recognition for effort.* No one learns 100 percent of the time. Some risk is usually involved. We can help by acknowledging learners' effort and by respecting their persistence. Any comment that says, "I like the way you try," can help learners understand that we value their effort. With positive expectations for their learning, comments of this sort can diminish learners' performance anxiety.

- *Emphasize learning from mistakes.* Help adults see a mistake as a way to improve future learning. When we help them learn from a mistake, we directly show them how thinking and trying are in their best interest and that we are confident they will learn.

- *Work with the learner at the beginning of difficult tasks.* Sometimes a learner might be momentarily confused or not know what to do next.

As a form of early scaffolding, our proximity and minimal assistance can be just enough for the learner to find the right direction, continue involvement, and gain the initial confidence to proceed with learning.

- *Affirm the entire process of learning.* We need to acknowledge all parts of the learning endeavor—the studying, the practicing, the cooperating, and so forth. If we wait for the final product—the test results, the project, or any other final goal—we may be too late. In addition, we will have shown that we only value the end, rather than both the means and the end. Learning does not follow a linear progression: there are often wide spaces, deep holes, dead ends, and regressions. Real encouragement says the task of learning is itself important and emphasizes the intrinsic value of the entire learning process.

Establishing Challenging and Attainable Learning Goals

One of the strongest influences on self-efficacy is how the learner interprets and sets the goal for learning, a process that directly influences their expectancy for success (Brophy, 2004). In an intensive course, it is quite possible that a learner could initially like a subject, feel positive toward the instructor, believe she is very effective in the subject, and still not expect to succeed because there is not enough time available to achieve the learning goals. For adults, the decision to invest time in a learning activity may be as important as the decision to invest money or effort (Lowe, 1996).

When expectancy for success is high, and adults can commit to reaching the given learning goals, there is usually an increase in their performance and motivation (Locke and Latham, 2002). When their expectancy for success is low, adults tend to protect their well-being by remaining withdrawn or negative. Instructors often interpret this as apathy or resistance, but for the learners it is usually self-protection, more to do with realistic doubt than with being irascible. In such instances, clearly demonstrating that the learning goal is possible to achieve can be a significant, positive influence on learners' attitudes.

Strategy 17: Make the Criteria of Assessment as Fair and Clear as Possible

Although assessment is thoroughly discussed in Chapter Seven, it is necessary to pay attention to assessment here as an attitudinal issue, because discussion of learning goals and assessment procedures go hand in hand in the beginning of most intensive courses. For most adults, how they are assessed will play a crucial role in determining their expectations for success.

If learners understand the assessment criteria and agree to them as fair, they will know which elements of performance are essential. Assessment criteria help them gauge the relationship between their effort and the learning outcomes of that effort. Therefore, they can more easily self-assess and self-direct their learning as they proceed (Angelo and Cross, 1993).

As the cliché in assessment theory goes, "There are no more secrets!" We want learners to know from day one what assessment looks like, how it's done, and by what criteria their work is appraised. If we sincerely want learners to succeed, they should not have to guess about what is expected of them. From the first day of class, we need to provide examples of concrete learning outcomes—past tests, papers, projects, and media—that we have already evaluated using the same criteria, thus giving learners realistic illustrations of how we have applied them. At this time, we also want to allow for questions and take seriously the suggestions from learners about their assessment.

As you may already have noted, there is a direct connection between this strategy and Strategy 15, using relevant models to demonstrate expected learning. Former students whom you have brought to class or exemplars of their past work have the power to demystify the assessment criteria for current students and inspire their peers to relevant accomplishments. Constructing a syllabus, as described in Strategy 10 in Chapter Four, also bears mention, because the syllabus is where assessment is discussed and outlined, giving students a written understanding of related criteria.

Strategy 18: Help Learners Understand and Plan for the Amount of Time Needed for Successful Learning

In a study exploring why adults leave college before completing their degrees in accelerated and traditional programs, lack of time was the dominant reason in both programs (Wlodkowski, Mauldin, and Campbell, 2002). Adults in this study repeatedly made reference to competing priorities, such as work and family. In general, they did not have enough time to meet the demands of course work, care for their families, and also perform their jobs. A quote from one woman in the study amplifies how overwhelming school can be for adults: "I felt like I was going in four directions at the same time and just finding enough time to drive to school was becoming a problem" (p. 7).

It is often very difficult for adult learners to estimate the amount of time a given course, assignment, or practice regimen might take. Some will overestimate. Some will underestimate. Others will procrastinate, as busy people often do. If a learning activity will require a significant amount of time, it is best for learners to know this, so that they can plan more effectively, avoid procrastination, and begin to set *proximal goals*—goals that make sense and are achievable in the near future with reasonable effort (Brophy, 2004).

As instructors we can, when appropriate, help learners break down or segment their larger or more time-consuming learning goals into subgoals in order to have the sense of self-efficacy to achieve them. For example, we can describe the steps, responsibilities, and timelines for completing a project or reaching proficiency with a particular skill. We can facilitate learners' progress by requesting that they submit representative work, such as rough drafts, outlines, and completed problems or exercises, on given dates to provide feedback and support as they move toward accomplishing their learning goals. In addition, as discussed in Strategy 4 in Chapter Four, cooperative learning is another way for learners to use their mutual support and combined efforts to productively manage time constraints.

Strategy 19: Use Learning Contracts

For individual students, learning contracts can be an excellent means of establishing attainable learning goals. In adult education they have been widely used to foster self-direction, volition, relevant learning, improvement of learning performance, and expectancy for success among adults (Berger, Caffarella, and O'Donnell, 2004). Learning contracts can accommodate individual and cultural differences in regard to experience, perspective, and capabilities (Lemieux, 2001).

Learning contracts tailor the learning process to the individual and provide maximum flexibility in regard to learning content, pace, process, and outcome. They usually detail in writing what will be learned, how the learning will be accomplished, the period of time involved, and the evidence and criteria to be used in assessing the learning. Learners can construct all, most, or part of the contract, depending on the learner's and instructor's knowledge of the subject matter, the resources available, the restrictions of the program, and so on. For example, what is learned (the objective) may not be negotiable, but how it is learned may be wide open to individual discretion.

The contract document usually consists of the categories shown here (Berger, Caffarella, and O'Donnell, 2004):

1. *Learning goal.* (What are you going to learn?) For further elaboration see Strategy 5.

2. *Choice of resources, strategies, and activities for learning.* (How are you going to learn it?)

3. *Target date or timeline for completion.*

4. *Evidence of accomplishment.* (How are you going to demonstrate your learning?)

5. *Evaluation criteria and validation of learning.* (What criteria will be used to evaluate the learning, and how and by whom will the evidence of learning be evaluated and confirmed?)

The following is an example of a learning contract. It covers a specific skill to be accomplished in a short period of time in an undergraduate communication skills course.

Sample Contract: Paraphrasing Skills

Learning goal: apply and learn paraphrasing skills for actual communication situations.

Learning resources, and activities: view videotapes of paraphrasing scenarios. Complete one hour of role-playing paraphrasing situations with peers.

Target date or timeline for completion: one week (dates specified).

Evidence of accomplishment: participate in paraphrasing exercises under the instructor's supervision and monitoring.

Evaluation criteria and validation of learning: contribute appropriate paraphrasing responses to 80 percent of the communications from peers. Eighty percent of the responses should reflect the meaning of these communications, as assessed by the instructor.

Composing a learning contract is a learned skill, and with an intensive course, there may be less time to write and negotiate learning contracts. From the outset, however, learners will need clear guidelines for developing contracts with diverse examples of a variety of learning processes (writing, researching, calculating, and so on) and outcomes (papers, projects, case studies, and so on) (Berger, Caffarella, and O'Donnell, 2004). The most challenging part of composing a learning contract is writing the description of the evaluation criteria and validation of learning. Students often need coaching and flexibility from the instructor to construct this element.

Creating Relevant Learning Experiences

As discussed in Chapter Two, for adults to see learning as truly relevant, it has to be connected to who they are, what they care about, and how they perceive and know. If we were to base this book on personal experience alone, we would say the quickest path to boredom and resistance among adult students is teaching an irrelevant lesson to them. Conversely, the fastest avenue to securing their interest and involvement is teaching a relevant lesson to them. Due to our human instinct for survival, our brains just do not tolerate what does not seem to matter to us (Ahissar and others, 1992). As soon as we get a blip on our mental radar of something that strikes us as aimless or senseless or insignificant, we are on our way out biopsychologically. Gone. Those eyeballs glazing over are the real thing. The strategies that follow give us a set of practices to relevantly respond to the learning preferences and differences among diverse adults.

Strategy 20: Use the Entry Points Suggested by Multiple Intelligences Theory as Ways of Learning About a Topic or Concept

Sometimes one of the weaknesses of intensive courses that are taught through standardized modules—preset instructional objectives and learning activities for all faculty who teach the course—is that they offer limited ways to learn about a topic or concept. Often they do not present other possible ways of learning that might be more culturally relevant and accommodating of different intelligences.

We subscribe to the definition of intelligence, offered by Howard Gardner (2006), as the ability to solve problems or to fashion products that are valued in one or more cultural or community settings. Problems may range from creating an end to a mystical story to finding a physics equation that describes the interaction among subatomic particles. Fashioning products entails anything from making delicious food to creating musical compositions to designing computer software. The range appears to be nearly infinite and highlights the reality that intelligence cannot be conceptualized separately from the contexts in which individuals live. There are multiple ways to be capable and to demonstrate intelligence.

According to Gardner, people have the capacity for at least nine intelligences (see Table 5.2). People differ in the strength of these intelligences, however. Some perform best when asked to manipulate symbols of various sorts (linguistic and logical-mathematical intelligences), whereas others are better able to demonstrate their understanding through a hands-on

TABLE 5.2

Gardner's Multiple Intelligences

Intelligence	Example	Core Components
Linguistic	Novelist, journalist	Sensitivity to the sounds, rhythms, and meanings of words; sensitivity to the different functions of written and spoken language
Logical-mathematical	Scientist, accountant	Sensitivity to and capacity to discern logical and numerical patterns; ability to handle long chains of inductive and deductive reasoning
Musical	Composer, guitarist	Ability to produce and appreciate rhythm, tone, pitch, and timbre; appreciation of the forms of musical expressiveness
Spatial	Designer, navigator	Capacity to perceive the visual-spatial world accurately and to perform transformations on one's initial perceptions and mental images
Bodily-kinesthetic	Athlete, actor	Ability to know and control one's body movements and to handle objects skillfully
Interpersonal	Therapist, politician	Capacity to discern and respond appropriately to communicate the moods, temperaments, motivations, and desires of other people
Intrapersonal	Entrepreneur, spiritual leader	Access to one's own feelings and inner states of being, with the ability to discriminate among them and draw on them to guide behavior; knowledge of one's own strengths, weaknesses, desires, and intelligences
Naturalist	Botanist, zoologist	Capacity to recognize and classify plants, animals, minerals, grasses, and objects or phenomena in nature
Existential*	Cosmologist, philosopher	Capacity to conceptualize phenomena and questions beyond sensory evidence, such as the infinite or the genesis of morality

*At the time of this writing, Gardner (2006) has provisionally identified this intelligence.
Source: *Adapted from Viens and Kallenbach, 2004; Moran, Kornhaber, and Gardner, 2006.*

approach (spatial and bodily-kinesthetic intelligences). Rather than possessing a single intelligence, people have a *profile of intelligences* that combine to complete different tasks. The keen ability of the Inupiat hunter to discern sea, stars, and ice from a small boat on the Arctic Ocean meets an intellectual challenge as profound in its own way as that faced by a systems analyst deciphering a federal budget at a computer terminal. The crucial question is not how intelligent is one but how is one intelligent?

In general, the higher education system is heavily biased toward linguistic—and, to a lesser degree, logical-mathematical—modes of instruction. Because people learn in ways that are identifiably distinctive, determined to a large extent by their profiles of intelligences and unique cultural backgrounds, the broad spectrum of learners would be better served if learning involved "rich experiences in which students with different intelligence profiles can interact with materials and ideas using their particular combinations of strengths and weaknesses" (Moran, Kornhaber, and Gardner, 2006, p. 27).

Rich learning experiences are activities in which students personally engage with material rather than trying to understand it only in abstract and decontextualized ways, such as by listening to a lecture. These activities usually include projects, research, and problem solving that are collaborative, allowing students to learn from one another's unique profiles of intelligences as well as their own. For example, a rich learning experience could be a project in which students use sociological concepts to analyze and assess a local political campaign as they work for particular candidates. As they collaboratively study the financing (logical-mathematical and linguistic intelligences), strategizing (linguistic and interpersonal intelligences), and goals (intrapersonal and existential intelligences) of the campaign, the project will deeply engage their diverse profiles of intelligences.

Howard Gardner (1993) and others (Viens and Kallenback, 2004), using multiple intelligences theory to teach adult literacy, propose that most topics can be approached through a variety of "entry points." These engagement activities, roughly speaking, map onto the nine multiple intelligences and grant relevant access to a range of learners. Gardner and his colleagues advocate for thinking of any topic as a room with at least five doors, or entry points. We have used this approach for intensive courses and found that these entry points usually accommodate the wide range of cultural backgrounds and profiles of intelligences found among a diverse group of postsecondary students. Let us look at these five entry points one by one, considering how each might be used to approach a concept in the natural sciences—photosynthesis.

> A *narrational entry point* presents a story or narrative account about the concept in question. In the case of photosynthesis, a learner might describe with appropriate vocabulary this process as it occurs among several plants or trees relevant to his environment, describing differences as they are noted.

A *logical-quantitative entry point* approaches the concept by invoking numerical considerations or deductive and inductive reasoning processes. The student could approach photosynthesis by creating a timeline of the steps of photosynthesis and a chemical analysis of the process.

A *foundational entry point* explores the philosophical and terminological facets of a concept. This approach is appropriate for people who like to pose fundamental questions of the sort that one often associates with young children and philosophers. A student using a foundational corridor to photosynthesis might examine an experience that was transformative for herself or a relevant individual, family, or institution, and compare that experience with the process of photosynthesis, assigning parallel roles as they fit (source of energy, catalyst, and so on).

With an *esthetic entry point,* the emphasis falls on sensory or surface features that appeal to learners who favor an artistic approach to life. In the case of photosynthesis, the student could look for visual, musical, or literary transformations that imitate or parallel photosynthesis, and represent them in artistic formats (for example, a painting, dance, mime, video, cartoon, or dramatic sketch).

The last is an *experiential entry point.* Some people learn best with a hands-on approach, dealing directly with the materials that embody or convey the concept. Such individuals might, for example, carry out a series of experiments involving photosynthesis.

For intensive courses, especially those that are project driven, using two or three of these entry points early in the course improves the chances that diverse learners with different ways of knowing and differing intelligence profiles can find relevant and engaging ways of learning. The use of technology, such as films, the Internet, and interactive software, can further enhance these efforts.

Our experience with these entry points is that they generally provide a more effective instructional approach than learning styles theories do for engaging culturally different adult learners. Learning styles appear to vary across tasks and situations (Cassidy, 2004). For example, in ethics a person might prefer knowing a moral principal before applying it to his life circumstances, but in the realm of education he might prefer using a particular teaching method and seeing its results before understanding the theory behind it. Exhibit 5.1 presents one more example of a concept approached from five entry points.

EXHIBIT 5.1

Learning Activities Based on the Five Entry Points from Multiple Intelligences Theory

Concept: All living things are systemically related.
Related principle: All human behaviors affect the earth.

Entry Point	Example
Narrational	Report incidents that show effects of human behavior on distant places. Identify behaviors according to whether they harm or benefit the planet. Based on interests generated, select relevant reading materials.
Logical-quantitative	Choose a harmful but necessary human systemic influence, such as carbon emissions. After finding data that quantify the effects from this systemic influence, search for cultural, economic, and political factors (from a country of interest) that inhibit or exacerbate this influence.
Foundational	Reflect on your influence on the local environment. Consider which behaviors improve the environment and which pollute it. Examine the beliefs and values that appear critical to each set of behaviors. Create a personal environmental philosophy.
Esthetic	Choose from the following options: create a sketch, a photo journal, or a video to depict relevant systemic relationships in your environment.
Experiential	Create mini-environments in a yard or terrarium. Experiment with such influences as temperature, water, pollutants, and pets. Observe and report their effects on various life forms.

Source: *Adapted from Wlodkowski, 2008.*

Strategy 21: Use the K-W-L Strategy to Introduce New Topics and Concepts

The *K-W-L strategy* is an immediate way to make a new topic or concept relevant to adult learners, based on their prior knowledge (Ogle, 1986). This method engages their anticipation and curiosity with three questions—What do I already *know*?, What do I *want* to know?, and What have I *learned*? Adults have a storehouse of experiences that can give extraordinary meaning to novel ideas. The K-W-L strategy offers a simple and direct way to probe their vast reservoir of knowledge.

During the first phase of the strategy, the learners identify what they *know* about the topic. Whether the topic is the gross domestic product, phobias, or acid rain, this is a nonthreatening way to list some of the unique ways adults understand the topic. It allows for multiple perspectives and numerous historical contexts. Just think of what the possibilities might be for a diverse group of adults initiating a unit on immigration law. The discussion of what adults *know* about a topic can involve drawing, storytelling, describing critical incidents, and making predictions.

In the second phase, the learners suggest what they *want* to know about the topic. This information may be listed as questions or as subtopics for exploration and research. For example, if the topic were immigration law, some questions might be: Where do most immigrants come from today? Where did most come from ten years ago? Fifty years ago? What was the last significant immigration law enacted by Congress? And so on. These questions can serve as ideas for using the five entry points discussed in Strategy 20. For example, a student could use a narrational entry point to look at immigration history or the experiential and logical-quantitative entry points to conduct research on recent immigration patterns.

In the last phase, the learners identify what they have *learned,* which may comprise the answers to their questions; important related information; and new information that counters, confirms, or deepens their prior knowledge.

● ● ●

In this chapter, we have looked at numerous ways to help students build more positive attitudes toward learning in intensive courses. When your subject is relevant and adults want to learn what is before them, you have an excellent beginning for a successful learning experience. In order to foster such an appealing motivational environment, it is important for the learners' attitudes to be positive—toward you, the subject, their own self-efficacy, and the specific learning goal. Selecting and carrying out the strategies from this chapter early in your instructional design can create this advantage.

Chapter 6
Enhancing Meaning in Learning

"Nothing contributes so much to tranquilize the mind as a steady purpose—a point on which the soul may fix its intellectual eye."

MARY SHELLEY (2009)

FOR LEARNERS, PAYING attention is the first step in making meaning. Focused attention becomes *engagement* when it is persistent and joins with emotion, primarily interest, as well as metacognitive processes, such as learning strategies, to involve the person in learning. This combination of behavioral (persistence), emotional (interest), and cognitive (strategy) processing makes engaged learning more likely to be retained (Woolfolk, 2007). Furthermore, academically engaged adult learners are more likely to be successful in higher education (National Survey of Student Engagement, 2007). Without engagement, learning does not have a chance to have deeper meaning—to infuse the experience with a steady purpose that matters to learners and is relevant to their beliefs and values.

Because interest has such a powerful influence on adult engagement in learning, we will take a close look at this emotion. One understanding of interest is that it results from our basic curiosity. We feel interested when we find things that are unique or novel, or possess elements of unpredictability or surprise. Whether it is solving a puzzle or hearing a captivating story, each experience will have its moments of novelty and surprise to pique our curiosity and evoke our interest.

Individual or personal interest emerges when a person sustains engagement in a learning experience and acquires positive feelings about, knowledge of, and value for its content, wanting to reengage with that particular content or activity whenever other opportunities arise (Brophy, 2004). Students often exhibit individual interest in a topic when it encompasses their cultural values or social concerns. Personal significance is often a bridge to deeper meaning for learners. For example, if you ask the question, "Why is psychology important?," students might be curious in an abstract sort of way. But if you ask, "How has psychology helped or hindered people in our families?," students are now more likely to join their curiosity with more penetrating understanding.

Research indicates that individual interests as a context for learning have benefits for the learner, which include greater resourcefulness while learning and perseverance to work in the face of frustration (Renninger and Shumar, 2002; Prenzel, 1992). Luis Moll's research with Mexican American families identifies *funds of knowledge*, which comprise valued information from the work, home, and spiritual lives of family and community members that can be rich resources for adult individual interests (Moll, Amanti, Neff, and Gonzalez, 1992). Below are a few questions that may be helpful to bring out these funds of knowledge from among culturally diverse adult learners (Ginsberg, 2007):

- How does your life in your community differ from your life in college? (Follow-up questions could then probe those differences.)

- What is important in your culture or family that you would like your instructors to know about?

- What are some of the skills or talents in your home or community that you value or are proud of?

- What interesting or important topics do you talk about at home that you seldom talk about in your courses?

Enhancing Meaning Through Engagement and Challenge

Engagement is not a one-dimensional process. It varies from just barely paying attention with low cognitive and emotional involvement, such as when listening to an important but boring lecture at which you have to constantly shift in your seat to stay alert and repeatedly remind yourself to pay attention, to deep and total absorption, such as when interviewing a respected and controversial leader in a profession to which you aspire. During the interview, time has flown by and you've been so focused on her responses that you might have forgotten to ask the questions you needed to. The latter scenario is an example of *vital engagement*, which is "characterized both by experiences of flow (enjoyed absorption) and by meaning (subjective significance)" (Nakamura and Csikszentmihalyi, 2003, p. 87). For enhancing meaning among adult learners, vital engagement is an ideal state of learning that involves *challenge*; it creates a valued relationship to learning that stretches learners' capacities while completely occupying their interest and participation.

Challenge is an opportunity for engagement that offers such possibilities as deeper understanding, more refined thinking, more complex perceptions, better performance, higher goal attainment, new knowledge, and improved skills. Challenge occurs when we have to apply current knowledge or skills to situations that require further extension or development of them. Engaging in challenging learning activities is among the best and most productive ways to learn (Donovan, Bransford, and Pellegrino, 1999; Mezirow, 2000; Nakamura and Csikszentmihalyi, 2003).

Maintaining Learners' Attention

The strategies in this chapter are organized according to the degree of engagement they tend to enhance. In intensive courses, with their long blocks of time when interest is more likely to wane and adults may feel fatigued from prior work, these strategies can be a kindness as well as a necessity. We begin with those strategies to be used when engagement may be waning—those we can use to gain and maintain adult learners' attention.

Strategy 22: Provide Frequent Response Opportunities for All Learners

Paying attention in a class that may last as long as four hours can defy human will, even for those students who are interested and value what they are learning. As Friedrich Nietzsche (1920) wrote, "Even the gods struggle in vain against boredom." However, if learners have response opportunities and know they are going to respond in a given class session, they have an incentive for focusing their attention. Along with personal interest, awareness of the social consequences of their responsiveness helps them pay attention. Response opportunities are any chances that an instructor or learning activity provides for learners to participate or perform publicly (Kerman, 1979). These include answering questions, giving opinions, demonstrating skills, and reacting to feedback. Some guidelines for effectively using response opportunities are as follows:

- Announce to the learners that you would like to have as many people participating as possible, but that it is OK to "pass." This gives everyone a choice, keeps the discussion or activity safe, and particularly respects those adults who have not been socialized to respond in front of groups. It also creates an expectancy that keeps students prepared and alert. People do not like to be caught off-guard.

- When asking a question or announcing an opportunity to perform a task, wait at least three seconds or more before selecting a respondent (Tobin, 1987). This technique allows everyone to consider the possible answer or skill to be demonstrated. It gives learners a chance to organize themselves mentally and emotionally for their responses.

- When you are looking for a volunteer, ask for a show of hands and wait three to five seconds after the first volunteer raises a hand before selecting a respondent. This technique has the same advantages as the previous one, and it increases the number of possible respondents from which to choose. If we tend to call on the first few volunteers, we often unwittingly "teach" the rest of the learners not to volunteer.

- For longer responses and demonstrations of some duration, alert the rest of the learning community that they will be asked to respond in some fashion to what they have observed. For example: "After Jawed has presented his case study, I'd like to ask a few of you to give him your evaluation of which consultant skills were critical to his success with his client." This method invests the entire learning community in the task at hand and affirms their responsibility to their peers.

- Sometimes use light, humorous, unpredictable methods for selecting a respondent. For example: "The next people to get a chance are all those with birthdays in February," or "Well, let's see who had toast for breakfast. OK, we've got three volunteers." Or ask someone, "What's your favorite color? Blue; that's great. Now check in your group to see who is wearing the most blue, because that's who will begin the next problem for us."

- During any task for which learners are working on their own or in small groups, move among them as an available resource and observer. Depending on the situation, you can comment, question, react, advise, or quietly observe. This can prevent learners from feeling isolated in their work and will let you provide more response opportunities for them.

Strategy 23: Help Learners Realize Their Accountability for What They Are Learning

People tend to take more seriously the learning for which they are held accountable (Good and Brophy, 2003). They are more likely to find the will to remain attentive when they know that the knowledge and skills they will eventually demonstrate are directly dependent on their learning experiences. However, adults can construe accountability as a coercive force for paying attention. If you mention exams and final projects as being related to their learning tasks, for example, they may feel threatened. Their anxiety is real. We have all felt it. Therefore, we use accountability to enlist learners' attention only when necessary and in an empathic manner, not as a menacing manipulation.

One of the best ways to ensure that we are using accountability appropriately is to be careful that the components of the curriculum or instructional design are interdependent and necessary for achieving and assessing the learning goal. In this way, the learners know that *all* the learning activities are valuable and will help them develop the competencies they will acquire and exhibit. They will be reassured that there is no busywork and that each learning experience contributes to the desired result.

Show learners that your learning program is efficiently designed to build the requisite skills and knowledge for which they will be held accountable. Use syllabi, outlines, models, diagrams, and key concepts to briefly preview the integrated plan and related learning goals. Indicate how you will assess learners (tests, projects, and so forth) and how the assessment is functionally dependent on the learning process and content. This will help learners understand that their concentration is necessary every step of the way. Intersperse lectures and demonstrations with the *think-pair-share* process (Barkley, Cross, and Major, 2005). This is a short processing method to increase student attention and involvement. The instructor asks learners to *think* briefly about what has been stated or observed and then to *pair* up with someone to *share* their reflections for a few minutes. For example: "Please take a minute to think about how this material relates to your own life. Then turn to a partner and have a brief conversation about your reflections." This is a collaborative way to engage students during any passive learning experience with a thoughtful procedure that invites their perspectives and dialogue. After completion of this procedure, you can begin a whole-group discussion; solicit comments, list insights, take questions, or move on to the next segment of the lecture or demonstration.

Strategy 24: Provide Variety in the Processes of Instruction and in Learning Materials

People tend to pay more attention to things that are changing than to things that are unchanging. However, to use variety simply for the sake of variety is not a good idea, because learning often requires continuing concentration for further understanding and retention (Sweller, van Merrienboer, and Paas, 1998). That is why microscopes and photographs are so valuable to people in the pursuit of knowledge. They can hold an image steady for our examination and reflection. However, even with these methods we may need to refocus attention so students can restore their interest and energy, but we need to do so without making that change so extreme that it distracts learners from the subject at hand. *Processes of instruction* (sometimes called modes of instruction) include both the ways in which instructors interact with learners and the instructional activities in which learners can participate while they are learning. For example, lecturing, discussing, showing a video, and playing a simulation game are four different processes of instruction. *Learning materials* are the physical resources used to instruct, such as films, books, and computer software. Variety in instructional processes and materials will usually gain the attention of adults. Some suggestions follow:

- Vary the modality of learning between auditory, visual, and experiential modes. For example, learning through listening to recordings (auditory), learning through finding information on graphs (visual), and learning with hands-on experiments (experiential).

- In regard to visual media, it seems that the clearer and simpler the text or diagram, the more effective it is. Parsimoniously using visual aids to draw attention to new or critical information increases their effectiveness (Delahaye and Smith, 1998). Please be careful with PowerPoint, one of the most pervasive technological tools used today. Although it is an attractive format for outlines, models, and diagrams, it can reduce complicated, nuanced issues to overly simplified headings and bullet points (Young, 2009). Varying the intensity of any stimuli (size, shape, color, loudness, and complexity) has also been found to attract learners' attention (Day, 1981).

- Diversify the processes of instruction, designing interactions so that learners think or act differently from one activity to another. For example, they might move from listening to a mini-lecture (no more than twenty minutes) to solving a problem, they might watch a video and then discuss its contents, or they could work alone and then work in small groups. Each of these cases involves different forms of thinking, acting, and communicating. Every time adults alter the process of learning, they use different mental and physical resources, which prevents fatigue and maintains energy. Sometimes, for intensive courses, a change may work as well as a break or a rest.

Strategy 25: Introduce, Connect, and End Learning Activities Attractively and Clearly

A class session is analogous to a sporting event during which each team receives clearly delineated opportunities to exercise its skills. Baseball gives a team three outs to score; football allows four downs to go ten yards. In sports, these units of participation have obvious beginnings and endings to simplify transitions, to focus spectators' and players' attention, and to keep the game running clearly and smoothly. Similarly, a learning activity is significantly enhanced when it is distinctly introduced and clearly connected to previous and future learning activities.

Just as a football kickoff tells the crowd, "Pay attention, the action is about to begin," an attractive introduction to a lesson or activity gives learners the same message.

- *Ask provocative questions.* For example: "How many of you have ever…?" or "What do you think would happen if…?"

- *Call on learners to become active.* Ask them to help, to move, to observe, to assess, and so on.

- *Create anticipation.* For example: "I have been looking forward to doing this activity with you since our course began," or "This next set of problems is really tricky; let's see how we do."

Connecting learning activities is a real art. Because of longer class sessions in an intensive course, instructors make more transitions per class than in a conventional course. Fluid segues help maintain learners' attention and maximize instructional impact. The following are some helpful techniques:

- *Use organizational aids.* As mentioned earlier in this chapter, handouts, outlines, models, and graphs can connect concepts, topics, key points, and essential information.

- *Chunk information.* Working memory is limited to recalling about five to nine unrelated items of information. When we put such information into patterns or chunks, as we do with telephone numbers, we can more easily remember them (Driscoll, 2005). Looking for commonalities and chunking information into categories, such as advantages and disadvantages, similarities and differences, and so on, will help adult learners remember the information as they move on to the next part of the lesson.

- *Indicate to what the new activity relates.* For example: The new activity might continue to build on a previous skill or it might help further demonstrate a concept.

- *Make directions and instructions for the next learning activity as clear as possible.* This technique applies to introducing as well as connecting learning activities. People often stop paying attention simply because they are confused about what they are supposed to do.

- *Check for understanding.* Any time we provide important information—whether it is a concept or a procedure, and especially if what comes next is dependent on this information—we should take a few moments to see if everyone understands. Checking for understanding is usually a simple question, such as, "Are these directions clear enough?" or, "Do you understand how this example fits the concept we've just discussed?"

Closure refers to how we end a learning activity and help learners feel a sense of completion. Some helpful means to this end are as follows:

- *Review the basic concepts or skills achieved during the learning activity.* For example: "Before we move on, let us review the main ideas we have discussed thus far."

- *Allow for clarification at the end of the learning activity.* For example: "Now that we have finished this section, are there any questions about what we have done?"

- *Request feedback, opinions, or evaluation.* For example: "Perhaps the best way to end this exercise would be to share with one another what we have learned from cooperating in this task."

Making Learning Interesting

At this point, we need to remember that *attention, interest,* and *engagement and challenge* may overlap and can occur simultaneously. Whatever gets students' attention may become interesting, and what is interesting could naturally be a part of an engaging and challenging learning activity. Individually and in combination, these factors contribute to the motivational condition of *meaning.* This section describes strategies that can make learning in intensive courses more compelling. We begin with strategies to evoke the personal interests of adult learners.

Strategy 26: Relate Learning to Learners' Interests and Values

By integrating learning activities with adults' current interests and values, we provide them with a constant stream of relevant material. We are exposing them to experiences that will naturally connect to their desire for understanding. In general, the most stirring examples, analogies, supporting evidence, and current events are those that vividly touch on what people already find interesting.

Values represent the important and stable ideas, beliefs, and assumptions that consistently affect a person's behavior (Taylor, Marienau, and Fiddler, 2000). Someone who values politics does not merely vote: that person probably also joins a political organization, donates some amount of money to political causes, writes to political representatives about selected issues, reads about political matters, acts on behalf of political candidates, and frequently talks about politics with friends. Every adult has some strong values. The following topics are areas with which many adults associate firmly held values (Loden and Rosener, 1991):

Politics	Friends	Authority
Ethnicity	Money	Gender
Work	Age	Sex
Leisure	Death	Love
Education	Health	Possessions
Family	Race	Culture
Sexual orientation	Personal tastes	Literature
Clothes	Music	Religion Spirituality
Manners	War, peace	

When these topics become part of the learning experience, adults' emotional responsiveness is likely to increase. On some occasions there may be disagreement or controversy. Please remember that the more learners feel included, and the more they understand and use the participation guidelines (see Strategy 8 in Chapter Four), the more likely they will be able to maintain mutual respect. We have adapted some of Pat Griffin's excellent suggestions for instructor communication during controversial, value-laden discussions (1997):

• *Giving information.* At times, offering factual information in the form of statistics or documented facts is useful. This is often an important way to address misconceptions.

• For example: A learner states that gay men are child molesters. The instructor responds, "That's a frequently held notion that's received a lot of attention over the years. However, police records show that over 90 percent of sexual abuse against children involves heterosexual men molesting female children." Notice that the first statement tends to deflect any listener reaction that this idea belongs only to the learner who made the remark, which helps diminish defensiveness.

- *Conceptualizing.* Feelings can overwhelm people and cause them to shut down or lose focus. The introduction of useful questions can give people a way to understand their feelings and a means to proceed more productively. For example, several learners are arguing back and forth about the degree of racism that continues to exist in the United States. The instructor says, "We have some differences of opinion here. What questions might provide insights or clarify the differences between these viewpoints?" Learners could break into small groups to generate questions, and the instructor could list their questions.

- *Working with silence.* Sometimes silence reflects fear or discomfort. Silences can actually provide a powerful learning opportunity and deepen dialogue. On such occasions, we can ask learners to write down their feelings and thoughts at that moment and then to turn to a partner to share what they are comfortable with communicating. This activity gives learners a chance to acknowledge and clarify their reactions. Sometimes something as simple as commenting on the silence takes the discussion to a deeper level. For example, two adults begin to argue vigorously about the role of the federal government in health care. As their confrontation tails off, silence envelops the learning group. The instructor says, "I'm not sure what this silence means. Why don't we each take a few minutes to write down what we are thinking or feeling right now. Then, to the degree that you're comfortable, talk about it with a partner before we come back to the entire group."

- *Redistributing.* At times, we need to make space for other adults to participate in a discussion.

- For example, the instructor says, "Before we hear from you again, Lynn, I'd like to see if some of the people who haven't had a chance to speak would like to say something."

- *Accepting the expression of feelings.* For some instructors and adult learners, the expression of intense feelings in a learning environment is an unusual experience. At times like this, how we react as instructors will strongly influence all learners' feelings of security and respect. There is no formula. Usually, our reactions are spontaneous. In our own teaching, at such times we have tended to acknowledge and validate learners' expressions of strong feelings. Sometimes appreciation is also appropriate. Ultimately, we need to guide learners to the next phase of learning.

For example, a learner begins to cry as he tells the class about the difficulties his mother endured at school because of a severe disability. The instructor says, "Jamal, that's still a painful memory for you (acknowledgment). It's difficult to see those we love suffer (validation). Thanks for giving us a chance to learn from your own experience (appreciation). Now let's take a look at how we might influence a situation like this as administrators (learning connection)." (It's never this tidy!)

• *Addressing conflict.* There are times when we need to encourage the expression of conflicting ideas. Learner dialogue related to conflicting ideas is an important part of transformative learning (see Transformative Learning section toward the end of this chapter). In productive conflict, all learners have a voice; they are assured their right to express differing perspectives. Mutual respect is maintained, and the participation guidelines are in effect (see Strategy 8 in Chapter Four).

Strategy 27: Clearly State or Demonstrate the Benefits of a Learning Activity

People usually want to know more about anything that benefits them. They often want to be better, quicker, and more creative in doing what they value. There are many things they want to save and gain, such as time and money. Most adults want to overcome their limitations in regard to health, endurance, and speed. Any learning that offers the possibility of acquiring a desired advantage is usually interesting to them.

The most important questions for the instructor are, what real benefits to adults does the planned learning experience offer, and how can I make the benefits apparent and available to them? If we can answer these questions clearly, we have a vital opportunity to increase their interest. For example, it would be difficult for an aspiring technician to remain indifferent to an instructor who introduced learning how to use a new tool by saying, "This instrument can repair 90 percent of all malfunctions in this system."

• • •

The remaining strategies in this section offer ways to evoke situational interest, interest that develops among students because what they are learning has surprising information, unexpected relevance, animating images, or a stimulating narrative. They are probably most applicable to direct instruction, such as presentations and demonstrations, but the first—using humor—is almost always welcome.

Strategy 28: While Instructing, Use Humor Liberally

Humor has many qualities, and being interesting is one of them. People love to laugh. They will be a little more interested in anyone or anything that provides this possibility. Humor offers enjoyment, a unique perspective, and unpredictability—qualities that are attractive and stimulating to most human beings. Probably nothing else can so easily break the potential tedium of a late-night, four-hour class.

But how does one develop a sense of humor? How does an instructor incorporate humor into learning activities? We continue to find the suggestions of Joel Goodman (1981) to be a helpful guide:

- People are more humorous when they feel safe and accepted.

- Laugh with people (which includes), not at them (which excludes).

- Humor is an attitude. Be open to the unexpected, insane, silly, and ridiculous that life offers daily.

- Do not take yourself too seriously. How easily can you laugh at yourself?

- Don't be a perfectionist with humor. It will intimidate you. No one can be witty or funny 100 percent of the time. (Talk shows are a living testament to this.)

- If you look for humor, humor will find you.

Strategy 29: Use Examples, Analogies, Metaphors, and Stories

Examples not only stimulate learners' thinking but also provide an indication to learners about how well they have comprehended what has preceded those examples (Gage and Berliner, 1998). For learners, being given an example is the "moment of truth" for personal meaning—the point at which the information, concept, or demonstration is clarified, applied, or accentuated. Good examples give learners a way to focus new learning so that it is clearly illustrated in their own minds.

We must also realize that when learners construct their own good examples, they create meaning that reflects language and imagery more firmly anchored in their world than what we as instructors usually have to offer. When learners can give their own fitting examples for something newly learned, deeper learning is at hand.

Because adults are experientially rich learners with considerable mental powers of abstraction, they readily appreciate analogies and metaphors. Metaphors allow us to reach meanings not possible with simpler academic language. For example, to say, "At seventy-three, she saw that he looked very old" is logically clear, but to say, "At seventy-three, his demeanor left her feeling as though she were in the presence of a ashen skeleton" adds insight and transports meaning to a much deeper and more emotional level.

Stories, especially when they are well told, imaginative, and unpredictable, are extremely interesting. Used wisely and relevantly, they can captivate a group of learners. People also use stories to give meaning to their own lives. The natural cohesiveness of a story facilitates both retention and recall. If learning is deepest when it engages most parts of the brain, as some scientists claim, then sharing a compelling story is a fundamental way of learning, as old as language and as important as fire (Zull, 2002).

Strategy 30: Invite Learners to Anticipate and Predict

Because of our need to survive, we constantly anticipate and predict. Whether we are attending to the direction another car will go or the next topic of conversation with a friend, we regularly assess our environments for what we think will happen next. The upside of this phenomenon is that whenever we predict or estimate something, we become interested—hooked, you might say—in finding out how it will turn out. For example, there are five capitals in the United States that begin with the letter A. One of them is Atlanta, but what are the rest? If you've even thought of a city that begins with the letter A, you're into this. You want to know what the other four capitals are and may even put this book aside to find out. This sort of question is the mainstay of many trivia games but also the stuff of good novels, films, and plays. So when we build anticipation or ask learners to predict an outcome in any subject, from accounting to marriage counseling, we have encouraged their interest.

Strategy 31: Use Concept Maps to Develop Interest in Ideas and Information

Concept maps are graphic diagrams that organize and represent relationships between concepts and their components, and between ideas and information, with visual, concrete connections. They can give us a model for how we understand an academic topic. Any interesting idea or question can be the focus of a concept map. Concept maps can be linear or nonlinear and individually or collaboratively constructed on paper, a board, or a computer screen. They allow adults, especially those more visually oriented, to construct mental models that reflect the unique set of relationships an idea can generate in their minds. Concept maps are particularly effective with English language learners (Chularut and DeBacker, 2004).

The example in Figure 6.1 illustrates *mindmapping*, a concept mapping technique that gives adults the freedom to create the graphics and form the associations themselves (Buzan, 1991). Mindmapping begins with a key word or image in the center of the page (in this case, the word "economics"), followed by extensions expanding outward. Arrows and lines connect secondary ideas to each other; the more important concepts are drawn nearer to the center. Single words are suggested for each line.

Mindmapping and other concept-mapping techniques can involve arrows, asterisks, question marks, geometric shapes, three-dimensional drawings, and personal images. Multiple colors can enhance a mindmap as a mnemonic tool. Such variations encourage learners to create relevant, comprehensive views of connected information that will make recall more accessible (Nesbit and Adesope, 2006).

FIGURE 6.1

Example of Mindmapping

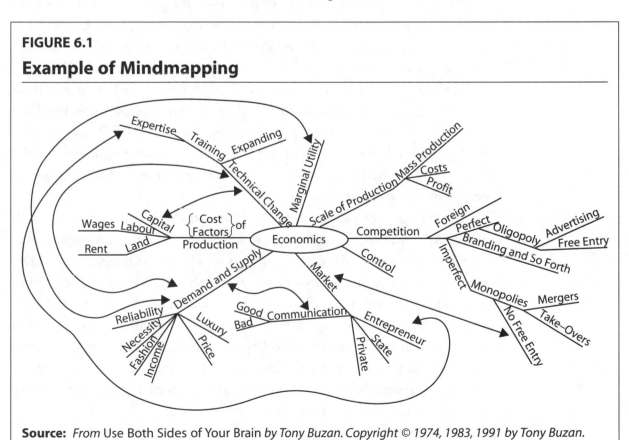

Source: *From* Use Both Sides of Your Brain *by Tony Buzan. Copyright © 1974, 1983, 1991 by Tony Buzan. Used by permission of Dutton, a division of Penguin Group (USA) Inc.*

Deepening Learning with Engagement and Challenge

The strategies in this section such as Using Case Studies are entire teaching methodologies which may require combining learning processes, including cooperative learning, researching literature, solving problems, and synthesizing ideas. By their nature, they offer considerable challenge for students, requiring complex and substantive involvement that takes time (from hours to weeks) and usually results in a learning product, such as a project or research report.

These strategies offer ways to learn that respect the multiple perspectives and variety of prior knowledge found among diverse adults. All the strategies are highly interactive processes, using the reflection and dialogue of other learners to construct knowledge. The challenges these strategies generate do not compel learners to simply participate; rather, they engage learners in ways that help them realize why what they are learning is important and what competent performance looks like (Donovan, Bransford, and Pellegrino, 1999).

These strategies create a life of their own for students in an intensive course. They are composed of procedures that engage the learner with questions, thoughts, and actions to propel learning toward deeper meaning and accomplishment. A case study strategy (see Strategy 35 below), for example, usually starts with an analysis of the case, which naturally leads to reflection and discussion, followed by an attempt at resolution. The sequence for a research strategy (see Strategy 34 below) is often to observe, analyze, predict, test, and reflect on results. When the strategies in this section are carried out optimally, learners experience *flow*, the joy of complete engagement.

At its most ideal, a state of flow while learning allows us to feel totally absorbed, with no time to worry about what might happen next and with a sense that we are fully participating with all the skills necessary at that moment. There is often a loss of self-awareness, which sometimes results in a feeling of transcendence or a merging with the activity and the environment (Csikszentmihalyi, 1997). Writers, dancers, therapists, surgeons, pilots, and instructors report feelings of flow during engrossing tasks in their repertoire of activities. In fact, when interviewed, they report that flow experiences are among the major reasons why they enjoy and continue to do the work they do.

Flow can be found across cultures, which suggests that humans may have developed this sense in order to recognize patterns of action that are worth preserving (Massimini, Csikszentmihalyi, and Delle Fave, 1988). Whenever they happen, flow experiences have remarkably similar characteristics (Nakamura and Csikszentmihalyi, 2003):

- *Goals are clear and compatible.* Playing games like chess, tennis, and poker induce flow, but so can playing a musical piece or designing computer software. As long as our intentions are clear and our emotions support them, we can concentrate even when the task is difficult. For any flow experience to occur, cultural relevance is an inescapable necessity.

- *Feedback is immediate, continuous, and relevant as the activity unfolds.* We are clear about how well we are doing. Each move of a game usually tells us whether we are advancing or retreating from our goal; as we read we *flow* across lines and paragraphs and pages. In a good conversation, words, facial expressions, and gestures give immediate feedback. In learning situations, there should be distinct information or signals that allow us to assess our work.

- *The challenge is in balance with our skills or knowledge but stretches existing capacities.* The challenge is manageable but pulls us toward further development of our knowledge or skills. Flow experiences usually occur when our ability to act and the available opportunity for action correspond closely. If challenges get significantly beyond our skills, we usually begin to worry; and if they get too far away from what we're capable of doing, fear can emerge. To use a cliché, we're in over our heads. Conversely, when the challenge is minimal (as with any type of busywork), even if we have the skills we will feel apathetic. When the challenge is more moderate but our skills still exceed it, we are likely to become bored. However, if the activity is a valued hobby, such as cooking, we might actually feel relaxed.

When flow merges with meaning it becomes *vital engagement*, one of the pinnacles of what living can be. This phenomenon occurs when we are enjoyably absorbed in such valued, socially useful tasks as work, teaching, or learning. For example: vital engagement can occur during a class activity such as problem solving, when there is a "felt conviction" by learners that the task is part of something "inherently important," such as art, science, or education (Nakamura and Csikszentmihalyi, 2003, p. 100).

Flow is very possible while learning or teaching. One in five people experiences flow often, as frequently as several times a day (Csikszentmihalyi, 1997). The purpose of this handbook for teaching intensive courses is to provide a no-frills approach to making teaching and learning lifelong pursuits of vital engagement. Most of us have a favorite subject in which we flourish as we learn. As instructors we want to expand the range of those subjects for adults so that there is a consistent conjunction of joy and meaning as they learn across a broader horizon. The strategies that follow are ideal for meeting this purpose.

Strategy 32: Use Critical Questions to Engage Learners in Challenging Reflection and Discussion

When ideas and experiences feel comfortable, seem self-evident, and make sense, we tend not to think any more about them. With a more critical orientation, however, we examine ideas and experiences for inconsistencies and consider them from alternative perspectives, with sensitivity to possible bias, overgeneralization, and social injustice. Critical questioning promotes high-level cognitive processing, stimulating us to analyze, infer, synthesize, apply, evaluate, compare, contrast, verify, substantiate, explain, and hypothesize. Such questions are generative, causing us to reflect on our own information and experience and having the potential to transform what we know into new meanings while we recognize the same capacity in others (Brookfield and Preskill, 2005).

Many adults may not be experienced with posing critical questions in their courses. Alison King (2002) has developed and extensively tested an instructional procedure for teaching postsecondary learners to pose their own critical questions. We have found that adult learners can effectively use this strategy in intensive courses either individually or in groups. Using this procedure, the teacher gives the learners a written set of question starters, such as, "What is the meaning of...?" and "Why is... important?" Learners use these question starters to guide them in formulating their own specific questions pertaining to the material to be discussed. Table 6.1 includes a list of these thoughtful question stems, which can be adapted to any subject by asking students to complete them with information relevant to that topic. The thinking processes these questions elicit are also listed in Table 6.1.

Learners can also use these question stems to help them generate their own critical questions following a presentation, class, or reading. For example, your class has read *The Hunchback of Notre Dame*, by Alexander Dumas. Students have agreed that they will each bring along two questions, based on the list in Table 6.1, regarding any aspect of the book that they find relevant to their own lives. Students break into dyads, and the partners share their questions:

1. Why is it important that much of the story and its climax take place in the Cathedral of Notre Dame? (Analysis of significance)

TABLE 6.1

Guiding Critical Questioning

Question Starter	Specific Thinking Skill
What is a new example of …?	Application
How would you use … to …?	Application
What would happen if …?	Prediction/hypothesizing
What are the implications of …?	Analysis/inference
What are the strengths and weaknesses of …?	Analysis/inference
What is … analogous to?	Creation of analogies and metaphors
What do we already know about …?	Activation of prior knowledge
How does … affect …?	Analysis of cause-effect
How does … tie in with what we learned before?	Activation of prior knowledge
Explain why …	Analysis
Explain how …	Analysis
What is the meaning of …?	Analysis
Why is it important …?	Analysis of significance
What is the difference between … and …?	Comparison-contrast
How are … and … similar?	Comparison-contrast
How does … apply to everyday life?	Application
What is the counterargument for …?	Rebuttal argument
What is the best …, and why?	Evaluation and provision of evidence
What are some possible solutions to the problem of …?	Synthesis of ideas
Compare … and … with regard to …	Comparison-contrast
What do you think causes …?	Analysis of cause-effect
Do you agree or disagree with this statement: …? What evidence is there to support your answer?	Evaluation and provision of evidence
How do you think … would see the issue of …?	Taking other perspectives
In terms of today's … how do you think …?	Taking other perspectives

Source: *King, 1994, p. 24. Used by permission.*

---

2. What are some of the differences between today's people who are homeless and the beggars portrayed in the novel? What are some similarities? (Comparison-contrast)

3. How does the romanticism of the author affect how the main characters act in this story? (Application)

4. In terms of today's understanding of disabilities, how do you think a modern story with a character like Quasimodo would be written? (Taking other perspectives)

With these questions, there is opportunity to infer, analyze, compare, contrast, and apply ideas as well as take other perspectives. Discussion of these questions has the potential to lead to better understanding and fuller awareness of social issues and may prompt students to modify their own thinking. As discussants, students will probably have to reflect more deeply, explain more thoroughly, offer further examples, and negotiate meaning. In an inclusive and respectful learning environment, these questions offer the possibility of an absorbing discussion—one of the most dynamic pathways to intrinsic motivation and new learning.

Strategy 33: Use Relevant Problems or Problem-Based Learning to Facilitate and Deepen Learning

A problem can be very broadly characterized as any situation in which a person wants to achieve a goal for which an obstacle exists (Voss, 1989). Problems, if they are relevant and within the range of an adult's capabilities, are both engaging and challenging. Most forms of research, creativity, and invention find their initial impetus in a relevant problem. Processes for solving problems are learned within a cultural context (Gay, 2000). Differences in perspective, communication, and ethical codes may influence how people conceive and approach a problem, from building a home to settling a divorce.

Our first approach to relevant problems is using the learner's concerns and interests. We want to match the learner with a problem and to mutually agree on a learning outcome. For example:

- In history, a learner who distrusts a historical viewpoint becomes a historian, reading primary material and writing her own historical account.

- In psychology or sociology, a learner who finds a psychological interpretation to be too theoretical and individualized conducts a study of sociological literature and research to offer a sociological analysis of the same phenomenon.

- In criminal justice, a learner sees a criminal problem as a systemic problem and investigates systems theory to recast the analysis of this issue.

Another method with a similar orientation is to figuratively situate the learner in a relevant problem:

- For such courses as accounting, math, or organizational planning, the problem might be stated: "You're the treasurer of a community organization, and you are losing X amount of money per month. With these assets, liabilities, dues, and so forth (actual figures would be given), what would you do?"

- For courses in ethnic studies, social policy, or law, the posed problem might be: "You are a twenty-one-year-old African American male; you have your first automobile accident, for which you are not at fault, and you have no other driving violations. Your insurance is cancelled. What recourse do you have to establish bias? You will need to understand actuarial records, predictive statistics, and resident state law to investigate this matter."

The second approach is *problem-based learning*, which is a more self-directed and constructive process, in which social context, discovery, and experience lead to new knowledge and skills (Lohman, 2002). Problem-based learning fits well into intensive formats because it is characterized by the use of real-life problems as a way for adult learners to learn critical thinking, collaboration, and the essential concepts and professional skills of a particular discipline. For example, professional educators in such programs as medicine and nursing have used problem-based learning to prepare learners for situations they will face in their work.

In order to illustrate the possible steps for problem-based learning, we have adapted an example from an inquiry course in arts and sciences at McMaster University, taught by P. K. Rangachari (1996). In this unit, learners are exploring the dimensions of health and illness in the modern world, in particular the interaction between providers and recipients of health care.

1. *Brainstorming.* The first meeting is a brainstorming session, during which learners discuss what they believe to be critical issues in health care. Distilled from this effort are such topics as bioethics, alternative medicine, technology in medicine, and funding for health care.

2. *The problem.* Working with the learners' list, the instructor writes a problem like the one that follows. This problem is based on the learners' expressed desire to discuss the appropriateness of specific procedures in medicine and, more specifically, the frequency with which certain surgical procedures are performed.

An article titled, "Study Finds Region Surgeons Scalpel-Happy" has appeared in the local tabloid. Naming names, the article identifies the hospital and notes that patients there are twice as likely to undergo a cholecystectomy, three times as likely to have a mastectomy, and five times as likely to have a hysterectomy compared to other regions in Ontario. The findings implicate the hospital surgeons to be an incompetent, money-grubbing, and misogynistic lot. The president of the hospital has demanded an explanation from the chief of surgery, and the chief is livid.

Possible *learning issues*, which are often the basis for the learning activities students carry out, include (1) a study of variability in the rates of surgical procedures based on demographics and hospital, (2) a profile of a surgeon, (3) an assessment of the surgery and technology identified in the problem, (4) a review of the cost and expense of surgical procedures, and (5) an examination of how to handle scandal. (Note the variety of entry points for multiple intelligences, discussed in Strategy 20 in Chapter Five.)

3. *Definition of learning issues and formation of study groups.* Learners receive the problem. They organize their ideas and previous knowledge related to the problem. They pose questions on aspects of the problem they do not understand or know, but that they wish to learn. Learners rank these learning issues in order of importance. Through dialogue and by personal preference they decide which issues to assign to small groups and which to individuals. In two weeks, learners will teach the findings related to these issues to the rest of the group. The instructor guides the learners toward resources and necessary research.

4. *Preparation for presentations.* During the two weeks prior to their presentations, learners meet, discuss, find and evaluate information, write their reports, and prepare for their presentations. To preserve continuity, the instructor holds an intervening session to discuss any issues that require clarification. Learners also share information and act as resources for one another. This process and the final presentation are structured according the guidelines for collaborative and cooperative learning (see Strategy 4 in Chapter Four). For readers who want to further investigate this approach, there are a number of other problem-based learning methods (Savin-Baden, 2003).

Strategy 34: Use Project-Based Learning to Deepen Understanding and to Engage Challenging, Authentic Topics

Project-based learning has evolved from problem-based learning. Although there is no single accepted definition of project-based learning, we prefer a definition that helps to separate this concept from problem-based learning (Markham, Larmer, and Ravitz, 2003). Project-based learning builds on learners' curiosity and interest, requiring students to develop knowledge and skills through an *extended inquiry process* involving authentic research that is central to the course, requiring learning products evaluated through performance-based assessment (see Strategy 42 in Chapter Seven).

Three criteria of project-based learning are:

• *Project-based learning builds on learners' curiosity and interest.* It isn't necessary for the learners themselves to identify the problem to be studied. However, they do need a relevant question which they are genuinely curious about which the instructor can provide. Also, there may be a resolution to the identified problem, but it is appropriate to have such alternative products as an artistic or dramatic presentation, a form of community service, clarification of understanding, related skill acquisition, or experiments leading to new insights and deeper questions.

• *The extended inquiry process involves authentic research.* Learners are going to take a considerable amount of time in the course and outside of it to collaboratively and actively investigate a question (or a problem) that has tapped into their personal curiosity or interests. When learners begin their inquiry, they will use primary sources and real-world information and data to share results with the people who might benefit from their findings, or take action themselves based on their findings.

• *The serious questions stimulating learning are central to the course rather than peripheral.* These questions engage students in the essential concepts, principles, and skills of a discipline or subject area. They require the use of ideas and tools that are central to the important learning contained in the course curriculum and objectives. For example, the project-based learning for an Accelerated MBA Capstone Course, as in Strategy 36 below, is an ongoing simulation covering the length of the course. Students are asked to answer the questions necessary to make decisions and to lead a multibillion-dollar industry. In order to answer these questions effectively, they have to research actual news articles, company reports, and other media that provide valuable information about production costs, market analyses, sales reports, finance operations, and human resources in an international market across three continents. With their collaboration and research they can construct business strategies on a day-to-day basis.

Because of its complexity and authenticity, project-based learning can challenge and engage diverse groups of adult learners with varying background knowledge, skill levels, and profiles of intelligences. In intensive courses, it is an excellent strategy for use with small learning cohorts (fifteen to twenty-five students) to grapple with important topics that need to be taught in depth. Project-based learning requires us as instructors to be co-researchers, coaches, and leaders who help students shape their projects and deepen the knowledge they acquire through their investigations. For those topics that remain important but are not a part of the project-based learning process, we can use direct instruction methods, such as short lectures, demonstrations, and textual readings.

Daniel Solorzano (1989) offers a documented example of a Freirean approach to teaching that fluidly meets our three specific criteria of project-based learning. We have outlined Solorzano's project, which could fit into the parameters of an eight-week intensive course, according to the three criteria:

Project-based learning builds on learners' curiosity and interest. In the late 1970s, Solorzano offered a course at East Los Angeles College that was jointly listed by the Sociology and Chicano Studies Departments to students who were mostly Chicanos from the local area. Through the examination of local papers and mass media, the instructor and students engaged in a dialogue that eventually centered on negative stereotypes of Chicanos and the Chicano-white culture clash presented in Hollywood gang movies. They arrived at two major questions that focused their interest and could drive further research: Why are Chicanos portrayed negatively in the mass media? and Whose interests are served by these negative portrayals of Chicanos?

An extended inquiry process involves authentic research. The class divided itself into three research groups and conducted research based on these questions over a number of weeks.

1. A library group researched contemporary and historical images of Chicanos in the media, using Hollywood trade papers, the *Readers' Guide to Periodical Literature*, and the *Social Sciences Index*.

2. A group researched public information data on youth gangs in East Los Angeles, using the area census on Chicanos, information from the sheriff's office and from the police department, sociological theories of gang and deviant behavior, and firsthand reports from gang members.

3. A group researched the film industry, including interviewing representatives of Universal Pictures and Warner Brothers Studios, Chicano community members, and groups working as consultants to moviemakers.

The serious questions stimulating learning are central to the course rather than peripheral. After their extensive research and in order to answer their two central questions, the students analyzed their data, examined related literature on stereotyping and bias, and applied relevant sociological principles from their readings. With this information, the teams collaborated to integrate their findings. Among these was the finding that the gang problem was blown out of proportion, with the percentage of Chicano youth joining gangs not 10 percent as reported in the media but closer to 3 percent. Another finding was that in films, Chicanos were stereotyped disproportionately in demeaning occupational roles, such as bandits, thieves, and gangsters. With further discussion and analysis, the learners believed they had evidence that the film companies were exploiting Chicano stereotypes to make a profit. Consequently, they initiated collaboration with other local organizations to create the Gang Exploitation Committee, an organization to confront and diminish such stereotypical filmmaking. As a postscript, Solorzano reports that no new Chicano gang movies appeared in the decade after he taught this class. Public protest and the mixed profitability of these films probably stopped their production.

This outstanding example of project-based learning shows its complexity and potential. It also reveals how students not only gained knowledge, skills, and a greater understanding of the systemic nature of this issue but also provided an authentic community service.

Because of the complexity of this strategy, and because some students will be unfamiliar with this approach to learning, learners often need an opportunity to learn about the components of project-based learning before more independently pursuing their projects. For this purpose, consider the following set of guidelines, which we have found quite helpful (Beyer, 1987):

1. Introduce the project by describing and demonstrating the steps of the process with a vivid, relevant example that is clearly outlined.

2. Have learners work in guided practice with a short and relevant process that captures one or more of the fundamental aspects of the project. For example, students could conduct brief interviews among themselves, following an outline prepared by the instructor.

3. Have learners take notes on their reflections while they are involved in the guided practice and discuss them collaboratively afterward.

4. As a result of their reflection, learners may make changes in planning for the project or the project itself that better align with their cultural

perspectives and profiles of intelligences. If necessary, learners may continue this guided practice by experimenting with how they have modified their project and again reflecting on the process.

In general, when students are not familiar with the procedures for a project and have had no chance for guided practice, we will need to coach them more closely throughout the process.

Strategy 35: Use Case Study Methods to Deepen Learning and to Engage Challenging, Authentic Topics

A case study integrates provocative questions in a narrative of real events. It requires learners to use their experience and knowledge to analyze, deliberate, and advance informed judgments from an array of perspectives and concepts. The hallmark of the case study is its authenticity. With real-life, concrete details, and characters expressing a personal voice, they put flesh and blood on otherwise abstract concepts.

Whether we have personally written the case or selected it from a text, it is very important that we have a thorough understanding of the case and its nuances before teaching it. Here are some useful questions on which to reflect while preparing the case for instruction:

What is your first impression of the case as an authentic story?

What are the different ways to interpret this case?

What are the teaching and learning issues?

What is culturally relevant in this case?

Can students construct principles and applications from this case?

Keep these questions in mind as you read the case in Exhibit 6.1, which was originally composed for use by faculty for discussion about improving college teaching. It describes the first day of a course in which students are working to improve their writing skills.

EXHIBIT 6.1

Case Study
"See You on Wednesday!"

by Deanna Yameen, Instructor and Critical-Thinking Specialist, Massachusetts Bay Community College, and Elizabeth Fideler, Recruiting New Teachers, Inc.

The first class meeting seemed to go smoothly enough. I went in, introduced myself, and reviewed the course syllabus and calendar. The students seemed pretty much like the students I taught at State

U.—maybe a little older. They asked the same questions about how long the paper should be and which books to buy. They made no comments about the journal assignment for the next class. They readily filled out my survey and class ended twenty minutes early.

I used the same survey I used at State U., with exactly the same directions: "I'm just looking for some information to get a feel for the class. Tell me (1) why you are taking the class, and (2) what you want me to know about you. Please be honest. You don't have to sign your name if you'd rather not." From reading their responses I know I'll have to reconsider what I am going to do on Wednesday. I can't assume that students have similar writing skills or academic goals to students at a state university. I may need to talk with someone more experienced with teaching students at this community college. *Take a look at the responses for yourself*:

I want to write very, very well.

I want you to know is that the main reason for me to learn, is because I wanna go to computer afterwards.

This is my first class in college. Since I graduated I wanted to try writing to see if I didn't have the ability.

I am an international student. Sometimes I don't speak or tell what I want to say well.

I want to how to use research information then write paper.

To enter nursing program, and have a good abilities.

You should know that I have a learning disable.

I have a Learning Disability in Reading and I think my writing is Poor.

I would like to prove to myself that I am now ready to be a serious student and that I can get an A in this class.

I failed out of school and it has taken me a long time to get the guts to try again. I really want to do well.

I have taken this course last semester and wrote three essay.

A lot of things come very easily to me but what does not I become easily frustrated which makes it that much harder. I have to read lips. I have trouble hearing.

I would like to learn how to get my thought down in an organized fashion.

I would like my writing to be impressive and express how I feel.

I would like to write a paper on my own that really makes sense.

I want to be able to write a good essay, or other papers I might have to write in my college days.

I want to be prepared for the other courses for my college education. I want to improve my writing skills.

I'd like to read different kinds of books and I want to try to like writing.

I want to learn to read and think about a situation or article and know what to write about.

Once you have determined which case to use, a practical next step is to be sure that learners comprehend the goals of the particular case study. In the instance of the case in Exhibit 6.1, possible goals could include the following:

- Increase understanding of how to improve teaching and learning among diverse learners.

- Improve understanding of how bias, class, privilege, and disability present themselves and influence teaching and learning.

- Learn how to find out more about learners at the beginning of a course so that teaching can be more effective and culturally responsive.

Opening the discussion of the case in a manner that invites wide participation and relevant commentary is important. Some ways to start include the following:

- Ask learners to freewrite for a couple of minutes after reading the case so they have something to offer based on reflection.

- Ask each learner to speak with a partner for a few minutes about key issues in the case before requesting individual responses.

- Ask each learner to comment on one element he or she felt was important in the case and record these remarks publicly. This lets everyone know there are a range of interpretations before discussion begins.

The kinds of questions the instructor asks during the discussion can serve different purposes. Some questions, for example, further analysis, challenge an idea, mediate between conflicting views, and compel students to generate principles and concepts. For the instructor, our role is one of a facilitator who provides opportunities for everyone to contribute, but who also has the responsibility to provoke and inform, cautiously avoiding the temptation to impose our own perspectives. At times, it may be effective to role-play certain aspects of the case—for example, leading off with, "Given your experience and the discussion today, what would be your first remarks to students on Wednesday? What would you specifically do as their instructor?"

Other times it may be beneficial to record key information on the board or a chart. Typically, after students have read the case, the pattern of learning moves incrementally from reflection and analysis to problem-solving hypotheses to students' application of their own learning and practices. Sometimes offering students a discussion outline with questions and probes for analysis and action can help them navigate through the case. A short outline follows for "See You on Wednesday!":

Suggested Discussion Outline

1. What kind of diversity appears to be represented in this case? *Probes*: What is a way to understand this kind of diversity that offers greater opportunity for learning for everyone? Do any issues of diversity in this case stir up your apprehension? Why?

2. How effective is the assessment strategy used to find out about the learners? *Probes*: How might you improve this assessment strategy? What alternative assessment strategies would you suggest?

3. What does the instructor do on Wednesday? *Probes*: If there were no time for further assessment, what would be your plan? How would you, as the instructor, inform the class about your understanding of the survey and what it suggested for you to do?

Closing the case discussion well is critical. Looking for "the answer" is often inappropriate. Part of the fun of a good case study is that learners, because of their different perspectives and different skills and knowledge, can construct an array of possible actions and solutions. It is necessary, however, to conclude the case-study process in a satisfying manner, which might include giving students the opportunity to reflect on what has been learned, to synthesize or identify new understandings, to air unresolved conflicts or questions, or to make plans for making changes or taking action. The following list provides some suggestions (Hutchings, 1993):

- Spend some time asking such questions as, "What new insights did you gain from this case study and its discussion?," "What are some new ideas with which you would like to experiment?," and "What resources would be useful to you?"

- As a group, brainstorm insights, personal changes in thinking or action, or new areas to explore as a result of the case study.

- Go around the group and allow each student to provide one insight, question, lesson, change, or benefit that has emerged as a result of the case study process.

Using case studies in technical fields, such as chemistry, may require a more structured approach, but the challenge remains to use this strategy in a manner that does not suppress the free flow of ideas and perspectives. Also, with the time available in intensive courses, we are wise to remember that adult learners, individually and collaboratively, are a rich resource for constructing relevant cases for course study.

Strategy 36: Use Role Playing and Simulations for New Learning and Adaptive Decision Making in Realistic and Dynamic Contexts

For real-life situations that are dynamic and with no clear "correct" answer, where our responses affect the context and the possible choice of responses that follow, we only learn and retain new knowledge for performing in those situations by *doing*—by acting in the situations themselves or learning in contexts that replicate them. According to Elkhonon Goldberg (2001), these situations, in which there is often no clear "correct" answer or response, require adaptive decision making. We do not have a recipe for what to do. We have to interpret the situation while it is happening and choose from a number of possible actions. When we drive a car, mediate an argument, or respond to an emergency, we are using adaptive decision making. In such situations, our analysis and critical thinking are occurring rapidly as responses to environmental feedback but without a clear best response at hand. We might have a goal, such as to get to a destination or resolve an argument; we have knowledge and skill to apply; we can make decisions and take decisive actions that lead to effectual consequences; but how and what to do are moment-to-moment choices, and there is no complete and final path of action.

When we use knowledge and skills effectively in these situations, we often say we have a feel for them. We have learned this knowledge and these skills such that they are part of our senses, cognitions, emotions, and physical being. This learning is an *embodiment of meaning* that allows us to effectively make adaptive decisions on a moment-to-moment basis (Caine and Caine, 2006). We need repeated immersion into real-life situations or their authentic replications, which we can navigate with our new knowledge while integrating feedback and engaging our senses, thoughts, emotions, and actions—our entire psychophysiological system. Role playing and simulations offer realistic ways for students to learn—to engage the knowledge and practice the skills necessary for adaptive decision making.

Role playing is acting out a possible situation by personifying another individual or by imagining another scene or set of circumstances. Role playing gives learners the opportunity to think in the moment, question their own perspectives, respond to novel or unexpected situations, and consider different ways of knowing (Meyers and Jones, 1993). Students can use this technique to practice a specific skill, such as providing an academic progress report in a parent-teacher conference; a collaborative skill, such as collective bargaining; or a problem-solving skill, such as conducting a biochemistry experiment.

Simulations, sometimes called simulation exercises, refer to situations in which a whole class is involved, with learners assuming different roles as they act out a prescribed scenario. Simulations allow adults to more deeply learn and practice multiple concepts and skills over a period of time that is shorter than the real-life experience. For example, in an intensive course, practicing skills for a six-month leadership training internship may occur in a six-week simulation scenario. Simulations immerse learners in a reality that mimics real life, allowing them to experience what might otherwise remain abstract in textual materials and conventional classes—power, conflict, discrimination, aggression, debt, stress, and expenditure of resources. When learners are able to experience perspectives, ideas, skills, and situations that approximate authentic environments in life, they have an opportunity to embody new meaning and to learn to be more proficient in the knowledge and skills relevant to a given role and its circumstances.

Simulations have become very popular in business education. As a format for learning, they are vastly improving as evolving technology makes them more creative and accessible for the classroom and for online learning. Depending on the degree of prescriptiveness and formality of the given scenario, role playing can blend into a simulation exercise. The main goal in either procedure is that the learner genuinely involve his or her intellect, feelings, and physical senses in a realistic context, such that the experience can engender new learning for adaptive decision making.

We offer the following series of guidelines, adapted from the work of Meyers and Jones (1993), for creating effective role-playing and simulation experiences:

• *Know how the role play or simulation conforms to your teaching situation.* Is it a good "fit," given who your students are, where learning is headed, and what learners expect to do? Avoid role plays and simulations that feel contrived or trivialize a significant issue or concept.

• *Plan well ahead.* Have some degree of confidence that your learners are sufficiently familiar and proficient with the concepts or skills to be practiced. Do they have adequate knowledge or background concerning the cultural or personal roles they may assume? If they are uncomfortable, can learners excuse themselves or observe until they are more at ease in playing their roles? Role plays often benefit from a student observer. The observer in the role-playing process provides feedback and guides the discussion that follows.

• *Be relatively sure students understand the roles and the scenario before you begin.* Allow for questions and clarification. Often it is helpful to write out a script with students in order to describe roles, attitudes, experiences, and beliefs. Developing a script with students helps deepen their familiarity with the roles.

• *Set aside enough time for the discussion that follows the role play.* The discussion and analysis are as important as the role play or simulation itself. The class might address such questions as: What are the different perspectives, reactions, and insights? What has not been dealt with that needs attention? Have the group's goals for learning been accomplished? How do we know? What about the process itself? How can it be improved?

• *When role playing seems potentially embarrassing or threatening, it is often helpful for the instructor to model the first role play and discuss it.* This may alleviate some initial hesitation and allow learners to see how other reasonably competent adults use mistakes to learn. In some cases, starting out slowly, with only those learners who are interested in role playing serving as initial models, can help work toward exercises involving all learners.

• *Freeze the action during a role play when necessary.* A pause in action can serve many purposes, providing students with more time, for example, to critique a perspective, explore reactions to a poignant comment, make beneficial suggestions to the actors, and relieve the tension.

For many students, a role play or simulation may be the only way to enter distant worlds or to try out actions initially too uncomfortable. The Master of Business Administration (MBA) program in the College for Professional Studies at Regis University in Denver responded to this challenge with an accelerated capstone course, depicted in Exhibit 6.2, that featured project-based learning through an eight-week simulation (Vaughan, 2006).

Strategy 37: Use Visits and Service-Learning in Authentic Settings to Provide Practice for Engendering New Learning and Adaptive Decision Making

Sometimes only the real thing can make learning meaningful and involve all of our senses and modes of engagement. Most service professions, such as teaching, social work, and nursing, involve clinical practice and internships. Over the years, the value of practice and learning in authentic settings has become apparent. What we want to emphasize in this strategy

---

EXHIBIT 6.2

Description of a Simulation for an Accelerated MBA Capstone Course

Faculty decided to make the capstone course a simulation that looked and felt like a real company. In collaboration with designers, they created an international shoe company, Mercury Shoes, for which students approaching graduation could serve as senior executives. In these roles, the students had a real-life business environment, with responsibilities to make decisions about strategic issues based on industry news, market data, stock quotes, quarterly budgets, employment resources, and so forth.

As in the real world, there were news articles, radio reports, and other media to provide valuable as well as distracting information. Students might get a news article about rising wages in an East Asian country or about new technology for inexpensively producing synthetic rubber. Because this information would affect their production and costs, they would have to further study financial and analyst reports; conduct market analyses; and update their knowledge about current company reports in sales, marketing, finance, operations, and human resources. In order to arrive at an effective business strategy, they would also have to be aware of government policies, economics, law, and ethical practices.

With their multibillion-dollar company reaching an international market in at least three continents, including manufacturing and service components, the context and complexity involved in students' decision making was realistic and substantial. Students received feedback from a simulated systemic framework about the intended and unintended consequences of their strategies and actions. In addition, they received coaching to probe their thinking and to facilitate further learning about working as business executives. At appropriate intervals, faculty provided guidance for students so that they could move forward with plans and strategies. With performance indexes and faculty evaluations as part of the assessment process, learners received further relevant information about their progress toward their academic and professional goals. With more than 3,700 students successfully completing this course to date, the capstone simulation continues today with ongoing supplements and refinements to make it an authentic and motivating process to foster new learning and embody new meaning.

Source: *Personal communication from Michael Vaughn and Arlo Grady, 2009.*

---

is what we would call "connected" visits—relevant real-life situations in which adult learners apply and reflect on what they are learning. Here are a few examples of course activities in which we have seen learning enter another stratum of meaning because it takes place in real-life environments:

- Interviewing immigrant families in their homes for courses in education, nursing, and communication

- Tutoring students in a variety of subject areas

- Working with politicians and activists for courses in the social and political sciences

- Service-learning for courses in social justice

In order to employ this strategy, the questions for us as instructors are the following: Can learners make a real-life connection to the subject I am teaching? If so, is there any way that I can create a placement or visitation in which they can apply what they are learning? If so, can they make that connection in a way that responsibly serves the community they are visiting? Am I giving learners an opportunity for embodiment of meaning through some degree of continued involvement that allows for practice of and reflection on new learning? Elise Burton (2003) provides an exceptional example of this strategy with her description of a service-learning experience for an intensive course in which adults engaged new learning in a powerfully different cultural setting in Guatemala.

Strategy 38: Use Invention, Artistry, and Enactment to Render Deeper Meaning and Emotion in Learning

Using invention and artistry are ways to create something with which to express oneself; to respond to a need or desire; to react to an experience; and to make connections between the known and the unknown, the concrete and the abstract, and the worldly and the spiritual—and among different people, places, and things. Through art and invention, adults attempt to answer such questions as: What do I want to express? What do I want to create? What is a better way? What do I imagine? What do I wish to render? What does…mean to me?

We discuss invention and artistry together because the conceptual and subjective differences between them are difficult to discern, and because both should be integral to learning and not, as is so often the case with art, separate entities in education. Both invention and artistry are forms of knowledge for potential use in every subject area. Each of these proficiencies is open-ended and entails kindling an awareness of creative possibility while attaining educational goals. They are also compatible with the aesthetic and experiential entry points from multiple intelligences theory (see Strategy 20 in Chapter Five).

To provide an example of invention, we recall an intensive course in which a small cadre of adult learners who were struggling to comprehend systems theory decided to invent a game that could teach the fundamental concepts and principles of this theory to others. The game board was a narrow roll of cloth, which, when extended, created a serpentine figure across the width of a small room. Along its path were stations at which players (learners in the course) were to be interviewed, asked to complete activities, and required to draw graphic models of systemic processes. The game became so popular as a teaching device that the university library acquired it as a resource.

Our experience has been that learners across many cultures welcome the invitation to infuse their academic work with artwork, such as sketches and poetry. We have also found that projects that include works of fiction, playwriting, visual art, musical composition, songwriting, and performance art offer adults access to some of the most profound understandings in their learning.

When learners enact the physical and emotional properties of an idea, the concept becomes more salient because the physical senses and emotional associations make the idea more directly compelling (Cozolino and Sprokay, 2006). This is what happens when learners in adventure courses explore the meaning of challenge, such as by crossing river rapids attached to a single rope with a pulley. However, the classroom is available for more tranquil enactment. For example, an adult basic education instructor conducting a course in earth science might request that learners physically represent the planets and their movements in order to understand the solar system. There are myriad possibilities with this approach.

Transformative Learning

When the strategies in this section are carried out optimally, learners are likely to experience flow. Some of these same strategies, such as employing project-based learning, case studies, and simulations, may also help them to experience *transformational learning*. Transformative learning, a theory developed by Jack Mezirow (2000), refers to learning that results in a deep change in our beliefs, assumptions, or perspectives, making them more discriminating and able to construct opinions that will prove more true to guide our actions. Daniel Solorzano's project (1989), described in Strategy 34, is a prototypical example of transformational learning, exhibiting its four essential characteristics: relevant experience, critical self-reflection, reflective discourse, and effective action.

Although it has long been recognized that adults can experience profound changes through learning (Freire, 1970), transformative learning theory advocates that instructors of adults be cultural activists who promote agency among learners through reflective discourse and action. Such instructors strive to facilitate the authority of learners, keeping in mind four pedagogical principles:

- Introduce *a relevant experience*, prior or current, that solicits learners' desire to make meaning because they find it dissonant.

- Collaborate with learners and use *critical self-reflection* to consider the information and ideas generated.

- Facilitate *reflective discourse,* a discussion in which learners are able to redefine meaning for themselves based on the reciprocal sharing of information and insights with peers.

- Initiate *effective action,* determined in collaboration with learners.

As an illustration of these principles, we return to the example discussed in Chapter Three of Beverly Daniel Tatum's course The Psychology of Racism (1992), in which her instructional approach influenced the transformation of her students' perspectives and behavior. Their points of view, moral judgment, and personal goals were significantly changed. When Tatum taught this particular course, class size averaged twenty-four students, most of whom were European Americans, and who ranged in socioeconomic background from very poor to very wealthy. The course was designed "to provide students with an understanding of the psychological causes and emotional reality of racism as it appears in everyday life" (p. 2).

Beyond providing the reading material and media for the course, Tatum created opportunities for learners to experience situations in which they might witness the realities of racism firsthand. These *relevant experiences* included visiting supermarkets in neighborhoods with different racial compositions to compare costs and quality of goods and services, and going apartment hunting as mixed racial partners. Students kept journals for *critical reflection* on their experiences, using their writing as an opportunity to examine their own underlying beliefs and assumptions about racism and to generate their own understandings of these experiences.

Further, Tatum gave students the opportunity for *reflective discourse*—a chance to engage in dialogue with peers and to search for a clearer understanding and interpretation of their experiences. With such self-generated knowledge, learners were inclined to use their own agency to explore possibilities for change and ways to take *effective action.*

Students worked collaboratively in small groups to develop realistic action plans to interrupt racism. They also had the opportunity to privately tape interviews of themselves regarding their racial views and understandings at the beginning of the course and at the end of the course. After reviewing these two tapes, they wrote about their perceived changes in racial understanding.

The instructor, Tatum, accepted the validity of students' experiences, thinking, and judgments; facilitating learning in such a way that students made their own meaning and came to their own conclusions. Evaluations indicated that most students left the course transformed, personally behaving in their lives with new awareness and self-understanding.

• • •

When learners experience something that is relevant and disorienting, and when they have the time and support to understand their feelings and to gain insight into personal beliefs, they are at the portal of a new perspective. The implications of transformative learning for intensive courses, especially those in the liberal arts and social sciences, are profound. As an adult learning theory, it allows us as instructors to be facilitators of social change: to bring adult learners to a more critical consciousness with which they can generate their own meanings and actions for a more socially just world.

Chapter 7

Engendering Competence Among Learners

"So much of childhood socialization in school is aimed at intellectual competence…at helping children to compete successfully against their peers, gain public recognition for solo work, and demonstrate mastery by rapid response rates, quick articulation of ideas, and high scores on standardized tests. But these often turn out to be the very competencies that interfere with successful aging and learning,…where collaboration, relationship building, slowness and deliberateness, risk taking, and irreverence are the coin of the realm; where work and play, restraint and expressivity, discipline and improvisation are joined."

SARA LAWRENCE-LIGHTFOOT (2009)

ASSESSMENT IS TRICKY, especially in intensive formats in which the instructor gives a course grade, which is likely to be permanent, often in less than five weeks. How can anyone—either the instructor or the learner—know with some degree of certainty that real learning, the kind of learning that is beneficial to a person with adult responsibilities, has not only occurred but can be accurately measured in this amount of time? And, just as important, does the final grade reflect the learner's competence in the course? Does it represent what the learner should proficiently retain to be effective when applied to what he or she values? We have found that even experienced, effective instructors frequently struggle with decisions regarding assessment and grading. That is certainly the case for us. We begin this chapter by offering a perspective on competence, assessment, and grading that respects their importance to adult motivation and learning, explores their complex relationship, and explains how to strategically plan for their implementation in an intensive course.

The quest for competence starts with something as simple as a baby looking for a toy behind a pillow and ends in later life with what Erik Erikson called *generativity*, our desire to leave an enduring and beneficent legacy. Across cultures, this human need for competence is not acquired, but rather already exists and can be strengthened or weakened through learning experiences. Of the four motivational conditions of the motivational framework, competence is the most powerful for adults (Plaut and Markus, 2005). All people want to be effective at what they value.

For people with a European American background, competence usually is associated with acting as an *independent* self, distinct from others. Although there are many exceptions and wide variance, individual proficiency in learning for achieving what's best for one's personal interests is a popular norm for this group. For people from an East Asian background, competence is usually linked to acting as an *interdependent* self, whose actions are conjoined with and related to the actions of others (Plaut and Markus, 2005). For example, one study found that Korean adults, who had cultivated self-directedness in their learning without remaining interdependent with their group, were seen as immature and self-centered by other group members (Nah, 2000).

The quest for a *balanced sense of competence* is often found among people who actively pursue social and environmental responsibility as an ethical commitment. The emphasis in this book is on finding ways to support adult competence while illuminating the socially conscientious aspects of the individual's increased effectiveness.

Relating Assessment to Competence

In postsecondary education, assessment exerts a powerful motivational influence on adults because it is the socially sanctioned procedure for communicating about their competence. Our comments, scores, grades, and reports affect learners in the present and the future. Assessment often leaves a legacy for adults, directly or indirectly, by having an impact on their careers, vocational opportunities, professional advancement, and acceptance into various schools and programs. When assessment is authentic and reflects adult learners' effectiveness, it is most likely to be intrinsically motivating.

Assessment supports competence when it is *authentic*—connected to adults' life circumstances, frames of reference, and values. For example, if a case study were used as an authentic assessment, it would require learners to respond to a situation that mirrors their work or community life with the resources and conditions normally existing there. A real-life context for demonstrating learning enhances that learning's relevance for adults, appeals to their pragmatism, and affirms their rich background of experiences. By contrast, one can easily see how an impersonal multiple-choice exam might seem tedious and irrelevant to most adults.

Effectiveness, as defined for assessment, is the learners' awareness of their mastery, command, or accomplishment of something they find to be important in the *process* of learning or as an *outcome* of learning. Therefore, both the processes and the results of learning are significant information for adults. How well am I doing? and How well did this turn out? are a critical pair of questions for adult learning activities. In the example of the case study, to judge the quality of their thinking as they *process* the case, the adults would likely want feedback about how well their responses relate to the issues in the case study. In addition, when learners have settled on their responses to the case, they would also want to assess the quality of this *outcome* for its merits. Motivation is elicited when adults realize they have competently performed an activity that leads to a valued goal. Adults' awareness of their own competence affirms their need, which is present across cultures, to act purposefully in their world as they understand it.

Relating Grading to Competence

Although they do not accurately predict educational achievement or occupational competence, grades receive very high status in U.S. society, and most people believe they are valid indicators of learning (Ginsberg and Wlodkowski, 2009). For the majority of adults, low grades are threatening and stigmatizing. Generally low grades decrease adults' sense of competence and future motivation to learn. Not surprisingly, when adults receive low grades in their beginning courses in postsecondary education, they are significantly at risk to leave.

Nationally, grade inflation has been a trend for several decades, and B rather than C is the average grade in college today (Rojstaczur, 2009). There is compelling evidence that the source of the problem is the lack of validity of grades. Quantification of a grade point average (GPA) does not necessarily indicate students' learning with accuracy or objectivity. So many factors and forces enter into grading that ranking students based on grades from different subject areas, different teachers, and often different institutions is not a sufficiently valid process. A GPA on a transcript is really a conglomerate that doesn't specify its criteria or content.

Looking specifically at grading in accelerated courses, we have evidence that the average GPA of adult students is higher than the average GPA of younger students in traditional programs at the same university (Wlodkowski, 2000). When we explored this phenomenon in discussions with adult educators from thirty-four colleges at an international conference, we found their responses to be insightful and realistic. This is not rigorous research. However, we think the reasons why these educators estimated that adults received higher grades in their accelerated and intensive courses as well, sheds light on what an instructor may experience when grading adult students in intensive courses. A summarization of their comments follows:

- Adults are more oriented toward grades as a reflection of their capabilities than younger traditional students are and pressure faculty for higher grades.

- Employers use grade averages to determine tuition support. Higher grades mean a higher percentage of financial support. This influences faculty grading.

- Adjunct faculty, the majority of instructors for many adult programs, don't see grades as reflective of true performance and are more casual in issuing grades.

- Traditional faculty use more multiple-choice and other testlike measures that lead to lower grades in traditional courses.

- Faculty in adult programs use more projects and collaborative activities as the basis for their grading, which leads to higher grades because the work reflects the best thinking of the group, and there is a chance to revise the work before it is graded.

- Faculty in adult programs identify more with their students and experience more anxiety in giving lower grades.

Our response to these complexities and the conundrum of grade validity is to focus not on grades per se but on grading practices—how we arrive at a grade and what those practices do to support learning, competence, and intrinsic motivation (see Strategy 46 below). No matter what the scale (for example, A, B, C, and so forth), grades should be clearly specified and based on reasonable standards that students can use to guide their learning. Before we describe the motivational strategies that address assessment and effective grading practices, we want to identify what to avoid—those grading practices that diminish learner motivation. Douglas Reeves (2008) has identified three practices he considers toxic for student motivation, which we find applicable to intensive courses:

1. *Assigning zero credit for a missing assignment while using a numbering system such as 100 points to determine the course grade.* This is essentially a punitive practice that dramatically lowers a student's chances for a higher grade. This practice diminishes student motivation and does little to improve learning, when what really benefits learning is the completion of the assignment.

2. *Averaging all scores throughout a course to arrive at a final grade.* This practice implies that all learning is equal and that performance early in the course is as important as performance later in the course. Because much of complex learning is developmental, sequential, and the result of practice and revision, this approach to grading is typically reductive and unfair. Students' first papers, early tests, and beginning projects are the means by which they learn from their errors and make improvements based on feedback and guidance. It is also the way the real world works: we construct and then refine a product to achieve quality, or learn and then practice a skill to become proficient.

3. *Using a single test, assignment, or project that determines almost all of the student's grade but is based on less than a third of the learning in the course.* In addition, for high-stakes testing or projects, there have to be preceding formative tests or first and second drafts of the project so that students can receive feedback, revise, and refine their learning without penalty.

We add a fourth grading practice to avoid: using selected-response tests that rely on factual recall at the expense of intricate thought (Woolfolk, 2007). Such assessments as multiple-choice, true-false, and short-answer tests are attractive to instructors because they are easy to score and average. But if they only measure retention of superficial information, they promote cramming, because students can rapidly cover and retain this sort of inert knowledge for a short period of time (such as the duration of an intensive course). In a few weeks, and often in a few days, a student has forgotten this information. He has, however, captured the grade and finished the course, and little else may matter. The irony is that we as instructors have been complicit in this entire process.

Assessment and Grading Strategies to Engender Competence

The assessment and grading strategies described in this chapter as well as Strategy 19 in Chapter Five, which advocates the use of learning contracts, can be used in various combinations to eventually determine a student's course grade. As a set of interdependent practices, they align with the guiding principles for assessment of adult learning, which suggest that adults become more competent, feel more confident, and look forward to being assessed when assessments are as follows (Kasworm and Marienau, 1997):

- Related to goals they understand, find relevant, and want to accomplish

- Reflective of growth in learning

- Indicative of clear ways to improve learning without penalty

- Expected

- Returned promptly

- Permeated with instructor and peer feedback that is informative and supportive

- Used to encourage new challenges in learning

Strategy 39: Provide Effective Feedback

Feedback, information that learners receive about the quality of their work, is the most powerful communication that instructors can regularly use to develop learners' competence, whether or not they are being graded. Knowledge about the learning process and its results, comments about emerging skills, notes on a written assignment, and graphic records are forms of feedback that instructors and learners use. Feedback appears to enhance the motivation of learners because it allows learners to evaluate their progress, locate their performance within a framework of understanding, maintain their efforts toward realistic goals, self-assess, correct their errors efficiently, self-adjust, and receive encouragement from their instructors and peers.

Morris Keeton and his colleagues (Keeton, Sheckley, and Griggs, 2002) emphatically support the finding that feedback is a critical influence for enhancing practice and deepening adult learning. In studies at Harvard, students and alumni overwhelmingly reported that the single most important ingredient for making a course effective is getting rapid instructor response on assignments and exams (Light, 1990). In general, feedback is at its best when it is informative—when it identifies "what is good and why, as well as what needs to be improved and how" (Brophy, 2004, p. 72). However, feedback can be complex, and nuance makes a difference. The following paragraphs further describe characteristics to make feedback more effective:

• Effective feedback *provides evidence of the learner's effect relative to the learner's intent.* This feedback is most often based on criteria, standards, and models on which the learner and instructor have agreed (Wiggins, 1998). Students can compare their work against a standard: a superbly written executive letter, a museum sculpture, or a rubric for critical thinking. They are then in a position to understand what they have done and how it compares to their own goals or a specific product. They can be clear about the criteria against which their work is being evaluated and can more explicitly indicate what needs to be done for further effective learning.

• Effective feedback *avoids being controlling.* Feedback is more likely to enhance intrinsically motivated learning when it tells learners about their effectiveness and supports their self-determination (Deci and Ryan, 1991). Controlling feedback demands compliance. For example: "You're doing as you should be doing, meeting the standards for organization and evidence that I've set for writing in this course." Feedback that is more supportive of the learner's self-determination might sound something like this: "Your writing is well organized and vivid; I appreciate how well you've supported your rationale with facts and anecdotes." The difference is subtle but can be extreme in its impact.

• Effective feedback is *specific and constructive.* Most people prefer specific information and realistic suggestions for how to improve (Brophy, 2004). For example: "I found your insights on government spending compelling. To emphasize your conclusion, you might consider restating your initial premise in your last paragraph." When you are giving feedback, it is important to keep in mind how much the learner wants to or ought to decide on a course of action relative to the feedback. In general, the more an adult learner can self-assess and self-adjust, the more intrinsically motivated he or she will be.

• Effective feedback can be *quantitative.* In such areas as athletics, quantitative feedback has definite advantages. It is precise and can provide evidence of small improvements, and small improvements can have long-range effects. A popular form of this feedback is deciding what percentage of learning performance is correct or appropriate. Percentages are calculated by dividing the number of times the learning performance occurs correctly by the total number of times the performance opportunity occurs, as in batting averages and field goal percentages.

- Effective feedback is *prompt*. Promptness characterizes feedback that is quickly given as the situation requires, but is not necessarily immediate. Sometimes a moderate delay in feedback enhances learning because such a delay is simply culturally sensitive or polite. For example, after a public performance, waiting for learners to reduce their anxiety or talk with peers seems entirely appropriate.

- Effective feedback should be *frequent when practice is vital to the desired learning goal*. Frequent feedback is probably most helpful when new learning is first being acquired, when practice can clearly lead to improvement of skills. Studies indicate, for example, that deliberate practice with feedback when a person first learns to read, play the piano, or golf has strong positive effects on new learning (Coyle, 2007). When multiple errors become established, improving a skill is more difficult because feedback may seem confusing and progress too slow. It isn't that practice doesn't help at this point—it just takes more practice to help.

- Effective feedback is *positive*. Positive feedback places emphasis on improvements, progress, and correct responses rather than on deficiencies and mistakes. It increases learners' intrinsic motivation, feelings of well-being, and sense of competence, and helps them form positive attitudes toward their instructors. Adults prefer positive feedback, because when they are trying to improve, negative feedback that emphasizes errors and deficiencies can be discouraging.

In addition to the specific characteristics of feedback just listed, some refinements in the delivery of feedback may be helpful. For many skills, *graphing or charting feedback* can encourage learners' motivation because it makes progress more concrete and shows a record of increasing improvement. Consider *asking learners what they would like feedback on*, especially when working with diverse groups. Their needs and concerns may be different from ours, and the knowledge gained from such a discussion can make the feedback more relevant and motivating. Learners' *readiness to receive feedback* is also important. If people are resistant to feedback, they are not likely to learn or self-adjust. For example, this may mean holding off on feedback until we can arrange a personal conference or until learners are more comfortable with the learning situation.

Checking to make sure the feedback was understood can be important, especially for complex feedback or situations in which the adult is an English language learner. In fact, everything we have said about feedback so far could also apply to *group feedback*. Whether the group involved is a team, a collaborative group, or an entire class, feedback on total performance can influence each individual. Because group feedback consolidates members' mutual identification and sense of connection, it helps enhance group cohesiveness and morale. As a final point, please remember that sometimes the best form of feedback is simply to encourage adults to move forward to the next, more challenging learning opportunity.

Strategy 40: Promote Equity in Assessment Procedures

It is difficult to avoid bias in any test or assessment procedure that uses language, because the words and examples used in the evaluation sway the learner toward a particular cultural perspective. This is especially true for paper-and-pencil tests. We should always examine the assumptions embedded in the materials we create or select for assessment, because we do not want to penalize anyone for not having been fully socialized in a particular culture or not being oriented to a dominant perspective. We know adult learning is derived from multiple sources and varied life experiences. So when we are developing our assessment instruments and curricular materials, it is important to consider the following issues:

- *Invisibility*. Is there a significant omission of women and minority groups in assessment materials? This implies that certain groups are of less value, importance, and significance in our society.

- *Stereotyping*. When groups or members of groups are mentioned, are they assigned traditional or rigid roles that deny diversity and complexity within different populations?

- *Selectivity*. Is bias perpetuated by offering only one interpretation—or allowing only one interpretation—of an issue, situation, or group of people? Such bias in assessment may prevent tapping into the varied perspectives and knowledge of learners.

- *Unreality*. Do assessment items lack a historical context that acknowledges—when relevant—prejudice and discrimination? Glossing over painful or controversial issues obstructs authenticity and creates a sense of unreality.

- *Linguistic bias*. Do materials reflect bias in language? For example, are masculine examples, terms, and pronouns dominant?

Even directions for tests can be biased. This is especially detrimental for English language learners, who benefit from test instructions that are direct and simple. Whenever possible, it helps to avoid the passive voice and ambiguous comments. Test instructions should be in short sentences with clear and explicit guidelines. Students should also be allowed adequate processing time to understand questions and directions.

It is fair and reasonable to provide assessment accommodations for learners with disabilities and for English language learners (Kornhaber, 2004). For example, they may need to be assessed in a small group or individually. Modifications may include extra time to complete tests; presentation of assessment materials in audio or video; and allowances for different ways of responding, such as dictation or using an interpreter.

Please also keep in mind Strategies 15 and 17 in Chapter Five, which advocate using relevant models to demonstrate expected learning and making criteria of assessment as fair and clear as possible. These strategies are essential to promoting equity in assessment for all students.

Strategy 41: Use Formative Assessments to Improve Learning and Instruction Essential to Course Goals

When not used for grades or evaluation scores, ongoing assessments are an excellent instructional method for understanding what adults are learning, how they are thinking, what their progress is, which learning problems to address, what to offer them as feedback, and how to improve our teaching (Donovan, Bransford, and Pellegrino, 1999). Applied in this manner, these are *formative assessments* that guide instruction and identify areas that learners may need to deepen, improve, practice, revise, or strengthen in terms of their understanding and skill development.

For example, in an accounting course at an urban college, the assessment requires learners to make recommendations based on a cost-volume-profit analysis for a manufacturing company's production and sale of a new product. Students' recommendations and calculations reveal both their conceptual and computational understanding of this analysis. They have had time to practice it, and the instructor could have chosen to grade their work. However, due to the professional value of this analysis and the linguistic diversity of his students, the instructor prefers to use this assignment as a formative assessment to give each learner feedback about his or her understanding of this analysis, offer each one suggestions for further practice, and use the information from this assessment to improve his teaching of this form of appraisal.

Many instructors are experiencing greater linguistic diversity among adult learners than ever before. Often English language learners need more practice and feedback during learning in order to accommodate the linguistic forms and Eurocentric context of the courses they take. Formative assessment is one more strategy for meeting linguistically diverse adults where they are in a way that benefits all learners.

Our experience with formative assessments suggests that most students like them, appreciate the feedback, and see them as a way to improve instruction and to engage as a community of learners. It may seem counterintuitive to use formative assessments in intensive courses because their duration is short. However, the expanded hours per class can allow for this type of assessment and follow-up with feedback by the instructor, either in the same block of time or through e-mail before the next class.

Strategy 42: Use Authentic Performance Tasks as Part of Assessment so Learners Will Know They Can Proficiently Apply New Learning to Their Real Lives

Although authentic performance tasks go hand in hand with problem-based learning and project-based learning (Strategies 33 and 34 in Chapter Six), they can stand alone as effective assessment procedures. They are among the oldest forms of assessment and have been routinely used in adult education for many years (Fenwick and Parsons, 2000). Today we have a more sophisticated understanding of authentic performance tasks and their central idea: that assessment should resemble as closely as possible the ways adult learners will express in their real lives what they have learned in a course. For example, we would assess students learning computer programming skills by asking them to write or debug source codes of computer programs.

The closer assessment procedures come to allowing learners to proficiently demonstrate their learning in the environment where they will eventually use that learning, the greater will be learners' motivation to do well. Providing the opportunity for learners to complete an authentic task is one of the best ways to conclude a learning activity because it indicates competence, develops self-confidence, and promotes *transfer of learning—retaining and using new learning in everyday applications beyond the course.*

According to Wiggins (1998), an assessment task, problem, or project is authentic if it has the following characteristics:

- *It is realistic.* The task replicates how people's knowledge and capacities are "tested" in their real world.

- *It requires judgment and innovation.* People have to use knowledge wisely to solve unstructured problems, just as a carpenter remodeling part of a house must do more than simply follow a routine procedure.

- *It asks the learners to "do" the subject.* Rather than recite or demonstrate what they have been taught or what is already known, the learners have to explore and work within the discipline, as when they demonstrate their competence for a history course by writing history from the perspective of particular people in an actual historical situation.

- *It replicates or simulates the contexts that adults find in their workplaces, communities, or personal lives.* These contexts involve specific situations and their demands: for example, managers learning conflict resolution skills could apply them to their work situations, with consideration of the actual personalities and responsibilities involved.

- *It assesses the learners' ability to use an integration of knowledge and skill to negotiate a complex task effectively.* Learners have to put their knowledge and skills together to meet real-life challenges, often involving adaptive decision making (see Strategy 36 in Chapter Six). This characteristic is analogous to the difference between taking a few shots in a warm-up drill and actually taking shots in a real basketball game.

- *It allows appropriate opportunities to rehearse, practice, consult resources, and get feedback on and refine performances and products.* These opportunities are so important. Learning and, consequently, assessment are not one-shot enterprises! As emphasized in Strategy 41, much of learning is formative, whether its purpose is understanding how to repair plumbing, write a publishable article, or bake a pie. We put out our first attempt and see how it works, reads, or tastes. We repeatedly move through a cycle of *perform, get feedback, revise, perform.* That's how most high-quality products and performances are attained—especially in real life.

Strategy 43: Use Assessment Options Based on Howard Gardner's Multiple Intelligences

As we said in Chapter Five (Strategy 20), adults have different profiles of intelligences. When they have the opportunity to select an assessment process that reflects their particular intellectual strengths, they are likely to feel encouraged and motivated to demonstrate their competence. Table 7.1, adapted from *Multiple Intelligences and Adult Literacy* (Viens and Kallenbach, 2004) and *Teaching and Learning Through Multiple Intelligences*

TABLE 7.1

Assessment Menu for the Multiple Intelligences

Intelligence	Assessment Processes
Linguistic	Tell or write a short story to explain …
	Keep a journal to illustrate …
	Write a poem, myth, play, or editorial about …
	Create a debate to discuss …
	Create an advertising campaign to depict …
	Create a talk show about …
	Write a culminating essay to review …
Logical-mathematical	Complete a cost-benefit analysis of …
	Write a computer program for …
	Design and conduct an experiment to …
	Create story problems for …
	Conduct a mock trial to …
	Induce or deduce a set of principles on …
	Create a timeline for …
	Create a crossword puzzle for …
Musical	Create a song that explains or expresses …
	Revise lyrics of a known song to …
	Collect music and songs to …
	Create a dance to illustrate …
	Create a music video to …
	Create an advertisement to illustrate …
Spatial	Create a piece of art that demonstrates …
	Create a poster to …
	Create a videotape, collage, or photo album of …
	Chart, concept-map, or graph …
	Design a flag or logo to express …
	Create a scale model of …
	Create a mobile to …
Bodily-kinesthetic	Perform a play on …
	Invent or revise a game to …
	Role-play or simulate …
	Use puppets to explore …
	Create a sequence of movements to explain …
	Create a scavenger hunt to …
	Create a poster session or exhibition to …

TABLE 7.1 *Continued*

Intelligence	Assessment Processes
Interpersonal	Participate in a service project that will … Offer multiple perspectives of … Collaborate to resolve a local problem by … Teach a group to … Use what you've learned to … Conduct an interview or a discussion to change or influence …
Intrapersonal	Create a personal philosophy about … Discern what is essential in … Explain your intuitive hunches about … Explain your emotions about … Explain your assumptions in a critical incident … Keep a reflective journal to …
Naturalist	Discover and describe the patterns in … Create a typology for … Relate and describe the interdependence of … Observe and describe … Using observations and field notes, describe your learning about … Use a field trip to analyze …

(Campbell, Campbell, and Dickinson, 2004), is categorized by type of intelligence and coordinated with assessment processes that are likely to allow learners to demonstrate this particular intellectual strength.

In addition to accommodating multiple intelligences, the assessment menu in Table 7.1 allows for a range of learning and performance that requires deep understanding—the ability to design, teach, discern, explain, analyze, write, create, and so on. For example, a learner in a science course might design an experiment to analyze the chemicals in the local water supply, and write an editorial based on the results for the local paper. These assessments allow for imaginative experiences that let adults use their unique perspectives, preferences, and strengths. Furthermore, with these assessments, adults can develop deeper connections between new learning and their cultural backgrounds and values.

Strategy 44: When Using Rubrics, Make Sure They Assess the Essential Features of Performance and Are Fair, Valid, and Clear

Rubrics are used to make judgments for evaluation. A rubric is a guideline for evaluating a learner's work. It provides the criteria that determine how acceptable or unacceptable a given performance is. Instructors assign grades or scores according to the rubric. Although many instructors do not use rubrics formally, they do use them on an intuitive basis. They make evaluations of a learner's work based on experience and knowledge, but often without explicit language. For example, the instructor might say, "This writing is excellent, insightful, and entertaining" without specifically saying why or what makes the writing so successful. Barbara Walvoord's definition (2004, p. 19) speaks well to a rubric's advantages and limitations: "A rubric articulates in writing the various criteria and standards" that an instructor "uses to evaluate" a learner's work. "It translates informed professional judgment into numerical ratings on a scale. Something is always lost in the translation, but the advantage is that these ratings can now be communicated and compared."

Rubrics answer a question that counts for many adults: What are you going to use to judge me? As a set of scoring guidelines for evaluating learners' work, a rubric strongly directs their learning. To perform this service clearly and proficiently, a rubric should answer the following questions (Wiggins, 1998, p. 154):

By what criteria should performance be judged?

What should we look for to judge performance success?

What does the range in quality of performance look like?

How do we determine validly, reliably, and fairly what score should be given and what that score should mean?

How should the different levels of quality be described and distinguished from one another?

If rubrics answer these questions while they focus on the essentials of performance, learners can assess themselves using rubrics to improve before the instructor evaluates their performance. Then rubrics can enhance motivation, because they significantly increase the probability of learners' achieving competence in a subject. However, rubrics need models and indicators to make each level of quality readily understandable. And they need to be created or revised with input from learners if they are to be culturally sensitive. For example, if we use *smiles frequently* as one indicator for *very good* presentation style, we penalize someone who tends to be droll or someone from a culture in which smiling frequently is more an indication of anxiety than of ease. Excellent rubrics are valuable but flawed assistants in making judgments about learning—flawed because language at best renders, but never duplicates, experience.

EXHIBIT 7.1

Rubric for Expressing an Idea Clearly

Rating	Descriptor with Indicators
Exemplary = 4	Clearly communicates the main idea or theme and provides support that contains rich, vivid, and powerful detail.
Competent = 3	Clearly communicates the main idea or theme and provides suitable support and detail.
Acceptable with flaws = 2	Clearly communicates the main idea or theme, but support is sketchy or vague.
Needs revision = 1	The main idea or theme is not discernible.

Exhibit 7.1 is a sample rubric for judging the clear expression of a main idea in an essay. (Other rubrics would be necessary for evaluating other dimensions of performance in the essay, such as critical thinking or writing skills.) This rubric gives at least one example to help understand Grant Wiggins's guidelines (1998) for creating effective rubrics. In this case, these guidelines (found below) apply to the rubric in Exhibit 7.1.

An instructor evaluating a set of essays with the rubric in Exhibit 7.1 will also use a model such as an essay from a previous class, with an exemplar for the descriptor of each performance level as she follows these guidelines:

- Use the rubric to accurately discriminate the essential features of performance for expressing an idea clearly in each essay. This makes the rubric valid.

- Rely on the rubric's descriptive language (what the quality or its absence looks like), as opposed to relying on merely evaluative language, such as "excellent writing," to make the discrimination and communicate it to students. For example, it is preferable to say, "The personal experiences you use to illustrate the concept of authenticity are rich, vivid, and powerful," rather than, "Your writing in this paragraph is excellent."

- Use the rubric to consistently make fine discriminations across four levels of performance. When a rubric can be repeatedly used to make the same discriminations with the same sample of performances, it is reliable. (To maintain reliability, use rubrics with no more than six levels of performance.)

- Make sure learners can use the rubric and its descriptors (and the model for writing their essay) for each level of performance to self-assess and self-correct their work.

- See that the rubric has parallel language: each descriptor should generally match the others in terms of language used.

- See that the rubric is coherent and that it focuses on the same criteria throughout.

- See that the rubric is continuous. The degree of difference between each descriptor as indicated by its rating or level of performance is discernable by its language and that difference tends to be equal.

You may also wish to see how these guidelines have been followed to construct the two rubrics found in the comprehensive syllabus for the Introduction to Research course in Exhibit 4.2 in Chapter Four. If you choose to develop rubrics to evaluate adult performance, please keep Strategy 40 in mind as a general guide for a more culturally responsive approach to their construction.

Strategy 45: Use Self-Assessment Methods to Provide Insights and Deepen Learning

In addition to self-assessment in which learners compare their work against rubrics and make self-adjustments, other reflective assessment methods enable adults to better understand themselves as learners and participants in a complex world. These methods make use of the immersion that learners experience when intensive courses meet for large blocks of time. Self-assessment of this type provides a means for learners to merge their identities and values with what they are learning. This kind of self-assessment can strengthen their competence and bridge formal learning with their subjective world.

Jean MacGregor (1994) advises instructors to build self-assessment into longer learning situations as an ongoing activity. We agree and appreciate using this strategy on a regular basis. Among the methods we have found most beneficial for intensive courses are journals and closure techniques.

Journals

Journals can take a number of forms. For example, students in a science course may use journals to synthesize lab notes, address the quality of their own work, and examine the group's emerging interests and concerns. Journals document risk, experimentation with ideas, and self-expression.

They are an informative complement to more conventional forms of assessment.

To increase their critical awareness and sensitivity to cultural differences, learners can use journals to address the following questions: From whose viewpoint am I seeing or reading or hearing? From what angle or perspective? What is the evidence, and how reliable is it? Whose purposes are served by this information?

A learner's journals can include interests, ideas, and issues related to course material and processes; recurring problems; responses to questions from the instructor; responses to questions generated by the learner; and important connections the learner is making. Providing time in class for learners to respond in their journals to readings, discussions, and significant questions builds community around the journal process and sends yet another message that the classroom is a place in which the skills of insight and making personal meaning are valued.

Journals require time and effort. Initially, it may be best for learners to pay less attention to the mechanics, organization, and logic of their writing; they should simply try to get their thoughts and feelings down on paper where they can learn from them. Having sufficiently incubated, this material can be reorganized and summarized later.

Closure Techniques

Closure activities are opportunities for learners to synthesize—to examine general or specific aspects of what they have learned, to identify emerging thoughts or feelings, to discern themes, to construct meaning, to relate learning to real-life experiences, and to decide what learning to use. In these activities, closure can become a way of building coherence between what people have learned in the course and their personal experience beyond it. The following are three methods we have found effective for constructing positive closure in intensive courses:

• "Head, Heart, Hand" is a closure activity that allows learners to integrate different dimensions of a learning experience. After learners have had a short time for reflection, the activity may be conducted as a small- or large-group experience in which all learners have a chance to hear one another's voices. Learners respond to one or more of the following prompts: for "Head," learners identify something they will continue to think about as a consequence of the learning experience; for "Heart," they identify a feeling that has emerged as a result of the learning experience; for "Hand," they identify a desired action they will take that the learning experience has stimulated.

- "Summarizing Questions" is an activity that enables learners to reflect on an entire course. The following are examples of summarizing questions adapted from *Embracing Contraries: Explorations in Learning and Teaching* by Peter Elbow (1986) and *Discussion as a Way of Teaching* by Brookfield and Preskill (2005):

> Which assumption of yours was most challenged by what you learned in this course? Has it changed? How?

> What have you accomplished in this course that you are proud of?

> How do your accomplishments compare with what you had hoped for and expected at the start?

> What is the most important thing you did during this course?

> What idea or skill was hardest to really "get"? What crucial idea or skill came naturally?

> What are a few ways you could have done a better job?

> What has this course helped you realize you have to work on most?

> What perspectives different from your own did you gain from this course that you now appreciate?

> Is there any way that you will act differently as a result of this course? If so, please describe it.

> What would you most like to say about being in this course?

- "Critical Incident Questionnaire" is a self-assessment approach we have adopted from the work of Stephen Brookfield (1995, p. 115). In teaching intensive courses, it helps us to be more responsive as instructors and helps learners be more reflective about their significant experiences.

The Critical Incident Questionnaire has five questions, each of which asks learners to write details about important events that took place while they were learning. For intensive courses, we prefer to use it at the end of each session that is three hours or longer. We print the questions on a form, leaving space below each question for learners' responses. Learners complete the questions anonymously and retain a copy of their answers for their own benefit.

We as instructors explore the questionnaire forms, looking for themes, patterns, and learners' concerns or confusions that need our responses or adjustments. We also look out for the parts of our learning and instruction that have been affirmed. We find hints and suggestions for areas to probe or deepen learners' understanding. Most important, we have found that this questionnaire gives us a more sensitive reading of the emotional

---

EXHIBIT 7.2

The Critical Incident Questionnaire

1. At what moment in this class session did you feel most engaged with what was happening?

2. At what moment in this class session did you feel most distanced from what was happening?

3. What action that anyone (instructor or learner) took in this class session did you find most affirming and helpful?

4. What action that anyone (instructor or learner) took in this class session did you find most puzzling or confusing?

5. What about this class session surprised you the most? (This could be something about your own reactions to what went on, or something that someone did, or anything else that occurs to you.)

---

reactions of learners and a greater awareness of those areas that may create controversy or conflict. However, we do realize that for some students, writing may inhibit their responses, and we acknowledge this shortcoming of the process to the group.

For the beginning of the class session immediately following the distribution of the questionnaire, we outline the questionnaire results in short phrases and have a dialogue with the learners about these responses. This tends to build trust, further communication, and deepen learning. What we like most is that this form of self-assessment can be so fluidly used to build community.

• • •

In general, we regard all the self-assessments we have described as formative assessments. Consequently, we do not grade them.

Strategy 46: Use Grading Practices That Enhance Learner Motivation

The following suggestions are an aggregate from both our professional experience and a review of the literature on grading. They are tailored to respect the structure of intensive courses in a way that provides students with fair and informative grades.

• Limit what is represented by grades to such indicators of learning achievement as formal assignments, performances, projects, and tests. Such factors as attendance, effort, participation, and attitude ought to be addressed through course requirements and participation agreements.

- Use criterion-referenced standards or rubrics to distribute grades. Grading on a curve does not allow all students to see how close they are to meeting standards of performance. If all students reach the same standard, it is okay for all to reach the same grade.

- Relate grading procedures to the intended learning goals. The emphasis we give to different topics or skills in a class should be reflected in the weight they have in determining the final grade. For example, it is possible that a particular skill or topic might be so important in a given course—such as constructing a lesson plan in an education course, conducting a study in a research course, or performing a particular experiment in a science course—that 40 percent of the course grade may be dependent upon learners' proficiency in it. Projects that integrate important skills and knowledge may reasonably exceed the 40 percent ceiling.

- Use summative and integrative assessments for grade calculations. Summative assessments provide a summary (and often an integration) of learning over a given period of time. Final exams and capstone projects are classic examples of summative assessments for an entire course. However, do not grade everything students do, and do not include all marks in the final grades. Sometimes it helps to provide feedback through formative assessments, with scores that are based on an evaluative scale but that are not counted toward the final grade.

- When possible, offer opportunities to improve grades. In an intensive course, even second chances are difficult to offer. Nevertheless, if there's a situation in which all students can have the same opportunity for further learning, retesting and revising are legitimate options. Some instructors, in the interest of fairness, require students who want to retake a test or revise an assignment to demonstrate that they have done additional work to merit the opportunity for a chance at an improved grade.

- Use care calculating numbers for final grades. Very low scores on tests or assignments can dramatically lower averages in ways that do not reflect students' actual learning achievements. In such instances, consider using students' median scores as a representation of learning. Also, consider giving students a chance to retest or revise the work. Or, alternately, let a future assignment that demonstrates the same learning as that in the former graded assignment count for extra credit.

- Discuss assessment and grading with students at the beginning of the course. The criteria for high-quality work should not be a mystery to students. It is extremely helpful for students to see the grading schemes and rubrics that you will use to judge performance and that can serve as models of superior performance. If discussion leads to awareness of bias or issues of fairness in the assessment or grading procedures, allow for the revision of grading criteria and schemes to make them more equitable.

Reward and Communication Strategies to Engender Competence

The remaining motivational strategies in this chapter also enhance competence but are frequently used apart from evaluation measures. These strategies can be used to reward or communicate meaningfully with students. Often they are rewards or communications given to students as the situation merits.

Strategy 47: Effectively Praise and Reward Learning

As we understand it, the definition of *praise* has the same meaning here as it has in conventional usage: to commend the worth of or to express approval or admiration (Brophy, 1981). It is an intense response on the part of an instructor, one that goes beyond positive feedback to include such emotions as surprise, delight, or excitement as well as sincere appreciation for the learner's accomplishment. ("That's a remarkable answer! It's comprehensive, insightful, and extremely precise.")

The use of praise as a strategy has a controversial history. Some scholars have opposed praise and rewards on principle, viewing them as bribes for doing something that is often in the learners' best interest or in the best interest of society (Kohn, 1993). Others are critical of praise because it may contribute to a hierarchical relationship between learners and instructors. Instructors distribute praise because they are the judges and experts who deem learners as praiseworthy. The critics see this kind of social exchange as likely to diminish the chances for co-learning and for a more egalitarian relationship with adult learners.

In general, to praise effectively we need to praise *well*, rather than necessarily *often*. The same could be said about rewarding effectively—in fact, praise is often considered to be a verbal reward (Pittman, Boggiano, and Ruble, 1983). Whether the reward is verbal (praise), tangible (money, promotions, privileges), or symbolic (grades, trophies, awards), there are guidelines that can ensure the positive effects of rewards on learner motivation. The six suggestions that follow are based on a continuing analysis by Jere Brophy (2004). Although Brophy has mainly conducted his research with children and adolescents, this material is congruous with findings from studies focused on young adults and adults learning in the workplace (Morgan, 1984; Keller and Litchfield, 2002).

Effective praise and rewards share these six characteristics:

1. *They are given with sincerity, spontaneity, variety, and other signs of credibility.* These characteristics may be more pertinent for praise than for other rewards. Rewards are often known ahead of time and given according to procedure. However, the affect with which a reward is given is critical to its impact on the learner. An insincerely given reward or statement of praise is an insult to an adult.

2. *They are based on the attainment of specific performance criteria.* This means that the learner has achieved a certain standard and clearly understands what particular personal behaviors are being acknowledged. This approach not only makes the reward or praise informational but also significantly increases the adult's chances of learning exactly which behaviors are important. For example, "Nice job" written on a paper is not as helpful as, "This paper does not have a single spelling, grammar, or syntax error. I appreciate the meticulous editing it so obviously reflects."

3. *They are adapted in sufficiency, quantity, and intensity to the accomplishments achieved.* Praise or rewards that are less than what is merited can be insulting and demeaning. Praise or rewards that are too much for what has been accomplished are excessive and disturbing. In fact, we have clichés to reflect adult embarrassment in response to inadequate or undeserved praise: "damning with faint praise" (too little praise) and "gushing over trivia" (too much praise).

4. *They are given to attribute success to the apparent combination of the personal effort, knowledge, and capabilities of the learner.* Emphasizing some combination these attributes (see Strategy 14 in Chapter Five) increases the learner's sense of responsibility and implies that the learner can continue such accomplishments in the future. For example: "Your design of this model is exceptional (capability). It meets all the criteria for strength, durability, and aesthetics. Would you mind sharing how you created it with the rest of the team? I think we could all learn from your approach (knowledge)."

5. *They are given contingent on success at a challenging task.* This makes the learner's task *praiseworthy* and testifies to the learner's competence. The praise implies that the learner overcame a real difficulty and deserves the recognition.

6. *They are adapted to the preference of the individual.* Again, this characteristic may be more applicable to praise than to rewards. Rewards are often given in a ritualistic manner, as in award ceremonies. In more collectivist cultures, such as many Asian societies, adults may prefer to receive praise indirectly as members of a social group that has been recognized, rather than directly as individuals. One study found that Chinese adults did not want to be used as "good examples for others," whereas a group of adults from the United States found that to be quite acceptable (Jones, Rozelle, and Chang, 1990). When in doubt, it is probably best to give praise privately.

There is a mnemonic device for remembering these six guidelines: 3S-3P, which stands for Sincere, Specific, Sufficient, Properly attributed, Praiseworthy, and Preferred. The mnemonic can be stated in a sentence: "Praise (or other rewards) should be Sincere, Specific, Sufficient, and Properly attributed for genuinely Praiseworthy behavior, in a manner Preferred by the learner." In general, it is important to remember that the subjective viewpoint of the learner and the context in which praise and other rewards are given will immensely influence their effect.

Strategy 48: Use Incentives to Develop Motivation for Valued Learning That Is Initially Unappealing

An *incentive* can be defined as an anticipated reward. It serves as a goal we expect to achieve as a result of some specific behavior. Incentives take many forms, such as recognition, money, relationships, and privileges. We use this concept to support intrinsic motivation and individual autonomy while learning. Incentives should be used as a means to assist adults in becoming more effective at what they personally value, rather than as a means to manipulate them.

We frequently use rewards for performing activities we value but find tedious, difficult, or perhaps even painful. We reward ourselves at certain points for performing such activities as exercising, dieting, studying, budgeting, cleaning, and practicing just about anything from dance steps to golf swings. The reward may be a piece of chocolate, a massage, a movie, a long-distance call, or a walk outside. Knowing these kinds of incentives are coming at the end of our tasks makes the tedium or effort more bearable.

There are at least two situations in which incentives may be a means to encourage adult participation in a valued learning activity:

1. *The learner has had little or no experience with the learning activity.* Perhaps she is learning how to use a new technology. The learner

anticipates there may be added value inherent in this technology but has not yet realized that value. In this case, the learner is likely to see the incentive as a reward for "trying out" or becoming competent with the new technology. In such a case the incentive might be a certificate designating proficiency with the new technology.

2. *The learner has to develop competence before the learning activity can become enjoyable or interesting.* Some sports, such as tennis and swimming, are good examples of this situation, as are learning to speak another language or use a personal computer or play the trumpet. There are so many things that are valuable to learn but just not that appealing to do until the learner has achieved at least a moderate level of competence. In such situations, incentives may be the only positive means to sustain effort until the necessary level of proficiency provides its own satisfaction. For the example of learning another language, when the class reaches a specific level of proficiency, it attends a cultural event together where this language is spoken.

When it comes to incentives, the paramount issues to consider are the learners' value for the activity or for what it leads to, the probability of increasing competence through the activity, and the cultural context.

Strategy 49: Emphasize When Learning Has Natural Consequences and Help Learners to Be Aware of Their Impact

Natural consequences are *changes in a person* resulting from learning (Vargas, 1977). Reading a book may have the natural consequence of producing new insights and expanded awareness in an adult. Just as exercises can strengthen muscles, finding solutions to arithmetic problems can strengthen math skills. Both consequences naturally result within a person from repeated performance. Emphasizing natural consequences is an effective motivational strategy, because it helps students more vividly understand the personal impact that results from their learning—their new competencies.

Understanding natural consequences encourages us as instructors to make learning active as soon as possible, so that adults can quickly experience personal changes—literally, new learning—to increase and maintain their motivation. For example, learning to speak and understand words and phrases in a new language, learning to send and receive e-mail, or learning to perform a chi-square analysis to determine significant differences for a personally relevant survey. The guiding question is, as a result of this learning activity, what does the learner know and what else can the learner do that is important for him or her to understand? In intensive courses, the sooner students realize that they have "changed," that they have concretely learned something new and important with which they can actually do something of value, the sooner they will develop sustainable motivation—motivation to learn that lasts throughout the block of time scheduled, and often for the entire course as well.

One can see that natural consequences and feedback go hand in hand. Sometimes instructors need to act as mirrors or magnifying glasses to reveal relevant consequences not readily apparent to learners. Suppose, for example, that a working adult takes a course in technical report writing. She achieves the standard of performance and successfully completes the course. But also as a result of the course she has learned to be more confident as a writer, enjoys writing more than ever before, sees improvement in personal letter writing, and will now pursue a career in which writing is a requisite skill. When the instructor takes some time at the end of this course to discuss with the learners what other outcomes beyond the learning objectives they may have achieved, she and other students have an opportunity to deepen their motivation and broaden their transfer of learning.

Discussion is not the only means of making natural consequences more conspicuous. Authentic performance tasks (Strategy 42) and simulations (Strategy 36 in Chapter Six) often reveal more than the learning objectives may encompass. Using self-assessment methods (Strategy 45) as well as videos to record progress and demonstrate before-and-after effects can also highlight a variety of natural consequences of learning for adults.

Strategy 50: Provide Positive Closure at the End of Significant Units of Learning

A significant unit of learning can be determined by length or importance. In terms of length, the ending of any course marks a significant unit of learning. In terms of importance, a significant unit of learning is any segment of learning that has some characteristic that makes it special: the level of difficulty or creativity; the type of learning structure or process (special equipment, materials, location, grouping, or task); or the presence of prominent individuals, such as an esteemed audience or speaker.

In all these cases, something notable is coming to an end. Positive closure enhances learners' motivation because it affirms the entire learning process, verifies the value of the experience, directly or indirectly acknowledges competence, increases cohesiveness within the group, and encourages the surfacing of inspiration and other beneficial emotions in the learners themselves. Positive closure can be a small gesture, such as thanking learners for their cooperation, or something much more extravagant, such as an awards ceremony. We have found that intensive courses, due to the large blocks of time in which students actively learn together, tend to facilitate the development of close ties among learners. Students appreciate celebrations, acknowledgments, and sharing, which are some of the best ways to achieve positive closure:

• *Celebrations.* For people all over the world, festivals and holidays are a joyous means of acknowledging the ending of seasons, religious observations, and harvests. Celebrations allow us to savor with learners their moment of accomplishment. This can be a pleasurable discussion, a party, a round of applause, sitting back and recalling special moments, or offering congratulations. Let the moment linger and enjoy it together. It is a happy occasion, not to be taken for granted. Celebrations are wonderfully inclusive: they allow people to feel pleasure for whatever they personally accomplished or valued during the learning experience.

• *Acknowledgments.* These can be simple statements of gratitude and appreciation or more formal and ritualized awards. The goal is to recognize noteworthy learner contributions or achievements during the span of the learning event. Depending on the situation, acknowledgments can be given by the instructor, the learners, or both.

• *Sharing.* Sharing is anything the instructor and learners do to show their caring and sensitivity to the special quality of the learning experience and those involved in it. Some have cooked dinner for their class. Some have told stories that reflected their special feelings or insights. Some have brought in personal collections or demonstrated their musical talents. Frequently, this type of sharing takes the form of a poignant final statement, which may include an eloquent poem or an inspirational quotation. When a learning experience has gone well, it deserves a fitting form of closure.

• • •

This chapter has presented strategies to engender competence. In postsecondary education, assessment and grading are the most frequently used processes to communicate competence to adult learners. As we have discussed them, it is obvious that they can also diminish learner motivation. As always, their meaning will be understood by learners through a cultural lens, reflecting personal, familial, and communal values of what particular grades and scores communicate. How many times have we seen an adult learner who receives a B and seems devastated by it while another student in the same class regards the same grade with joy. Why? Most of us as instructors seldom ever know. What this image does convey is that due to their emotional and lasting impact, assessment and grading are ethical processes and among our most profound responsibilities as educators.

Chapter 8

Designing Instruction for Intensive and Accelerated Courses

"Among the few places where time spent can be more important than what is accomplished are prisons and schools."

WILLIAM GLASSER (1986)

THE CONSIDERATION OF instructional time for accelerated and intensive courses may seem paradoxical, because although each class session is two to five hours longer than those of conventional courses, the overall length of these courses is shorter by as much as eight weeks or more. As instructors, we have to simultaneously stretch and condense our curricula. Some of us may ask, what do I do with students for four entire hours?, while asking in the same breath, how do I cover this curriculum in five weeks?

In our work with colleges that were initiating or transforming their programs into intensive and accelerated formats, these two questions were foremost in the minds of those faculty responsible for accommodating this significant change in their departments. We reviewed with them the research on quality discussed in Chapter One of this book and emphasized the instructional differences between intensive and more conventional courses, highlighting such elements as large instructional blocks of time, offering guidance for independent study outside of class, and planning and organizing in-class learning. We also provided them with examples of course syllabi, such as the one found with Strategy 10 in Chapter Four. We encourage you to keep these same components in mind while delving into the main subject of this chapter: how to design instruction for accelerated and intensive courses.

Neuroscientific research (Wlodkowski, 2008) supports what Donovan, Bransford, and Pellegrino generalized in 1999: "[K]nowledge of a large set of disconnected facts is not sufficient. To develop competence in an area of inquiry, students must have opportunities to learn with understanding. Deep understanding of subject matter transforms factual information into usable knowledge. … [C]ommand of concepts shapes their understanding of new information: it allows them to see patterns, relationships, or discrepancies" (p. 12). What this means for instruction is that concepts make factual knowledge meaningful. As such, they are the "glue" for binding information in patterns that make them relevant, understood, and retained.

What we have found is that many disciplines have overloaded the content that is required for learning in a course—extensive facts and research that are often unrelated and marginal to understanding the subject. This phenomenon occurs in the introductory courses in the biological, physical, and social sciences. A perusal of the mega-textbooks for these courses makes this situation obvious.

For retention and transfer of knowledge, however, "coverage" is less important than focusing on the key concepts of a discipline that tie significant facts together and make them understandable and usable. This principal should guide designing and teaching intensive courses. Instructors also need an instructional plan to teach concepts that is motivating and appropriate to the time parameters of intensive courses.

Part of the challenge is maintaining efficiency. Encouraging motivation takes interpersonal skills and time. Like a good conversation, motivation cannot be rushed. A helpful way to look at using a motivational strategy is to see it as an investment: it pays dividends, but often not immediately. Also, because what motivates people is often not part of the structure of the knowledge or skill they are learning, instructors have to plan for motivation in its own right. Motivation cannot be taken for granted. If we look at the motivational strategies described in the previous chapters, most of them address cultural and internal human conditions that influence and mediate learning, such as inclusion, attitude, meaning, and competence. Although many instructional design formats and course modules for adults do not address these influences, understanding them is essential to fostering motivated learning, and at the very least it is sensible to plan for them (King, 2005).

We have found the Motivational Framework for Culturally Responsive Teaching to be an effective model for analyzing and designing instruction for intensive courses (Wlodkowski and Westover, 1999). The framework and its related strategies enable us to combine a series of learning activities from the beginning to the end of an instructional sequence so that they create a network of mutually supportive motivational conditions. These conditions—inclusion, attitude, meaning, and competence—work in concert to elicit students' intrinsic motivation for learning for the entire learning sequence. Furthermore, using the motivational framework can help you design a complete lesson or learning unit for a large block of time (see Tables 8.2, 8.3, and 8.4 below). We recommend that you review the discussion of the motivational framework in Chapter Two before reading further sections of this chapter.

Motivational Self-Awareness as an Instructor

When you are preparing to use the Motivational Framework for Culturally Responsive Teaching, we encourage you to conduct an analysis of how well this approach fits with your philosophy and teaching style. Please take a few minutes to answer the questions outlined below and to reflect on your responses. Writing them out may clarify your thoughts. Using the motivational framework for designing and implementing instruction is generally incompatible with an authoritarian teaching style but is effective with a more collaborative and consultative approach.

1. What are three things you most often do to enhance learner motivation? What do these habits tell you about the kind of role you prefer as an instructor?

2. In general, what have been your own reactions to your experiences when you are a guide and facilitator of learning rather than a director or lecturer?

3. In respecting the perspectives of others as you teach, what tensions do you negotiate that are difficult to resolve?

4. What are your thoughts about the importance of teaching in ways that engage the motivation of *all* learners?

5. How do you think your learners would complete the following sentence: My instructor helps me feel motivated because he or she…

6. How have the previous chapters affirmed the way you teach?

7. How have the previous chapters encouraged you to consider any changes in your teaching? If so, what might be the best place to begin to make a few changes?

After reflecting on the previous questions, please review the strategies discussed in this book before proceeding to the instructional planning section of this chapter. Being well versed in these strategies is essential to designing instruction creatively. If some of these strategies seem unfamiliar to you, you may wish to identify them and refresh your understanding of them. Table 8.1 is a summary of the motivational strategies contained in the four previous chapters. It includes the four major motivational conditions and a list of related strategies and the purposes they serve. Reviewing the list of strategies in Table 8.1 will help indicate the possible strategies you can use when designing instruction for intensive courses. You can also use the table as a checklist of the strategies you are currently employing. For those strategies that are not part of your repertoire, consider the ones you would like to initiate. *Rank them in terms of their personal value to you as well as their probability of being successful.* Using these two criteria for selection will increase the likelihood that the new strategies you select will be effective and adaptable to your instructional situation.

TABLE 8.1

Summary of Motivational Strategies

Major Motivational Condition	Motivational Purpose	Motivational Strategy
Inclusion (beginning learning activities)	To engender a feeling of connection among learners	1: Allow for introductions. 2: Provide an opportunity for multidimensional sharing. 3: Concretely indicate your cooperative intentions to help adults learn. 4: Use collaborative and cooperative learning. 5: Clearly identify the learning objectives and goals for instruction. 6: Emphasize the human purpose of what is being learned and its relationship to the learners' personal lives and contemporary situations.
	To create a climate of respect	7: Assess learners' current expectations, needs, goals, and previous experience as they relate to your course or lesson. 8: Explicitly introduce important participation guidelines. 9: Acknowledge different ways of knowing and different levels of knowledge or skill to engender a respectful learning environment. 10: Create a clear, inviting, and inclusive course syllabus.

(Continued)

TABLE 8.1 *Continued*

Major Motivational Condition	Motivational Purpose	Motivational Strategy
Attitude (beginning learning activities)	To build a positive attitude toward the subject	11: Eliminate or minimize any negative conditions that surround the subject. 12: Scaffold complex learning.
	To develop self-efficacy for learning	13: Help learners to realize their personal control of learning. 14: Help learners attribute their success to their capability, effort, and knowledge. 15: Use relevant models to demonstrate expected learning. 16: Encourage learners.
	To establish challenging and attainable learning goals	17: Make the criteria of assessment as fair and clear as possible. 18: Help learners understand and plan for the amount of time needed for successful learning. 19: Use learning contracts.
	To create relevant learning experiences	20: Offer the entry points suggested by multiple intelligences theory as ways of learning about a topic or concept. 21: Use the K-W-L strategy to introduce new topics and concepts.
Meaning (during learning activities)	To maintain learners' attention	22: Provide frequent response opportunities for all learners. 23: Help learners realize their accountability for what they are learning. 24: Provide variety in the processes of instruction and in learning materials. 25: Introduce, connect, and end learning activities attractively and clearly.
	To make learning interesting	26: Relate learning to learners' interests and values. 27: Clearly state or demonstrate the benefits of a learning activity. 28: While instructing, use humor liberally. 29: Use examples, analogies, metaphors, and stories. 30: Invite learners to anticipate and predict. 31: Use concept maps to develop interest in ideas and information.

TABLE 8.1 *Continued*

Major Motivational Condition	Motivational Purpose	Motivational Strategy
	To deepen learning with engagement and challenge	32: Use critical questions to engage learners in challenging reflection and discussion. 33: Use relevant problems or problem-based learning to facilitate and deepen learning. 34: Use project-based learning to deepen understanding and to engage challenging, authentic topics. 35: Use case study methods to deepen learning and to engage challenging, authentic topics. 36: Use role playing and simulations for new learning and adaptive decision making in realistic and dynamic contexts. 37: Use visits and service-learning in authentic settings to provide practice for engendering new learning and adaptive decision making. 38: Use invention, artistry, and enactment to render deeper meaning and emotion in learning.
Competence (ending learning activities)	To engender competence with assessment and grading	39: Provide effective feedback. 40: Promote equity in assessment procedures. 41: Use formative assessments to improve learning and instruction essential to course goals. 42: Use authentic performance tasks as part of assessment so learners will know they can proficiently apply new learning to their real lives. 43: Use assessment options based on Howard Gardner's multiple intelligences. 44: When using rubrics, make sure they assess the essential features of performance and are fair, valid, and clear. 45: Use self-assessment methods to provide insights and deepen learning. 46: Use grading practices that enhance learner motivation.
	To engender competence with rewards and communication	47: Effectively praise and reward learning. 48: Use incentives to develop motivation for valued learning that is initially unappealing. 49: Emphasize when learning has natural consequences and help learners to be aware of their impact. 50: Provide positive closure at the end of significant units of learning.

Designing an Instructional Plan

Authors' Note: Although this section offers relevant information for instructional planning in general, those of us who teach in departments that use standardized modules or syllabi will find the next section on superimposing the motivational framework to be most useful for working with preexisting instructional plans.

The first step for designing an instructional plan is to clarify the learning goal. A clear understanding of the proposed learning outcome will suggest the best sequence of instruction and its relationship to a larger instructional unit (if there is one).

Once you thoroughly understand the learning goals, the next step is to determine the amount of time available to help learners accomplish them. This length of time will have a strong influence on the kind and number of motivational strategies you choose. For example, because processing a lengthy case study takes much longer than conducting a short role play, time constraints may dictate that you select the role play for the instructional plan.

The third step is to analyze the inherent structure of the material, knowledge, or skill students will learn. This structure may determine the order in which you will teach the content or the sequence of steps needed for students to adequately learn the material, as is often the case in teaching math or languages.

Another important step is to consider the assessment process. Often we mentally have to go back and forth between the flow of the content and the type of assessment we will use in order to plan the appropriate sequence of learning activities. The instructional plan should provide sufficient opportunities for engagement and practice, followed by an assessment that establishes and verifies learners' competence.

Among these steps, sequencing academic content may be the most challenging, because there is no single best way to order learning. Different pedagogical theories suggest different approaches. Some start with general concepts and move to the specific, whereas others initiate learning with a concrete experience and move to reflection, conceptualization, and active experimentation (Kolb, 1984). In the case of problem-based learning, the instructor begins with a relevant problem and generates a series of learning processes with students to understand and construct possible solutions to the problem (see Strategy 33 in Chapter Six).

In this book, we advocate following a motivational framework to teach content in a way that evokes intrinsic motivation to learn among diverse learners. We suggest teaching any significant learning objective in a course with activities based on the fifty motivational strategies to establish the conditions of inclusion, attitude, meaning, and competence, respectively. Although you might plan extensively for instruction, once learning has started there may be unexpected twists and turns. In these instances, if the potential for learning seems particularly strong, we suggest using the strategies on an "as-wanted" basis. For example, if students spontaneously bring up a current event, and it evokes strong interest throughout the class, you might introduce critical questions to deepen engagement at this moment (see Strategy 32 in Chapter Six).

Looking beyond pedagogical theory, there are some commonsense considerations from the field of instructional design to keep in mind (Dick, Carey, and Carey, 2004):

- Provide a context, outline, or graphic to use in organizing what students are to learn.

- Place prerequisite knowledge and skills in the sequence prior to the point where they must be combined with subsequent knowledge and skills.

- Place practical application of concepts and principles close to the point of the initial discussion of those ideas.

- Provide practice and review of skills and knowledge that are essential parts of tasks to be introduced later in the activity.

- Avoid overloading any task with elements that are too difficult to learn.

- Provide support or coaching for practice of required skills, concepts, and principles in areas where transfer is likely to occur.

For intensive courses, we usually plan for some kind of authentic performance task as early as possible in the beginning class sessions. We believe that becoming effective at something they value (competence) is such a high priority for adult learners that the sooner they experience it, the deeper their learning and motivation for the entire course will be. Therefore, once we ascertain the learning objectives and the content for a course, we imagine what kind of performance task could clearly reveal to learners that they are becoming more proficient at what they value. Once we settle on that performance task, we go back to sequence the content so that it can lead learners to successfully accomplish that task. For example, at the end of the first session of an intensive course on instruction, in which students have learned about motivation using critical questions and problem solving, we often provide an instructional scenario for learners to critique. We ask them to look for, describe, and then discuss with a partner which of the scenario instructor's actions might diminish student motivation. In discovering and explaining how the instructor may have diminished student motivation, many learners realize that their knowledge of motivation is genuinely increasing. In the course assessment after this class session, they often mention their performance on this task as an authentic indicator of new learning they want to continue.

Superimposing the Motivational Framework on an Instructional Module or Existing Instructional Plan

Our experience with predesigned instructional modules is that they offer well-organized course readings and assignments, comprehensive course objectives, and a variety of proposed activities and assessments from which the instructor can select. Their composition often does not, however, include motivation to learn as a priority. For instructors who teach from such modules or from prior instructional plans, one of the best ways to use the motivational framework to enhance learner motivation may be to *superimpose* it on the preexisting instructional plan. This approach uses the motivational framework as a template to guide an instructor's analysis of whether the previously completed instructional plan or module includes learning activities to establish the four motivational conditions of the framework.

In Exhibit 8.1, we have turned the four motivational conditions into functional questions to ask to represent the motivational framework as a template for analysis of instructional plans. By asking these questions as you peruse your module or instructional plan, you can estimate where its instructional activities fulfill the conditions of the motivational framework and where they do not. For those conditions that are not adequately met, you can develop new learning activities based on the motivational strategies related to the unfulfilled motivational conditions summarized earlier in Table 8.1.

The two main criteria for successful instructional planning based on the motivational framework are (1) the establishment of all four of the motivational conditions, and (2) having activities in each phase (beginning, during, and ending) of instruction to elicit intrinsic motivation among learners.

Most of the fifty strategies found in Table 8.1 are applicable *throughout* an instructional plan. For example, we might begin a module (or one of

---

EXHIBIT 8.1

Four Questions for Instructional Planning

1. *Establishing inclusion:* How does this learning sequence create or affirm a learning atmosphere in which instructor and students feel *respected* by and *connected* to one another? (Emphasis on beginning activities)

2. *Developing attitude:* How does this learning sequence make use of personal *relevance* and learner *volition* to create or affirm students' favorable disposition toward learning? (Emphasis on beginning activities)

3. *Enhancing meaning:* Are there *engaging* and *challenging* learning experiences that include students' perspectives and values in this learning sequence? (Emphasis on main activities during or ending the instructional plan)

4. *Engendering competence:* How does this learning sequence create or affirm an understanding that students have effectively learned something they *value* and perceive as *authentic* to their real world? (Emphasis on ending activities)

---

the units within it) with an authentic performance task (Strategy 42) to estimate learners' previous experience with the skill to be taught, or we might start with a role play (Strategy 36) to evoke the social need for the concept to be learned. The fact that these two strategies occur in the ending and during phases of Table 8.1, respectively, does not mean that they cannot be used in the beginning phase as well. The most important aspect of this approach is establishing the four motivational conditions, and the strategies are a means of achieving this essential goal.

You may also be wondering about the specific calibration for each time phase in an intensive class session: When does the "beginning phase" end and the "during phase" begin? When does the "during phase" end and the "ending phase" begin? There is no precise way to determine this, because course content is not linear and learning activities often overlap. In this respect, the time phases are analogous to the broad way in which we divide a day—morning, afternoon, and evening—imprecise segments of time that give order to our day and help us understand that some activities are more appropriate at certain times than at others.

The length of any time phase can range from a few minutes to a few hours, depending on the situation. For example, the beginning phase for a particular learning objective with a group of highly motivated learners may be very short. However, for a group of reluctant learners, the beginning phase for the same objective may have to be longer to develop inclusion and positive attitudes toward learning.

Our experience with superimposing the motivational framework on the design of preexisting modules for intensive formats is that the beginning phase is frequently too short, and the motivational conditions of inclusion and attitude are often not well developed. Creating a climate of respect and making content relevant to a group of diverse adults often takes some time. The benefits are well worth that time, however, because with a group that is becoming a community of learners, the quality of the dialogue, the depth of the thinking, and the candor of their perspectives make learning vital in ways that simply covering content does not.

Using the Motivational Framework as a Source for Designing a Modular Unit or Instructional Plan

The *source method* begins with intrinsic motivation as the *origin* for instructional planning. As with the superimposed method, we still have to accommodate the learning objectives, the structure of the content, and the time available. Most instructional units with a modular format are organized according to the time parameters of each class session (usually ranging from three to six hours). This is often the case with intensive courses as well. With the *source method*, whatever the length of the instructional unit, the design for the instructional plan considers intrinsic motivation and culture as essential to the entire process.

In order to plan instruction, we reflect on the learners' experience and prior knowledge, cultural characteristics such as age, gender, and ethnicity, and their motivation for the learning objectives. Next, we review the motivational strategies that will guide our choice of learning activities. We design these activities to accomplish the learning objectives, to be responsive to the learners' cultural characteristics and expected motivation, and to fit the structure of the content and the time available for learning. We use the motivational strategies to plan learning activities that create the four motivational conditions *and* accomplish the learning objectives.

Having selected the most relevant strategies for each phase (beginning, during, and ending), we then reflect on what learning activity will convey the essence of each strategy. Because instructional design is a creative process and an act of composing, ideas for activities will sometimes emerge before we select strategies, in which case the strategies are then applied as part of a reflection to confirm the motivational intent of the activities.

Faculty who teach intensive courses often divert from any set method of instructional planning. Creating an instructional plan from the framework and its related motivational strategies can be as varied a process as writing a story. However conceived, the plan should respect the cultural, structural, and temporal considerations for learning; establish the four motivational conditions; and guide the instructor and students to accomplish the learning objectives with an understanding of how they will be assessed.

Examples of Designing an Instructional Plan Using the Motivational Framework

Whether developed using the superimposed method or the source method, an instructional plan contains an alignment of motivational purposes with motivational strategies and their related learning activities that can be accomplished in a given time frame. The three examples of instructional plans that follow are single class sessions from accelerated and intensive courses in general education, business, and nursing. (Throughout these examples, the numbers of the motivational strategies correspond to those used in Table 8.1 and in Chapters Four through Seven.)

Example 1

An instructor is conducting a three-hour class session in the School for Professional Studies, a division of the university that serves primarily adult learners. This is a general education course titled The Modern American Novel. The topic for the evening is Alice Walker and her novel *The Color Purple*. The learners have been asked to finish reading the novel prior to this course session.

Type and number of learners: twenty men and women ranging in age from twenty-one to fifty-nine. There is considerable diversity of age, ethnicity, and race among the students in the class. Most of them have had at least a few general education courses before this one.

Learning objective: learners will communicate their perspectives and understandings of the novel through participation in discussion and a short written critique. (The instructor handed out writing samples and related rubrics that the group discussed at the first class session.)

The instructional plan for Example 1 is illustrated in Table 8.2. This example contains at least one motivational purpose for each of the four major motivational conditions. In this example, the instructor used eight motivational strategies out of a possible fifty. Because the example is only

TABLE 8.2

Instructional Plan for Example 1

Motivational Condition Timing	Motivational Purpose	Motivational Strategy	Learning Activity or Instructor Behavior
Inclusion (beginning)	To create a climate of respect	9: Acknowledge different ways of knowing and different levels of knowledge or skill to engender a respectful learning environment.	Acknowledge Alice Walker's feminist perspective and the controversial issues dealt with in the novel, including abuse, incest, violence, racism, and its vision of the liberation of women from men—areas in which different ways of knowing, strong feelings, and new learning may emerge.
Attitude (beginning)	To create relevant learning experiences	4: Use collaborative and cooperative learning. 6: Emphasize the human purpose of what is being learned and its relationship to the learners' personal lives and contemporary situations.	Divide the learners into small groups to share (to the extent they are comfortable) any situations in the novel that they relate to their personal experiences—areas that have a resonance with their own reality.
Meaning (during)	To deepen learning with engagement and challenge	32: Use critical questions to engage learners in challenging reflection and discussion.	Conduct a whole-group discussion with the following questions: *Probe for assumptions*: Based on your reading, what do you think are Alice Walker's assumptions about the relations between men and women? Women and women? Men and men? Please offer evidence from the book for each of these assessments. *Compare and contrast*: What are some of the similarities and differences between this book's perspective of humanity and what we've read by Flannery O'Connor? *Critically assess*: A hundred years from now, will this book remain a classic? With this in mind, what are the book's strengths and weaknesses?

TABLE 8.2 *Continued*

Motivational Condition Timing	Motivational Purpose	Motivational Strategy	Learning Activity or Instructor Behavior
	To maintain learners' attention	23: Help learners realize their accountability for what they are learning.	To encourage equitable responding, at times randomly select students, but only on those occasions when students have initially used *think-pair-share* to process the question.
Competence (ending)	To engender competence with assessment and grading	42: Use authentic performance tasks as part of assessment so learners will know they can proficiently apply new learning to their real lives.	Request learners to write a short critique of the novel as they might for a newspaper or news magazine.
		39: Provide effective feedback.	After learners have completed their critiques, pass out copies of the actual reviews of the novel from the *New York Times* and *Newsweek* in 1982.
		45: Use self-assessment methods to provide insights and deepen learning.	Ask learners to compare the reviews to their critiques, and then to select one review and write answers to the following questions: How has this review informed my thinking? How might my critique have informed this reviewer?
		39: Provide effective feedback.	Collect learner critiques and self-assessments. Return them with feedback at the next class meeting.

Source: *Adapted from Wlodkowski, 2008.*

illustrative, it is conceivable that more or fewer strategies could be employed. The particular learning activities or instructor behaviors are what the instructor would do to carry out the motivational strategies. Note that it is common for one activity to involve more than one strategy—as one does in this example, carrying out Strategies 4 and 6. In fact, one elaborate activity might represent as many as six strategies. Notice also that many of the motivational strategies can be used for more than one motivational purpose. For example, Strategy 4 (collaborative and cooperative learning) and Strategy 6 (emphasizing the human purpose of learning and its relationship to learners' lives) are used to create relevant learning experiences in the instructional plan, rather than for the motivational purpose of establishing inclusion, as was the case in Chapter Four. The placement of motivational strategies in the summary (Table 8.1) with a particular motivational purpose is theoretically sound but not absolute. Finally, a strategy can appear more than once in an instructional plan—Strategy 39 (provide effective feedback) does twice in this plan.

Example 2

An instructor is conducting a six-hour class session for a weekend course in business leadership. There is a one-hour lunch break.

Type and number of learners: eighteen men and women ranging in age from twenty to fifty. Most of the learners are European Americans who work full-time. All of the students are undergraduate juniors and seniors. They have had at least two previous courses in the business leadership program, and as a group average twelve years of work experience.

Learning objectives: upon completion of the class session, learners will:

1. Understand personal, professional, and systemic reasons for resistance to organizational change

2. Review their understanding of first-order change and second-order change

3. Apply theories and methods of participatory leadership to facilitate organizational change

4. Assess and select relevant ideas and methods to lead and facilitate organizational change in their professional work

The instructional plan for Example 2 is illustrated in Table 8.3. (This example is adapted from the instructional plan of Tim McGowan, director of program operations and faculty development at Edgewood College in Madison, Wisconsin.) This example contains at least one motivational purpose for every major motivational condition. Example 2 also illustrates in a number of instances combining two or more motivational strategies to fulfill a single motivational purpose. In fact, for the motivational purpose of deepening learning with engagement and challenge there are five strategies used (Strategies 32, 22, 4, 35, and 36). In longer class sessions, more strategies are often needed to sustain engagement.

TABLE 8.3

Instructional Plan for Example 2

Motivational Condition (Timing)	Motivational Purpose	Motivational Strategy	Learning Activity or Instructor Behavior
Inclusion (beginning)	To engender an awareness and feeling of connection among adults	1: Allow for introductions	Self Introduction—sharing biographical background and emphasizing the role of "change" in professional career. Ask learners to introduce themselves with a short description of a significant change they've experienced in the organizations where they work.
Attitude (beginning)	To create relevant learning experiences	20: Use the narrative entry point from multiple intelligences theory to learn about a topic or concept.	Display four quotes that reflect the complexity and importance of change. Authors include Florynce Kennedy, Barack Obama, Juana Ines de la Cruz, and John Patrick Shanley. Ask learners to pick a quote that offers insight for organizational change that they've experienced and to freewrite their responses. Then have learners break into small groups to share these reflections. After this process, ask groups to surmise and record the possible "lessons" about organizational change they can glean from their discussions. Each group reports out these lessons, which are recorded and displayed by the instructor for a whole-group discussion.
Meaning (during)	To deepen learning with engagement and challenge	32: Use critical questions to engage learners in challenging reflection and discussion. 22: Provide frequent response opportunities for all learners.	Select the lesson or lessons from the previous activity that most affirm resistance to change. Use the lesson(s) as a bridge for a whole-group brainstorm of the question, What are the possible strengths and weaknesses at play when employees resist organizational change?

(Continued)

TABLE 8.3 *Continued*

Motivational Condition (Timing)	Motivational Purpose	Motivational Strategy	Learning Activity or Instructor Behavior
	To make learning interesting	31: Use concept maps to develop interest in ideas and information.	Ask learners to construct a personal concept map of reasons for their resistance to organizational change and the possible advantages and disadvantages for themselves, their coworkers, and the organization.
		24: Provide variety in processes of instruction and in learning materials.	Introduce students to the concepts of "survival anxiety" and "learning anxiety" through a mini-lecture. Relate the concepts through discussion to first-order change and second-order change. Integrate them with the previously discussed reasons for resistance to organizational change.
	To deepen learning with engagement and challenge	4: Use collaborative and cooperative learning.	Use a jigsaw procedure to have students read and discuss an article on methods and authentic examples of participatory leadership.
		35: Use case study methods to deepen learning and to engage challenging, authentic topics.	Divide students into three groups. Pass out and process the case study, "Changing for Social Change," in which administrators are confronted with varied forms of resistance to making a nonprofit organization more responsive to social change. Ask students to use their experience and understanding of methods of participatory leadership, such as collaboration, collective vision, and shared leadership, to respond to the case study.
		36: Use role playing and simulations for new learning and adaptive decision making in realistic and dynamic contexts.	Selectively role-play scenarios from the case study in which conflict between the administrators and the workers seems evident. Use the role play as a way to embody methods for managing tension and anxiety during resistance to organizational change.

TABLE 8.3 *Continued*

Motivational Condition (Timing)	Motivational Purpose	Motivational Strategy	Learning Activity or Instructor Behavior
Competence (ending)	To engender competence with assessment and grading	39: Provide effective feedback.	Ask each group to report out its response to the case study. The other groups and the instructor offer feedback regarding the methods each group suggests. Probe each report for specific ideas (both preventive and reactive). Where appropriate, relate suggestions to survival and learning anxiety.
		45: Use self-assessment methods to provide insights and deepen learning.	Ask students to review the "lessons" they constructed from the earlier quotations exercise and to review the concept maps about their understandings of the advantages and disadvantages of resistance to change. After this review, ask students to reflect on and to respond in writing to these three questions: (1) What new and relevant insights did you gain from today's lesson? (2) What ideas or methods have authentic, pragmatic value for you for leading organizational change? (3) What are your lingering questions about resistance to organizational change?
	To engender competence with rewards and communication	26: Relate learning to learners' interests and values.	Focus a short discussion on students' lingering questions.
		50: Provide positive closure at the end of significant units of learning.	Conclude by having students in turn highlight one thing learned from the prior self-assessment that has value for them today.

The narrative entry point strategy (Strategy 20) has a number of sequenced activities aligned with it, which demonstrates that several learning activities can together carry out a single motivational strategy. *It is not necessary that every instructional behavior or learning activity in a learning sequence have listed next to it every possible motivational strategy corresponding to it.* Creating too specific a breakdown in instructional planning can become confusing and unnecessarily labor intensive (Gronlund, 1985). The instructional plan should be sufficient and effective if it lists the most important strategies and related activities, and if the necessary structural components of the concept or skill to be learned are evident and linked in the sequence of learning activities.

The instructional plan in Table 8.3 places heavy emphasis on relevance, especially as it applies to resistance to organizational change. The instructor uses quotations, critical questions, and concept maps to personalize the feeling of resistance. In longer class sessions, keeping learners active makes sense, but without relevance active learning can be superficial. The case study is the central activity, so that students can apply and practice ideas and methods from the theory of participatory leadership. The instructor uses role playing both to heighten relevance and to give students realistic practice with managing tension. The three questions used for self-assessment as well as the closure activity focus on the instructor's willingness to trust the learners' opinions concerning what learning they consider most valuable to retain and use.

Example 3

An instructor is conducting a three-hour clinical lab for first-quarter nursing students, who are enrolled in a clinical practicum course at a large urban university. The course emphasizes beginning nursing skills for performing individual health assessments.

Type and number of learners: seventeen students ranging in age from nineteen to forty. About a third of the students are Asian, many of whom are from the Philippines and China. A number of these students have been nurses in their countries of origin. The class is nearly 90 percent women.

Learning objectives: upon completion of the lab session, students will have the knowledge and skill to:

1. Define postural blood hypotension

2. Explain the three most common causes of postural hypotension

3. Distinguish between types of orthostatic (postural) hypotension

4. Correctly perform a postural blood pressure reading

3. We are engaged in challenging learning in which our experience and perspective can inform as well as be informed.

4. We are becoming more effective in something we value.

These four statements represent what is possible when adults learn in an environment where the four motivational conditions—inclusion, attitude, meaning, and competence—are pervasive. This does not mean that students bear no responsibility for their own motivation for learning. It does mean, however, that we as instructors have optimally exercised our professional skill to respect adult learners individually and culturally and to make instruction an experience that enhances their motivational resources. In the reciprocal exchange of teaching and learning, we have to take the lead. Just as a dinner host provides the best setting possible to elicit involvement and conversation among all guests, we provide the best learning situation possible to evoke motivation among all learners.

Assessing Motivation

It is as simple as this: the longer the intensive class session, the more likely learner motivation will bog down. In a longer class there are just more chances for distraction, fatigue, boredom, and the stressful realization that time in class is time spent away from family, work, and other adult responsibilities. Knowing when learners are or are not motivated provides a barometer for instruction to gauge when it may be necessary to use other motivational strategies. But how do we know if and when learners are motivated? At best, student learning is an indirect and only partial indicator of motivation.

A standardized, self-reported measure of motivation to learn is the Motivated Strategies for Learning Questionnaire (MSLQ), which has been widely used in postsecondary education (Garcia Duncan and McKeachie, 2005). The MSLQ is considered a reliable measure for getting feedback on student learning strategies and self-efficacy as well as for guiding decisions concerning course adjustments. Studies of adult learners have made use of its scale for measuring Intrinsic Goal Orientation to infer when their learning is intrinsically motivated (Bye, Pushkar, and Conway, 2007).

We often use the Motivational Framework Self-Report found in Exhibit 8.2 to understand how well our class or course is fulfilling the four motivational conditions of the framework. Learners rate each of the following items on a four-point scale, from (1) strongly disagree to (4) strongly agree.

The instructional plan for Example 3 is illustrated in Table 8.4. (This example is adapted from an instructional project conducted by J. A. Ferguson, K. M. Hoflack, N. R. Johnson-Crowley, and G. Altman in the School of Nursing at the University of Washington-Seattle.) The example contains at least one motivational purpose for every major motivational condition.

TABLE 8.4

Instructional Plan for Example 3

Motivational Condition (Timing)	Motivational Purpose	Motivational Strategy	Learning Activity or Instructor Behavior
Inclusion (beginning)	To create a climate of respect	7: Assess learners' current expectations, needs, goals, and previous experience as they relate to your course or lesson.	Assess students' previous experience with taking blood pressure, including the number of years of experience, frequency, settings, type of patients, and purposes.
Attitude (beginning)	To develop self-efficacy for learning	14: Help learners attribute their success to their capability, effort, and knowledge. 39: Provide effective feedback.	Assess students' understanding of taking and interpreting blood pressure readings. Provide feedback to students, attributing their performance to their knowledge, skill, and effort and highlighting what may need to be improved.
Meaning (during)	To maintain learners' attention	24: Provide variety in the processes of instruction and in learning materials.	Review and discuss a PowerPoint presentation and handout of principles of properly taking blood pressure (palpation, cuff size, positioning) and the interpretation of physiological changes influencing blood pressure readings (for example, crossing legs, activity prior to measurement, and so forth).
	To deepen learning with engagement and challenge	36: Use role playing and simulations for new learning and adaptive decision making in realistic and dynamic contexts. 4: Use collaborative and cooperative learning.	Students collaborate to practice in a nurse-patient role play to (1) take postural blood pressures, (2) interpret whether postural hypotension was present, and (3) develop a plan of care.

(Continued)

TABLE 8.3 *Continued*

Motivational Condition (Timing)	Motivational Purpose	Motivational Strategy	Learning Activity or Instructor Behavior
		32: Use critical questions to engage learners in challenging reflection and discussion.	To increase students' knowledge of factors influencing orthostatic hypotension, the instructor uses critical questions, such as "Why would you take a patient's blood pressure in both arms and thighs?" and "What are the possible reasons for recording a patient's blood pressure in the lying and sitting positions and averaging these numbers to obtain a mean blood pressure?"
Competence (ending)	To engender competence with assessment and grading	41: Use formative assessment to improve learning and instruction essential to course goals.	Distribute a lab questionnaire to assess knowledge specific to postural blood pressure. Review immediately and provide feedback to students, attributing their improved performance to their knowledge, skill, and effort, while giving any further information for what they may need to know to improve. Students discuss the assessments in small groups to deepen their learning and support one another.
		42: Use authentic performance tasks as part of assessment so learners will know they can proficiently apply new learning to their real lives.	Distribute a summative evaluation with authentic case studies involving fainting episodes and antihypertensive medications, with questions related to taking postural blood pressure and the interpretations of blood pressure readings. Collect and return these with grades and feedback at the next lab session.

In this clinical lab session, students are learning specific med procedures, and diagnoses. The instructor uses early assessmen for further learning in the lab session and to help students re their own knowledge and effort will contribute to their new lear collaborative approach to the nurse-patient role play allows practice the requisite skills and medical procedures. Collaborat allows the students to take advantage of knowledge in their g deepen further learning. Critical questioning by the instructo students both broaden and deepen their knowledge base. Fina formative assessment takes away the pressure of grades and students to see what they've learned as well as what they may r consider to improve their learning. The collaborative discussion assessments and feedback allow them to learn more and to feel sup by their peers.

Please note that in all three examples we have not shortene motivational purposes or strategies, writing them out in full as indi in the text. We did this to make the examples as clear and easy to fc as possible. However, most instructors as well as the authors have d oped shorthand of phraseology for the various purposes, strategies, learning activities to increase their efficiency in planning. These exam are meant to show what might be possible and what is structurally ne sary for instructional planning. They are not intended as precise mod to follow.

• • •

The more often you practice planning with the framework, the mo familiar the motivational conditions and their related strategies becom Such practice significantly lessens the time required for instructiona planning and makes the process more fluid. In our experience, mos instructors need to practice applying the framework about *six times* before their planning with it becomes more intuitive and automatic.

Ideally, for an intensive course, whether you are using the super-imposed method or the source method for instructional planning, learners have the following responses:

1. We are members of a learning community in which we feel a mutual sense of care and respect.

2. We are successfully learning something we find relevant and desirable.

EXHIBIT 8.2

Motivational Framework Self-Report

1. This class climate is friendly and respectful. (Inclusion)

2. This class is relevant to my personal or professional goals. (Attitude)

3. This class is challenging me to think. (Meaning)

4. This class contributes to helping me to be effective at what I value. (Competence)

5. The instructor in this class respects learners' opinions and ideas. (Inclusion)

6. In this class, I can use my experience and preferred ways of learning. (Attitude)

7. Most of the time during this class I feel engaged in what is going on. (Meaning)

8. I can actually use the information or skills I am learning in this class. (Competence)

Probably the best moment-to-moment method of assessing learner motivation is personal observation. However, biases and mood can influence what we perceive—for example, focusing on one reluctant learner can make the whole class appear bleak. It is also difficult to be sure that what we see is an indicator of motivation. For example, judging effort can be misleading. Culturally speaking, when tasks become difficult, some people are socialized to be calm and contemplative rather than to become intense and more active. Looking for vigor to assess motivation in learners can be deceptive. In the long run, we prefer to use persistence as an indicator of motivation. Even though the kind of behaviors may vary, motivated learners often continue to engage in actions aimed at accomplishing the task at hand. Other observable indicators of motivation to consider include when learners do the following (Stipek, 2002):

- Begin learning activities without hesitation

- Prefer the challenging aspects of tasks

- Spontaneously relate learning to outside interests

- Ask questions to expand their understanding beyond the learning at hand

- Go beyond required work

- Find joy in the process of learning—the studying, writing, reading, and so forth

- Express pride in their learning and its consequences

- Stay focused

- Become reluctant to stop when engaged

By continually observing to assess these indicators of motivation, we can adjust our instruction for the benefit of learners. As instructors we need minimum standards for the quality of motivation we observe in intensive courses. Such standards may be the percentage of people who willingly begin a learning task, the percentage of people who persist to overcome a learning obstacle, the percentage of people who appear relaxed and alert while learning, or some combination of these. We do not advocate the same standard for all instructors or subjects. The point is to have one—an observable standard—whether or not it's a percentage, that keeps us motivationally in touch with students. Possessing such standards enables us to be responsive, to flex rather than rigidly adhere to texts or modules, so that the way we teach brings to life the intensive classes we carefully design.

Chapter 9

Strengthening Instruction and Retention

"Poems come out of wonder, not out of knowing."

LUCILLE CLIFTON

THE CLASSROOM IS the central point of learning for nontraditional students. Because of the limited time they spend on campus, working adults view the classroom as their main place for engagement and interactions (Donaldson and Graham, 2002). Their primary college contact is their instructor, whether adjunct or full-time. Our relationship as instructors with adult learners is, therefore, the linchpin for their retention and their experience of the overall quality of their postsecondary education.

In general, there is very little research on the specific factors that affect the retention of adults in accelerated and intensive programs. Because the focus of this book is on instruction and the role of the instructor, we will examine these two influences to explore what the academic literature and our own experience reveal about their impact on adult learner retention.

The strongest research finding supports the conventional wisdom that adult learners with higher grades in accelerated or traditional colleges are more likely to persist and succeed at both types of institutions (Wlodkowski, Mauldin, and Gahn, 2001). This finding is indirectly supported by a longitudinal study of primarily traditional students by Ishitani and DesJardins (2002). They found that the higher a student's first-year GPA, the less likely that student was to drop out of college. Our own experience is that the first year of college, whether a working adult is just beginning or returning from an extended period away from college, is critical—a time when learners are most vulnerable to feeling unfamiliar and doubtful about their potential.

It is also important to note that "success" in college is a multifaceted experience for adults. For some, success is acquiring a particular certificate for areas ranging from medical technology to computer programming; for others, it is gaining an associate's degree without intending to get a bachelor's degree; while for yet another group of students, the bachelor's degree is hallowed in their dreams. In addition, there are those who see community college as a means of transferring to a four-year college; and let's not forget those who are going to college for little more than a particular course or a few credits. If you are teaching in a community college, it's probable that students with a wide variety of academic ambitions are with you in a single day.

Student Engagement with Peers, Faculty, and the College

Our awareness about the importance of student engagement for student retention is crucial to understanding our role as instructors. Findings from multiple studies conclude that helping nontraditional or traditional students feel connected to their institutions is key to keeping them enrolled and progressing toward their academic goals (Lederman, 2005). This form of student engagement includes social and academic relationships formed with peers, faculty, and the institution. As George Kuh and his associates write, "What students *do* during college counts more for what they learn and whether they will persist in college than who they are or even where they go to college" (2005, p. 8).

There are two key variables of engagement that influence student success. The first is the time and effort learners put into their studies. This factor relates to outcomes of student success including staying in school, getting good grades, and graduating. This component of engagement relates to the motivational conditions of inclusion and meaning, and encompasses students' participating in collaborative learning activities involving problem-solving, project-based learning, research, and so forth. Such activities help learners connect with their peers and faculty, possibly forming friendships or at least a sense of community. They make college a place where learners feel they belong and can manage challenging learning.

The second component comprises the ways colleges use resources and organize learning activities and services to compel learners to get involved and benefit from their participation (Kuh and Associates, 2005). This factor reflects how various opportunities and structures in the college encourage students, supporting their learning and demonstrating the institution's value for them as individuals. The college might do this by enabling students' participation in learning communities, cooperative groups, or peer teaching; by providing opportunities for service-learning, work with faculty, or field experience; or by helping students succeed academically, giving them opportunities to receive tutoring or help with their nonacademic responsibilities, such as work or family.

The course instructor is essential to fostering both of these components for working adults in intensive programs. At a college where one of us taught, the institution established a 24–7 online tutoring program for writing and math. This was a service for all students as part of their tuition and fees. However, once the tutoring was available, far fewer students than anticipated took advantage of it. Those who did use the support were most often the students who were already academically successful, whereas the less academically successful students seemed reluctant to seek assistance. When institutional researchers brought this phenomenon to the attention of the tutoring service, their representatives indicated that this response was typical of many colleges. Their advice was to request instructors to have all students in their courses use the tutoring service for their first paper to assist with such elements as grammar, organization, clarity, and exemplification. This early involvement would familiarize all the students in the course with the tutoring service and more of them would be comfortable using it.

From among the courses taught by those faculty members who required all students in their courses to use the tutoring service for their first paper, there were more students who used the tutoring service and a significant improvement in their writing when compared to the students in the courses in which faculty did not make such a request. We learned that it was not just having a tutoring program in place—it was how faculty encouraged students to use it that made the difference in improving student writing and grades.

For students, connecting with faculty takes many forms as it positively influences their persistence. Whether it is tutoring, advising, mentoring, community service, career planning, or navigating a college system, instructors are the hub for college services. In addition to enhancing academic performance, such guidance lets students know they belong to a caring and accessible community.

A research finding that has stood the test of time for over forty years suggests that nontraditional learners benefit, as all learners do, not only from strong teaching, support, and connection but also from high and clear expectations (Rosenthal and Jacobson, 1968). We can be supportive of students without coddling them. High expectations translate into actions on the part of the instructor that range from returning papers for revision when they are below acceptable standards to requesting a student-teacher conference when a student's work is falling off or incomplete. It's often more work and a bit of a balancing act, but nontraditional learners need to know we see their mistakes or difficulties as information to help them learn.

Professional Experience with Engagement and Retention

As we reviewed the literature and wrote this section on the instructor's role in retention, we realized that there are many intensive programs with imaginative and successful ideas for retaining working adults. However, these have not necessarily been researched or discussed in academic journals. Understanding the value of knowledge from one's craft, we offer examples of efforts to teach and retain working adults from our own experience in intensive and accelerated programs.

For five years, one of us was the director of an intensive urban doctoral program in educational leadership for working adults. This cohort-based program enrolled twenty-five to thirty students per year, all of whom had demanding full-time jobs, most of which were administrative and ranged from vice principal to superintendent positions. Students met with a team of five faculty members one weekend a month (except for December) for two eight-hour days and for one week in the summer. Completion of the program was targeted for the end of three years. All weekends were evaluated by the students and the faculty, with the results shared across the two groups.

What follows in Exhibit 9.1 is a compendium of some of the ideas and specific methods that have been scrutinized and highly rated through this process over the past five years. We found these methods provided an important understanding of possible ways to sustain learner motivation through long blocks of time, enhance complex learning, and retain students in an intensive program.

We describe each method, assigning it a strategy and a motivational condition. We also offer a brief rationale for its effectiveness. For the sake of brevity each strategy is numbered rather than defined. All strategies can be found according to their number in Table 8.1.

You will notice that most of these ideas and methods fit readily within the motivational condition of inclusion. We believe that the main reason

EXHIBIT 9.1

Methods for Engagement and Retention from Professional Experience

Method or Idea	Rationale
Faculty accessibility. Faculty are available to students before, during, and after each day of learning. (Strategy 3; Inclusion)	Ease of faculty contact and support sustains learning and retention.
Entry routines and rituals. Announcements, celebrations, and the outside world and work are regularly acknowledged; for example, students write down three things they need to put out of their minds in order to be fully present and dispose of the paper in a central basket. (Strategy 2; Inclusion)	This eases the transition from a hectic work world to a more focused and relaxed environment for learning.
Rotating food and cleanup groups. Revolving small groups of students are responsible for snacks, lunch, and cleanup. (Strategy 4; Inclusion)	This creates community and increases variety in the menu.
Name tents. On one side is the student's name and on the other side the name of a person who is responsible for part of the student's success in the program. (Strategy 6, Inclusion)	Name tents are potent reminders of who supports and advocates for the student's success.
Experience and skill matrix for the cohort. This depicts personal and professional experience and skills of each student that may be useful to members of the cohort—for example, math and writing skills; knowing world languages other than English; technology experiences; and so on. (Strategy 9; Inclusion)	Such matrices increase the resources available within the cohort and foster respect throughout the group.
Walk and talks. Students have opportunities to leave the classroom and talk with one another about various topics and new learning. (Strategy 4; Inclusion)	It is a long day. Getting outside to talk with peers about an academic subject increases community, learning, and alertness. It also promotes familiarity and identity with the campus environment.
Assignment keeper and historian. One student records what learners are responsible for and another student records significant notes and events within the cohort. (Strategy 6; Inclusion)	Helps students remember for what they are responsible. They experience an enhanced sense of continuity and identity beyond each weekend.
Clear written directions for assignments and activities. Students have a high degree of certainty and focus for their responsibilities. (Strategy 11; Attitude)	Given the responsibilities, complexities, and distractions of being a working adult as well as the length of the day, students appreciate receiving specific directions and knowing with certainty and structure what they need to do in their academic work.

(Continued)

Diverse as well as job-alike groups. Groups should often be diverse. However, sometimes it is better to group learners so that those who have similar jobs can apply and discuss their learning from perspectives that reflect similar responsibilities and contexts. (Strategy 7; Inclusion)	Adults are pragmatic learners.
At least once in the morning and once in the afternoon, providing strategies for a powerful learning experience. This learning experience is relevant, highly interesting, engaging, and challenging. (Strategies 32–38; Meaning)	Maintaining student involvement for eight hours requires a variation in the students' emotional state, so that it can peak as it might in the climax of a story or film. Satiation or an even emotional tempo will lead to boredom, even among the most interested learners.
Collaborative and cooperative learning groups outside of class. Students meet regularly among themselves to foster their own learning and completion of assignments. (Strategy 4; Inclusion)	Such group work diminishes a potential sense of isolation, builds community, and enhances learning.
Generating roles within class that can be continued outside of class in collaborative groups. Students learn how to act as conveners, facilitators, process observers, and recorders within class and can use these roles to maintain collaborative groups outside of class. (Strategy 4; Inclusion)	Such roles make expectations more clear and facilitate functioning groups outside of class.
Creatively approaching how work or absences can be made up. In a program of this length and magnitude, people will sometimes miss a class or an assignment. Life events happen and the instructor's empathy and flexibility make a significant difference for retention. For example, asking the student to co-teach for a segment of the next class can make up work and inspire other students. Or asking, "Who's not with us today and how can we look out for that person?" is both transparent and communally supportive. (Strategy 3; Inclusion)	Sometimes working adults need support to sustain their persistence.
Side-by-side writing. Students with writing challenges write with the instructor as he or she writes in her role as a faculty member. (Strategy 39; Competence)	Such work is a combination of tutoring and modeling that builds stronger relationships and a sense of academic identity.

students have rated these processes highly is that they demonstrate the instructor's as well as the program's value for them as individuals, which is essential to connection and retention.

Faculty Self-Directed Professional Development

Professional development for faculty in postsecondary education varies widely. Although a few schools with intensive formats offer professional development seminars, in many instances it consists of a one-day workshop each semester with a particular theme, such as assessment; a plenary speaker; and a few concurrent sessions (Davidson and McClintock, 2007). A session may be relevant and contain some good ideas, but it is usually left to the faculty to pursue the learning further, with little assistance from the institution. When adjunct faculty are invited, the day of the workshop may be inconvenient to their work schedules.

Our experience is that professional development in higher education, especially for adjunct faculty, is usually a personal responsibility. Faculty in intensive programs often teach the same course term after term. It is not uncommon that after a few years some of us *plateau*. Our instruction may be effective, but we are not that interested in instructional improvement. We are in a groove, and we know how to relate well to students, follow the text or module, and satisfactorily deliver the course to most learners. However, our enthusiasm for teaching may have lessened and we are relying more on habit than on vitality.

Whether or not this scenario is true for you, we want to make a case for regular, substantive professional development, not only because enthusiasm makes a major difference for student learning (see Chapter Three) but also because education is rapidly changing, with so much new to learn and apply. Professionally challenging ourselves is intrinsically motivating, a means to flow while teaching (Csikszentmihalyi, 1997). Here are some ideas for this purpose:

• *Become acquainted with the teaching and learning center of your college.* Although not every postsecondary institution has such a center, if available it provides resources, media, workshops, and such services as videotaping instruction to improve teaching and learning across the institution. Most of these centers are part of the Professional and Organizational Development Network in Higher Education (POD), which has an excellent Web site (http://www.podnetwork.org/) for faculty interested in professional development.

- *Consider joining the Commission for Accelerated Programs (CAP).* This is an organization with a Web site (http://www.capnetwork.org/) serving professionals who lead, teach, and conduct research in accelerated programs in higher education. Each year, CAP presents a national conference dedicated to serving students in accelerated programs. In addition, the American Association of Colleges of Nursing updates a regular bulletin on their Web site (http://www.aacn.nche.edu/index.htm) that addresses accelerated learning.

- *Consistently assess your instruction.* One thing about adult learners— they will tell you what they want from you as their instructor. Given their experience, they have many good ideas. Most colleges now regularly use an end-of-course evaluation of instruction, which can be very helpful and informative. However, sometimes these surveys do not address motivation. We usually use our own survey (see Exhibit 8.2 in Chapter Eight) in addition to the college's survey in order to organize more information around the Motivational Framework for Culturally Responsive Teaching. We also strongly suggest administering frequent, brief assessments to gauge instruction and make sure *all* learners are able to inform your practice and make their needs known to you. Usually both types of evaluations will provide cues for how to strengthen and develop your instruction.

- *Make friends with a colleague who loves teaching.* The enthusiasm of other instructors is contagious. Conversations about instruction are natural and easy. It is a pleasure to exchange great ideas and resources. Having a partner for collaboration, workshops, and conferences makes being an instructor that much more enjoyable. Perhaps most of all, you will have someone with whom you can be sincere about teaching.

- *Stay in touch with the cultures of your students.* With immigration and the shifts in populations in this country, the diversity in postsecondary education is constantly being transformed. Experience is the real teacher here, and conversation, mutual work, and a respectful willingness to learn can open many doors to a collective humanity.

Accelerated and Intensive Learning as They Are Evolving

Accelerated and intensive learning formats have become part of the status quo. There are real advantages to this—stability, higher academic status, a place at the executive table for institutional decision making, more resources, better technology for online learning, and predictability for student and faculty planning. There is evidence that intensive and accelerated programs can be effective with working adult learners in such disciplines as business management, general education courses, and second-degree programs in nursing, as well as in an online format (Wlodkowski, 2003; Wlodkowski and Westover, 1999; American Association of Colleges of Nursing, 2008; Wlodkowski and Stiller, 2005).

Evidence also suggests that accelerated programs are particularly effective with nontraditional learners and can, when they are enrolled to capacity, operate at significantly lower costs than conventional college programs (Wlodkowski, Mauldin, and Gahn, 2001; Center for Adult Learning in Louisiana, 2009). When we look at who is enrolled in accelerated programs, they tend to be women whose lower family income and race and ethnicity are underrepresented in four-year residential colleges. Because of their success, accelerated and intensive programs have been a model for reforms in conventional higher education, drawing into question the need for large bodies of full-time faculty; minimal advising and teaching roles; residential learning; expensive campus buildings; conventional faculty and student selection criteria; and the validity and reliability of college testing and admission measures, including the Scholastic Aptitude Test and the Graduate Record Exam.

The disadvantages associated with being part of the status quo are in some ways typical of most large institutional systems. As intensive programs have grown larger, there is the tendency to firmly set authority in technical, rational thought. To be more efficient, large accelerated and intensive programs bureaucratize, organizing themselves on the basis of spheres of competence (professional studies, institutional research, outreach, and so on), with specialized divisions of labor leading to a more impersonal hierarchy of departments and offices. These influences are compounded by a market orientation to recruiting students that uses advertising and focuses on the stated or not readily apparent needs of working adults to develop within them an attraction to their educational programs, much the same as a business draws customers to its own products.

As such, many intensive and accelerated educational programs, rely on individual self-selection to recruit students. This system draws those students who can most likely afford postsecondary education and pay its rising fees and tuition. As a national pattern of recruitment it can widen the educational, cultural, and income gaps in society (Rubenson, 1998), because higher income learners gain the employment benefits of an advanced education through accelerated and intensive programs while lower income students cannot afford to enroll. Deliberately or otherwise, constructing postsecondary education accessibility in this way, systematically accentuates individual ambitions over communal needs. With their promises of learning for career advancement and social mobility, accelerated and intensive programs may inadvertently set the stage for professional growth to trump the expressed need for social change, for making postsecondary education accessible to all income groups. (Wilson, 2009).

As Phyllis Cunningham (2000, pp. 574–575) writes from a sociological perspective, "The market is recognized as important to providing a discipline for organizing society but the type of economy should not be exploitive. Those whose standpoint is rational and psychological often allow technology to define the citizen's life world and promote individuality rather than communitarian values. ... This standpoint provides no way to critique social constructions for it denies power, thus irrationally insisting on sameness for all and believing in level playing fields." Such systems of education perpetuate postsecondary learning for the more privileged and diminish accessibility for low-income adults (Ginsberg and Wlodkowski, 2010).

One of the early hallmarks of accelerated and intensive learning programs has been to make postsecondary education accessible and attainable for nontraditional learners. However, we want to address two current systemic practices that contradict this mission. Because these practices foster a lack of institutional self-scrutiny, they have the potential to erode the legacy of equity that shaped the beginning of accelerated and intensive learning as an outgrowth of adult education.

The first is the failure to fund and conduct research that indicates the demographics of student enrollment, retention, and success within and across intensive postsecondary programs. Whom do accelerated and intensive programs actually serve? What are students' genders, income levels, races, and ethnicities? If we disaggregate the data, how well are specific groups persisting and succeeding? What are the trends from year to year? How do retention and graduation rates inform a system in which more students taking more courses more quickly generates profitable credit hours (Brookfield, 2003)? Although the American Association of Colleges of Nursing (2009) produces a fact sheet with numerous references to address these kinds of questions, no other organization or body of schools among the other accelerated and intensive programs makes this information readily available. There is some research by individual colleges within the Adult Learning Focused Institutions network, but we could not find comprehensive studies that explored these questions (Flint and Dodge, 2009). Nearly a decade ago, there was evidence that accelerated programs reached out to more historically underserved students than did four-year residential colleges, but we have no evidence that this is still the case.

The second practice that merits attention is an unexamined corporate orientation to education that uses corporate advisory boards, intense marketing, and the goal of providing a productive and efficient workforce as the rationale for the guidance and management of accelerated and intensive programs. Within private and for-profit colleges, accelerated programs often cite being "market driven" as part of their best practices (New Ventures of Regis University, 2007). Whereas the first documented use of accelerated learning was by the training division of the Bureau of Navigations to cope with the naval officer shortage during the First World War, leaders of accelerated programs today cite accelerated learning as a concept pioneered by corporations. (Besch, 2002; Bartlett, 2009). The creation of intensive courses goes back at least to the 1950s, when colleges shortened their classes to accommodate summer work schedules. Rather than question the corporate orientation to learning, or the pitfalls of free-market competition, or the devastating consequences of predatory capitalism, our experience is that there is a corporate orientation among the executive leadership for accelerated learning programs. This orientation, giving the impression that adults who want a better education can get one, in the absence of critical review or opposition, shifts responsibility for postsecondary education from a communal or government obligation to one for which the individual is held accountable, widening the educational gap between those already marginalized and those already privileged (Boshier, 2005). It also undermines teaching adults as a profession founded on caring and a dedication to social and personal transformation. As Arthur Wilson concludes (2009, p. 519), "[T]here is irony in raising such questions from within the academy, like biting the hand that feeds us. But, as I suggest, if we have lost control of this discourse, then we have lost control of our practice—or perhaps just simply forgotten this ever-so-important arena for the work of adult educators, as Americans seem to have."

A Need for Leadership to Serve Underserved Learners

In Chapters Two through Eight we have generally referred to accelerated and intensive learning as simply "intensive." In this chapter, however, we have returned to referencing them separately, because they operate differently in many postsecondary schools in terms of their organization. Accelerated learning programs tend to make up separate departments, divisions, or colleges within a larger university. Intensive programs, more often than not, are part of the regular departments, divisions, or colleges. Intensive programs are taught by full-time faculty far more often than are accelerated programs. Both programs tend to serve a nontraditional student population.

Accelerated and intensive learning programs also appear to be taking two different tracks in their evolution. As discussed earlier, both began for very utilitarian reasons. Because contact hours remained the same, intensive courses were more easily accepted and adopted by conventional colleges that appreciated an abbreviated summer schedule. Accelerated courses reduced both duration of the course and contact hours, were taught largely by adjunct faculty, were easily housed off-campus, had a sizable population of working adults who needed such a format, and were the more profitable alternative to conventional college programs, becoming the basic format in for-profit postsecondary schools. In addition, their larger profit margin kept them afloat in many private colleges that were struggling with fiscal debt.

Because both formats served working adults; increased accessibility for marginalized populations; allowed adults to continue their full-time employment; and, in the case of accelerated programs, flexibly reduced degree completion from eight to four years, they were compelling places to work for adult educators (Husson and Kennedy, 2003). In the 1980s, adult education was still a young and burgeoning discipline gaining a foothold in many universities. It was filled with egalitarian ideals, with leading thinkers, such as Paulo Freire, Phyllis Cunningham, and Jack Mezirow. Accelerated and intensive programs were pioneering experiential learning, flexible and large-block scheduling, and such alternative assessment practices as learning contracts and performance-based assessment. For many aspiring adult educators, these programs were the place to be, especially during the 1990s, when accelerated programs experienced rapid expansion (Donaldson and Graham, 2002).

Today, any postsecondary institution that seeks to enroll nontraditional students (nearly three-quarters of college students, most of whom are part- or full-time working adults) has to at least have online courses, intensive courses, and flexible scheduling. It is a matter of institutional survival. These programs are often quite conventional—condensing the same content into fewer weeks, using direct instruction, and employing such traditional assessment practices as multiple-choice and essay exams. Because there is so little research, it is difficult to gauge innovation among these programs. What is known is that at least for conventional higher education, the attainment rates among adults, first-generation college students, low-income students, and students of color are significantly lower than those of other students (Merisotis, 2009).

There is a trend within accelerated institutions to increase their development of online programs (Online Consortium of Independent Colleges & Universities, 2009). We could not find research within the last five years that indicated the numbers or percentages of low-income students and students of color who are enrolled in these online accelerated programs.

We can see that intensive and accelerated programs continue to expand but with little research or documented concern about their commitment to underserved learners. Given their historical legacy in adult education, we find it necessary, to ask, where is the leadership among accelerated and intensive programs to provide postsecondary education for underserved adult learners, who are mainly low income and students of color? At this time, we see three possible sources of leadership: community colleges, foundations, and the federal government. By virtue of their regional populations, especially in urban centers, community colleges serve low-income working adults, many of whom are students of color. We know of at least thirteen community colleges with accelerated programs, and we know that this number is growing (Commission for Accelerated Programs, 2009).

The Lumina Foundation for Education has supported a multiyear national initiative, Achieving the Dream: Community Colleges Count, to increase community college accessibility and success for groups that have traditionally faced significant barriers to academic achievement, including working adults, low-income students, and students of color (Lincoln, Goldberger, Kazis, and Rothkopf, 2009). The foundation has recently announced a goal to increase the proportion of Americans with high-quality degrees and credentials to 60 percent by the year 2025 (Lumina Foundation for Education, 2009). This mission is particularly directed at underserved nontraditional learners.

The Gates Foundation has also begun a new postsecondary initiative (Shaw, 2009). Also targeting the year 2025, this foundation's goal is to double the number of low-income students graduating from college and other post–high school programs. In addition, the federal government within the last few months has unveiled plans for a $12 billion federal investment to spur innovation to yield an additional five million community college graduates by 2020 (Viadero, 2009).

These efforts are encouraging and indicate the first stages of what may be a national consensus to provide more educational opportunity and support for working adults, especially those who have been marginalized by traditional institutions in higher education. Accelerated and intensive programs will be part of this initiative. Whether that is by default or through commitment will depend on each individual school. But there is a clear need for dedication among postsecondary schools with accelerated or intensive programs in order to more effectively support the needs of nontraditional learners who are poor.

It is our responsibility as instructors to hold ourselves accountable for this goal and to prepare ourselves to meet it. This calls for self-scrutiny, an understanding of our professional spheres of influence, and a deeper engagement with our institutions to be responsive to meeting the need for postsecondary education among low-income adult learners. There is a tendency to romanticize being a teacher in higher education. To most people unfamiliar with academic life, it seems a privilege and affords personal status. "What do you do?" "Oh, I'm an accountant. Now and then I teach a course at the university." Being careful not to stare, we watch for eyes widening and a small approving smile. But teaching in postsecondary education familiarizes us with its contradictions. The challenge before us is to make postsecondary education accessible for *every* adult learner, and to realize that at this time in history we can be agents for one of the largest transformations of postsecondary education since the Second World War, in ways that are needed and necessary for the values this country upholds.

References

Abercrombie, H. C., and others. "Cortisol Variation in Humans Affects Memory for Emotionally Laden and Neutral Information." *Behavioral Neuroscience*, 2003, *117*(3), 505–516.

Adams, M., Jones, J., and Tatum, B. D. "Knowing Our Students." In M. Adams, L. A. Bell, and P. Griffin (eds.), *Teaching for Diversity and Social Justice: A Sourcebook*. (2nd ed.) New York: Routledge, 2007.

Ahissar, E., and others. "Dependence of Cortical Plasticity on Correlated Activity of Single Neurons and on Behavioral Context." *Science*, 1992, *257*(5075), 1412–1415.

American Association of Colleges of Nursing. "Accelerated Programs: The Fast-Track to Careers in Nursing." *AACN Issue Bulletin*. [www.aacn.nche.edu/Publications/issues/Aug02.htm]. Apr. 2008.

American Association of Colleges of Nursing. "Accelerated Baccalaureate and Master's Degrees in Nursing." *AACN Fact Sheet*. Feb. 2009.

American Association of Colleges of Nursing. Washington, D.C.: http://www.aacn.nche.edu/index.htm.

American Association of State Colleges and Universities. *Access, Inclusion, and Equity: Imperatives for America's Campuses*. Washington, D.C.: American Association of State Colleges and Universities, 1997.

Anderson, L. W., and Krathwohl, D. R. (eds.). *A Taxonomy for Learning, Teaching, and Assessing: A Revision of Bloom's Taxonomy of Educational Objectives*. New York: Longman, 2001.

Angelo, T. A., and Cross, K. P. *Classroom Assessment Techniques: A Handbook for College Teachers*. San Francisco: Jossey-Bass, 1993.

Aslanian, C. B. *Adult Students Today*. New York: The College Board, 2001.

Astin, A. W. *What Matters in College? Four Critical Years Revisited*. San Francisco: Jossey-Bass, 1993.

Attewell, P., Lavin, D. E., Domina, T., and Levey, T. *Passing the Torch: Does Higher Education for the Disadvantaged Pay Off Across the Generations?* New York: Russell Sage Foundation, 2007.

Bandura, A. "Self-Efficacy Mechanism in Human Agency." *American Psychologist*, 1982, *37*(2), 122–147.

Bandura, A. *Self-Efficacy: The Exercise of Control*. New York: Freeman, 1997.

Barkley, E. F., Cross, K. P., and Major, C. H. *Collaborative Learning Techniques: A Handbook for College Faculty*. San Francisco: Jossey-Bass, 2005.

Barret, L. F. "Feeling Is Perceiving: Core Affect and Conceptualization in the Experience of Emotion." In L. F. Barret, P. M. Niedenthal, and P. Winkielman (eds.), *Emotion and Consciousness*. New York: Guilford Press, 2005.

Bartlett, T. "Phoenix Risen: How a History Professor Became the Pioneer of the for-Profit Revolution." *Chronicle of Higher Education*, July 2009, pp. A1, A10.

Bellah, R. N., Madsen, R., Tipton, S., and Sullivan, W. M. *The Good Society*. New York: Random House, 1991.

Berger, N. O., Caffarella, R. S., and O'Donnell, J. M. "Learning Contracts." In M. W. Galbraith (ed.), *Adult Learning Methods: A Guide for Effective Instruction*. (3rd ed.) Malabar, Fla.: Krieger, 2004.

Berliner, D. "The Development of Expertise in Pedagogy." Charles W. Hunt Memorial Lecture, American Association of Colleges for Teacher Education, New Orleans, Feb. 1988.

Besch, M. D. *A Navy Second to None: The History of U. S. Naval Training in World War I*. Westport, Conn.: Greenwood Press, 2002.

Beyer, B. K. *Practical Strategies for the Teaching of Thinking*. Needham Heights, Mass.: Allyn & Bacon, 1987.

Bong, M., and Skaalvik, E. "Academic Self-Concept and Self-Efficacy: How Different Are They Really?" *Educational Psychology Review*, 2003, *15*, 1–40.

Boshier, R. "Lifelong Learning." In L. M. English (ed.), *International Encyclopedia of Adult Education*. New York: Palgrave Macmillan, 2005.

Brookfield, S. D. *Becoming a Critically Reflective Teacher*. San Francisco: Jossey-Bass, 1995.

Brookfield, S. D. "A Critical Theory Perspective on Accelerated Learning." In R. J. Wlodkowski and C. K. Kasworm, (eds.), *Accelerated Learning for Adults: The Promise and Practice of Intensive Educational Formats*. New Directions for Adult and Continuing Education, no. 97. San Francisco: Jossey-Bass, 2003.

Brookfield, S. D., and Preskill, S. *Discussion as a Way of Teaching: Tools and Techniques for Democratic Classrooms*. San Francisco: Jossey-Bass, 2005.

Brophy, J. "Teacher Praise: A Functional Analysis." *Review of Educational Research*, 1981, *51*(1), 5–32.

Brophy, J. *Motivating Students to Learn*. (2nd ed.) Mahwah, N.J.: Lawrence Erlbaum, 2004.

Brothers, L. "The Social Brain: A Project for Integrating Primate Behavior and Neurophysiology in a New Domain." In J. Cacioppo and others (eds.), *Foundations in Social Neuroscience.* Cambridge, Mass.: MIT Press, 2000.

Burton, E. M. "Distance Learning and Service-Learning in the Accelerated Format." In R. J. Wlodkowski and C. E. Kasworm (eds.), *Accelerated Learning for Adults: The Promise and Practice of Intensive Educational Formats.* New Directions for Adult and Continuing Education, no. 97. San Francisco: Jossey-Bass, 2003.

Buzan, T. *Use Both Sides of Your Brain.* New York: Dutton, 1991.

Bye, D., Pushkar, D., and Conway, M. "Motivation, Interest, and Positive Affect in Traditional and Nontraditional Undergraduate Students." *Adult Education Quarterly,* 2007, *57,* 141–158.

Caffarella, R. S. *Planning Programs for Adult Learners: A Practical Guide for Educators, Trainers, and Staff Developers.* (2nd ed.) San Francisco: Jossey-Bass, 2002.

Caine, G., and Caine, R. N. "Meaningful Learning and the Executive Functions of the Brain." In S. Johnson and K. Taylor (eds.), *The Neuroscience of Adult Learning.* New Directions for Adult and Continuing Education, no. 110. San Francisco: Jossey-Bass, 2006.

Campbell, L., Campbell, B., and Dickinson, D. *Teaching and Learning Through Multiple Intelligences.* (3rd ed.) Boston: Pearson, 2004.

Cassidy, S. "Learning Styles: An Overview of Theories, Models, and Measures." *Educational Psychology,* 2004, *24*(4), 419–444.

Center for Adult Learning in Louisiana. *CALL: Investing in Louisiana's Adult Learners.* Alexandria: Louisiana Board of Regents, 2009.

Chirkov, V., Kim, Y., Ryan, R. M., and Kaplan, U. "Differentiating Autonomy from Individualism and Independence: A Self-Determination Theory Perspective on Internalization of Cultural Orientations and Well-Being." *Journal of Personality and Social Psychology,* 2003, *84,* 97–110.

Chiu, C., and Hong, Y. "Cultural Competence: Dynamic Processes." In A. J. Elliot and C. S. Dweck (eds.), *Handbook of Competence and Motivation.* New York: Guilford Press, 2005.

Chularut, P., and DeBacker, T. K. "The Influence of Concept Mapping on Achievement, Self-Regulation, and Self-Efficacy in Students of English as a Second Language." *Contemporary Educational Psychology,* 2004, *29,* 248–263.

Clifton, L. "Poems and Wonder." *Molasses: Slow Down to Savor Poetry.* [http://molasses.wordpress.com/2007/03/18/poems-and-wonder], 2007.

Commission for Accelerated Programs (CAP). Denver, Colorado [http://www.capnetwork.org/].

Commission for Accelerated Programs. "Accelerated Programs." [www.capnetwork.org/modules.php?op=modload&name=CAPDatabase&file=index&&letter=All&sortby=institutionname&], 2009.

Coyle, D. "How to Grow a Super Athlete." *New York Times Play*, Mar. 2007, pp. 36–41, 76–80.

Cozolino, L., and Sprokay, S. "Neuroscience and Adult Learning." In S. Johnson and K. Taylor (eds.), *The Neuroscience of Adult Learning*. New Directions for Adult and Continuing Education, no. 110. San Francisco: Jossey-Bass, 2006.

Cranton, P. "Types of Group Learning." In S. Imel (ed.), *Learning in Groups: Fundamental Principles, New Uses, and Emerging Opportunities*. New Directions for Adult and Continuing Education, no. 71. San Francisco: Jossey-Bass, 1996.

Cruickshank, D. R., and others. *Teaching Is Tough*. Upper Saddle River, N.J.: Prentice Hall, 1980.

Csikszentmihalyi, M. *Finding Flow: The Psychology of Engagement with Everyday Life*. New York: Basic Books, 1997.

Cunningham, P. M. "A Sociology of Adult Education." In A. L. Wilson and E. R. Hayes (eds.), *Handbook of Adult and Continuing Education*. San Francisco: Jossey-Bass, 2000.

Davidson, J., and McClintock, P. "Accelerated Online Faculty Development Seminars." Paper presented at the National Conference for Accelerated Programs in Higher Education, San Francisco, 2007.

Day, H. I. (ed.). *Advances in Intrinsic Motivation and Aesthetics*. New York: Plenum, 1981.

Deci, E. L., and Ryan, R. M. "A Motivational Approach to Self: Integration in Personality." In R. Dienstbier (ed.), *Nebraska Symposium on Motivation, Vol. 38: Perspectives on Motivators*. Lincoln: University of Nebraska Press, 1991.

Delahaye, B. L., and Smith, B. J. *How to Be an Effective Trainer: Skills for Managers and New Trainers*. (3rd ed.) Hoboken, N.J.: Wiley, 1998.

Denson, N., and Chang, M. J. "Racial Diversity Matters: The Impact of Diversity-Related Student Engagement and Institutional Context." *American Educational Research Journal*, 2009, *46*(2), 322–353.

Dick, W. O., Carey, L., and Carey, J. O. *The Systematic Design of Instruction*. (6th ed.) Boston: Allyn & Bacon, 2004.

Donaldson, J. F., and Graham, S. W. "Accelerated Degree Programs: Design and Policy Implications." *Journal of Continuing Higher Education*, 2002, *50*(2), 2–13.

Donovan, M. S., Bransford, J. D., and Pellegrino, J. W. (eds.). *How People Learn: Bridging Research and Practice*. Washington, D.C.: National Academy Press, 1999.

Driscoll, M. P. *Psychology of Learning for Instruction*. (3rd ed.) Boston: Allyn & Bacon, 2005.

Eisner, E. W. *The Educational Imagination*. (2nd ed.) Old Tappan, N.J.: Macmillan, 1985.

Elbow, P. *Embracing Contraries: Explorations in Learning and Teaching.* New York: Oxford University Press, 1986.

Ellis, A. "Rational-Emotive Therapy." In R. J. Corsini and D. Wedding (eds.), *Current Psychotherapies.* Itasca, Ill.: Peacock, 1989.

Fenwick, T. J., and Parsons, J. *The Art of Evaluation: A Handbook for Educators and Trainers.* Toronto: Thompson Educational, 2000.

Flint, T., and Dodge, L. "Ten Research Pillars in Support of ALFI." Track Session at the Council for Adult and Experiential Learning International Conference, Chicago, Nov. 2009.

Fong, M. "The Nexus of Language, Communication, and Culture." In L. A. Samovar, R. E. Porter, and E. R. McDaniel (eds.), *Intercultural Communication.* (11th ed.) Belmont, CA: Thomson Wadsworth, 2006.

Frankl, V. E. *Man's Search for Meaning.* Boston: Beacon Press, 2006.

Freire, P. *Pedagogy of the Oppressed.* New York: Continuum, 1970.

Gage, N. L., and Berliner, D. C. *Educational Psychology.* (6th ed.) Boston: Houghton Mifflin, 1998.

Garcia Duncan, T. G., and McKeachie, W. J. "The Making of the Motivated Strategies for Learning Questionnaire." *Educational Psychologist,* 2005, *40*(2), 117–128.

Gardner, H. *Multiple Intelligences: The Theory in Practice.* New York: Basic Books, 1993.

Gardner, H. *Multiple Intelligences: New Horizons.* New York: Basic Books, 2006.

Gardner, J. W. *On Leadership.* New York: Free Press, 1990.

Gawande, A. *The Checklist Manifesto: How to Get Things Right.* New York: Metropolitan Books, 2009.

Gay, G. *Culturally Responsive Teaching.* New York: Teachers College Press, 2000.

Gephart, W. J., Strother, D. B., and Duckett, W. R., eds. "Instructional Clarity." *Practical Applications of Research,* 1981, *3*(3), 1–4.

Ginsberg, M. B. "Lessons at the Kitchen Table." *Educational Leadership,* 2007, *64*(6), 56–61.

Ginsberg, M. B., and Wlodkowski, R. J. *Diversity and Motivation: Culturally Responsive Teaching in College.* (2nd ed.) San Francisco: Jossey-Bass, 2009.

Ginsberg, M. B., and Wlodkowski, R. J. "Access and Participation." In C. Kasworm, A. R. Rose, and J. Ross-Gordon (eds.), *Handbook of Adult and Continuing Education.* Thousand Oaks, Calif.: Sage, 2010.

Glasser, W. "Understanding Education: A Student's Perspective." Speech given at the Jewish Community Center, Milwaukee, Wis., Mar. 1986.

Goldberg, E. *The Executive Brain: Frontal Lobes and the Civilized Mind.* New York: Oxford University Press, 2001.

Goleman, D. *Social Intelligence*. New York: Bantam, 2007.

Good, T. L., and Brophy, J. *Looking in Classrooms*. (9th ed.) Boston: Allyn & Bacon, 2003.

Goodman, J. "Humor, Creativity, and Magic: Tools for Teaching and Living." Unpublished manuscript, Sagamore Institute, Saratoga Springs, N.Y., 1981.

Griffin, P. "Facilitating Social Justice Education Courses." In M. Adams, L. A. Bell, and P. Griffin (eds.), *Teaching for Diversity and Social Justice: A Sourcebook*. New York: Routledge, 1997.

Gronlund, N. E. *Stating Objectives for Classroom Instruction*. (3rd ed.) Old Tappan, N.J.: Macmillan, 1985.

Hill, C. E. *Helping Skills: Facilitating Exploration, Insight, and Action*. (2nd ed.) Washington, D.C.: American Psychological Association, 2004.

Hodgins, H. S., and Knee, C. R. "The Integrating Self and Conscious Experience." In E. L. Deci and R. M. Ryan (eds.), *Handbook of Self-Determination Research*. Rochester, N.Y.: University of Rochester Press, 2002.

Hoeller, K. "Adjunct Faculty at State's Two-Year Schools Deserve Equal Pay for Equal Work." *The Seattle Times*, May 8, 2009, p. A19.

Hoover, E. "The Millennial Muddle: How Stereotyping Students Became a Thriving Industry and a Bundle of Contradictions." *Chronicle of Higher Education*, 2009, *56*(8), A1, A28–A34.

Husson, W. J., and Kennedy, T. "Developing and Maintaining Accelerated Degree Programs Within Traditional Institutions." In R. J. Wlodkowski and C. K. Kasworm (eds.), *Accelerated Learning for Adults: The Promise and Practice of Intensive Educational Formats*. New Directions for Adult and Continuing Education, no. 97. San Francisco: Jossey-Bass, 2003.

Hutchings, P. *Using Cases to Improve College Teaching: A Guide to More Reflective Practice*. Washington, D.C.: American Association for Higher Education, 1993.

Ishitani, T., and DesJardins, S. "A Longitudinal Investigation of Dropout from College in the United States." *Journal of College Student Retention*. 2002, *4*(2), 173–201.

Jensen, E. *Teaching with the Brain in Mind*. (2nd ed.) Alexandria, Va.: Association for Supervision and Curriculum Development, 2005.

Johnson, D. W. "Social Interdependence: The Interrelationships Among Theory, Research, and Practice." *American Psychologist*, 2003, *58*, 931–945.

Johnson, D. W., and Johnson, F. P. *Joining Together: Group Theory and Group Skills*. (9th ed.) Boston: Allyn & Bacon, 2006.

Johnson, D. W., and Johnson, R. T. "An Educational Psychology Success Story: Social Interdependence Theory and Cooperative Learning." *Educational Researcher*, 2009, *38*(5), 365–379.

Johnson, D. W., Johnson, R. T., and Smith, K. A. *Active Learning: Cooperation in the College Classroom.* Edina, Minn.: Interaction, 1991.

Jones, A. P., Rozelle, R. M., and Chang, W. "Perceived Punishment and Reward Values of Supervisor Actions in a Chinese Sample." *Psychological Studies,* 1990, *35,* 1–10.

June, A. W. "Love of Teaching Draws Adjuncts to the Classroom Despite Low Pay." *Chronicle of Higher Education,* 2009, *56*(9), A1, A8, A10.

Kasworm, C. E., and Marienau, C. A. "Principles of Assessment for Adult Learning." In A. D. Rose and M. A. Leahy (eds.), *Assessing Adult Learning in Diverse Settings: Current Issues and Approaches.* New Directions for Adult and Continuing Education, no. 75. San Francisco: Jossey-Bass, 1997.

Keeton, M. T., Sheckley, B. G., and Griggs, J. K. *Effectiveness and Efficiency in Higher Education for Adults: A Guide for Fostering Learning.* Dubuque, Iowa: Kendall Hunt, 2002.

Keller, J. "Killing Me Microsoftly." *Chicago Tribune,* Jan. 5, 2003, p. 9.

Keller, J. M., and Litchfield, B. C. "Motivation and Performance." In R. A. Reiser and J. V. Dempsey (eds.), *Trends and Issues in Instructional Design and Technology.* Columbus, Ohio: Merrill Prentice Hall, 2002.

Kerman, S. "Teacher Expectation and Student Achievement." *Phi Delta Kappan,* 1979, *60,* 716–718.

King, A. "Inquiry as a Tool in Critical Thinking." In D. F. Halpern and Associates (eds.), *Changing College Classrooms: New Teaching and Learning Strategies for an Increasingly Complex World.* San Francisco: Jossey-Bass, 1994.

King, A. "Structuring Peer Interaction to Promote High-Level Cognitive Processing." *Theory into Practice,* 2002, *41*(1), 33–39.

King, K. P. "Distance Education." In L. M. English (ed.), *International Encyclopedia of Adult Education.* New York: Palgrave Macmillan, 2005.

Kinsella, K. "Instructional Strategies Which Promote Participation and Learning for Non-Native Speakers of English in University Classes." *Exchanges,* 1993, *5*(1), 12.

Kohn, A. *Punished by Rewards.* Boston: Houghton Mifflin, 1993.

Kolb, D. A. *Experiential Learning: Experience as the Source of Learning and Development.* Englewood Cliffs, N.J.: Prentice-Hall, 1984.

Kornhaber, M. L. "Assessment, Standards, and Equity." In J. A. Banks and C. A. M. Banks (eds.), *Handbook on Research in Multicultural Education.* (2nd ed.) San Francisco: Jossey-Bass, 2004.

Korvick, L. M., Wisener, L. K., Loftis, L. A., and Williamson, M. L. "Comparing the Academic Performance of Students in Traditional and Second Degree Baccalaureate Programs." *Journal of Nursing Education,* 2008, *47,* 139–141.

Kuh, G. D., Kinzie, J., Schuh, J. H., Whitt, E. J., and Associates. *Student Success in College: Creating Conditions That Matter*. San Francisco: Jossey-Bass, 2005.

Lambert, N. M., and McCombs, B. L. "Introduction: Learner-Centered Schools and Classrooms as a Direction for School Reform." In N. M. Lambert and B. L. McCombs (eds.), *How Students Learn: Reforming Schools Through Learner-Centered Education*. Washington, D.C.: American Psychological Association, 1998.

Larkins, A. G., McKinney, C. W., Oldham-Buss, S., and Gilmore, A. C. *Teacher Enthusiasm: A Critical Review*. Hattiesburg, Miss.: Education and Psychological Research, 1985.

Lawrence-Lightfoot, S. *The Third Chapter: Passion, Risk, and Adventure in the 25 Years After 50*. New York: Farrar, Straus, and Giroux, 2009.

Lederman, D. "Improving Student Retention and Persistence." *AGB Priorities*, 2005, *26*, 1–15.

Lemieux, C. M. "Learning Contracts in the Classroom: Tools for Empowerment and Accountability." *Social Work Education*, 2001, *20*(2), 263–276.

Light, R. *Explorations with Students and Faculty About Teaching, Learning, and Student Life*. Vol. *1*. Cambridge, Mass.: Harvard University Press, 1990.

Lincoln, C., Goldberger, S., Kazis, R., and Rothkopf, A. J. "Courageous Conversations: Achieving the Dream and the Importance of Student Success." *Change*. [www.changemag.org/Archives/Back%20Issues/January-February%202009/full-achieving-dream.html], Jan.–Feb. 2009.

Locke, E., and Latham, G. "Building a Practically Useful Theory of Goal Setting and Task Motivation." *American Psychologist*, 2002, *57*, 705–717.

Loden, M., and Rosener, J. B. *Workforce America! Managing Employee Diversity as a Vital Resource*. Homewood, Ill.: Business One Irwin, 1991.

Lohman, M. C. "Cultivating Problem-Solving Skills Through Problem-Based Approaches to Professional Development." *Human Resource Development Quarterly*, 2002, *13*(3), 243–261.

Lowe, J. "Time, Leisure, and Adult Education." In A. C. Tuijnman (ed.), *International Encyclopedia of Adult Education and Training*. (2nd ed.) New York: Pergamon Press, 1996.

Lumina Foundation for Education. "Goal 2025." [www.luminafoundation.org/goal_2025/], December 3, 2009.

MacGregor, J. "Learning Self-Evaluation: Challenges for Students." In J. MacGregor (ed.), *Student Self-Evaluation: Fostering Reflective Learning*. New Directions for Teaching and Learning, no. 56. San Francisco: Jossey-Bass, 1994.

Mager, R. F. *Developing Attitude Toward Learning*. Belmont, Calif.: Fearon, 1968.

Markham, T., Larmer, J., and Ravitz, J. *Project Based Learning Handbook: A Guide to Standards-Focused Project Based Learning for Middle and High School Students*. (2nd ed.) Novato, Calif.: Buck Institute for Education, 2003.

Massimini, F., Csikszentmihalyi, M., and Delle Fave, A. "Flow and Biocultural Evolution." In M. Csikszentmihalyi and I. S. Csikszentmihalyi (eds.), *Optimal Experience: Psychological Studies of Flow in Consciousness*. New York: Cambridge University Press, 1988.

McKeachie, W. J. "Good Teaching Makes a Difference—And We Know What It Is." In R. P. Perry and J. C. Smart (eds.), *Effective Teaching in Higher Education: Research and Practice*. New York: Agathon Press, 1997.

Merisotis, J. P. "It's the Learning, Stupid." *The Howard R. Bowen Lecture*. Lecture given at Claremont Graduate University, Claremont, Calif., Oct. 2009. [www.luminafoundation.org/about_us/president/speeches/2009-10-14.html].

Merriam, S. B., Caffarella, R. S., and Baumgartner, L. M. *Learning in Adulthood: A Comprehensive Guide*. (3rd ed.) San Francisco: Jossey-Bass, 2007.

Meyers, C., and Jones, T. B. *Promoting Active Learning: Strategies for the College Classroom*. San Francisco: Jossey-Bass, 1993.

Mezirow, J. "Transformative Learning: Theory to Practice." In P. Cranton (ed.), *Transformative Learning in Action: Insights from Practice*. New Directions for Adult and Continuing Education, no. 74. San Francisco: Jossey-Bass, 1997.

Mezirow, J. "Learning to Think Like an Adult: Core Concepts of Transformation Theory." In J. Mezirow and Associates (eds.), *Learning as Transformation: Critical Perspectives on a Theory in Progress*. San Francisco: Jossey-Bass, 2000.

Moll, L. C., Amanti, C., Neff, D., and Gonzalez, N. "Funds of Knowledge for Teaching: Using a Qualitative Approach to Connect Homes and Classrooms." *Theory into Practice*, 1992, *31*, 132–141.

Moran, S., Kornhaber, M., and Gardner, H. "Orchestrating Multiple Intelligences." *Educational Leadership*, 2006, *64*(1), 22–27.

Morgan, M. "Reward-Induced Decrements and Increments in Intrinsic Motivation." *Review of Educational Research*, 1984, *54*(1), 5–30.

Morrison, G. R., Ross, S. M., and Kemp, J. E. *Designing Effective Instruction*. (5th ed.) Indianapolis: Wiley, 2006.

Morrison, T. *New York Times Magazine*, Sept. 11, 1994, p. 73.

Nah, Y. "Can a Self-Directed Learner Be Independent, Autonomous, and Interdependent? Implications for Practice." *Adult Learning*, 2000, *18*, pp. 18–19, 25.

Nakamura, J., and Csikszentmihalyi, M. "The Construction of Meaning Through Vital Engagement." In C. Keyes and J. Haidt (eds.), *Flourishing: Positive Psychology and the Life Well-Lived*. Washington, D.C.: American Psychological Association, 2003.

National Survey of Student Engagement 2006 Annual Report: *Engaged Learning: Fostering Success for All Students*. [http://nsse.iub.edu/NSSE_2006_Annual_Report/index.cfm], Jan. 2007.

Nesbit, J. C., and Adesope, O. O. "Learning with Concept and Knowledge Maps: A Meta-Analysis." *Review of Educational Research*, 2006, 76(3), 413–448.

New Ventures of Regis University. *Accelerated Program Growth Stages and Best Practices*. Arvada, Colo.: Regis University College for Professional Studies, 2007.

Niedenthal, P. M., Barsalou, L. W., Ric, F., and Krauth-Gruber, S. "Embodiment in the Acquisition and Use of Emotion Knowledge." In L. F. Barrett, P. M. Niedenthal, and P. Winkielman (eds.), *Emotion and Consciousness*. New York: Guilford Press, 2005.

Nietzsche, F. W. *The Antichrist*. New York: Knopf, 1920.

O'Brien, J. G., Millis, B. J., and Cohen, M. W. *The Course Syllabus: A Learning Centered Approach*. (2nd ed.) San Francisco: Jossey-Bass, 2008.

Ogle, D. "The K-W-L: A Teaching Model That Develops Active Reading of Expository Text." *The Reading Teacher*, 1986, 39, 564–576.

Online Consortium of Independent Colleges & Universities. "About OCICU." [www.ocicu.org/default.asp].

Pintrich, P. R. (ed.). "Current Issues and New Directions in Motivational Theory and Research." *Education Psychologist*, 1991, 26, 384.

Pittman, T. S., Boggiano, A. K., and Ruble, D. N. "Intrinsic and Extrinsic Motivational Orientations: Limiting Conditions on the Undermining and Enhancing Effects of Reward on Intrinsic Motivation." In J. M. Levine and M. C. Wang (eds.), *Teacher and Student Perceptions: Implications for Learning*. Hillsdale, N.J.: Erlbaum, 1983.

Plaut, V. C., and Markus, H. R. "The 'Inside' Story: A Cultural-Historical Analysis of Being Smart and Motivated, American Style." In A. J. Elliot and C. S. Dweck (eds.), *Handbook of Competence and Motivation*. New York: Guilford Press, 2005.

Prenzel, M. "The Selective Persistence of Interest." In K. A. Renninger, S. Hidi, and A. Krapp (eds.), *The Role of Interest in Learning and Development*. Hillsdale, N.J.: Lawrence Erlbaum Associates, 1992.

Professional and Organizational Development Network in Higher Education (POD). Nederland, Colorado, (http://www.podnetwork.org/).

Rangachari, P. K. "Twenty-Up: Problem-Based Learning with a Large Group." In L. Wilkerson and W. H. Gijselaers (eds.), *Bringing Problem-Based Learning to Higher Education: Theory and Practice*. New Directions for Teaching and Learning, no. 68. San Francisco: Jossey-Bass, 1996.

Ratey, J. J. *A User's Guide to the Brain: Perception, Attention, and the Four Theatres of the Brain*. New York: Pantheon, 2001.

Reeves, D. B. "Effective Grading Practices." *Educational Leadership*, 2008, 65(5), 85–87.

Renninger, K. A., and Shumar, W. "Community Building with and for Teachers: The Math Forum as a Resource for Teacher Professional Development." In K. A. Renninger and W. Shumar (eds.), *Building Virtual Communities: Learning and Change in Cyberspace*. New York: Cambridge University Press, 2002.

Rich, A. Lecture given for the 164th Anniversary of Susan B. Anthony's birthday, Scripps College, Claremont, Calif., Feb. 1984.

Rizzolatti, G., Fogassi, L., and Gallese, V. "Mirrors in the Mind." In *The Jossey-Bass Reader on the Brain and Learning*. San Francisco: Jossey-Bass, 2008.

Rogers, C. R. *Freedom to Learn*. Columbus, Ohio: Merrill, 1969.

Rogoff, B., and Chavajay, P. "What's Become of Research on the Cultural Basis of Cognitive Development?" *American Psychologist*, 1995, *50*, 859–877.

Rojstaczur, S. "Grade Inflation at American Colleges and Universities." [http://gradeinflation.com/], March 10, 2009.

Rosenthal, R., and Jacobson, L. *Pygmalion in the Classroom*. New York: Holt, Rinehart and Winston, 1968.

Rossiter, M. "Radical Mutuality and Self-Other Relationship in Adult Education." In S. B. Merriam, B. C. Courtenay, and R. M. Cervero (eds.), *Global Issues and Adult Education: Perspectives from Latin America, Southern Africa, and the United States*. San Francisco: Jossey-Bass, 2006.

Rubenson, K. *Adults' Readiness to Learn: Questioning Lifelong Learning for All*. Proceeding of the Adult Educational Research Conference, no. 39. San Antonio: University of the Incarnate Word and Texas A&M University, 1998, 257–262.

Ryan, R. M., and Deci, E. L. "When Rewards Compete with Nature: The Undermining of Intrinsic Motivation and Self-Regulation." In C. Sansone and J. M. Harackiewicz (eds.), *Intrinsic and Extrinsic Motivation: The Search for Optimal Motivation and Performance*. San Diego: Academic Press, 2000.

Ryan, R. M., and Deci, E. L. "Overview of Self-Determination Theory: An Organismic Dialectical Perspective." In E. L. Deci and R. M. Ryan (eds.), *Handbook of Self-Determination Research*. Rochester, N.Y.: University of Rochester Press, 2002.

Samovar, L. A., Porter, R. E., and McDaniel, E. R. (eds.). *Intercultural Communication: A Reader*. (11th ed.) New York: Wadsworth, 2005.

Savin-Baden, M. *Facilitating Problem-Based Learning*. Berkshire, England: Open University Press, 2003.

Schuetze, H. G. "Financing Lifelong Learning." In P. Jarvis (ed.), *The Routledge International Handbook of Lifelong Learning*. New York: Routledge, 2009.

Schultz, W., and Dickinson, A. "Neuronal Coding of Prediction Errors." *Annual Review of Neuroscience*, 2000, *23*, 473–500.

Scott, P. A. "Attributes of High-Quality Intensive Courses." In R. J. Wlodkowski and C. K. Kasworm (eds.), *Accelerated Learning for Adults: The Promise and*

Practice of Intensive Educational Formats. New Directions for Adult and Continuing Education, no. 97. San Francisco: Jossey-Bass, 2003.

Scott, P. A. "Attributes of High-Quality Intensive Course Learning Experiences: Student Voices and Experiences." *College Student Journal,* 1996, *30,* 69–77.

Shaw, L. "Foundations Put $6.1 M into Boost for Community College Numbers." *The Seattle Times,* Oct. 15, 2009, p. B4.

Shelley, M. "Women's Voices: Quotations by Women." *About.com: Women's History.* [http://womenshistory.about.com/library/qu/blqushel.htm], December 2009.

Shor, I. "Education Is Politics: Paulo Freire's Critical Pedagogy." In P. McLaren and P. Leonard (eds.), *Paulo Freire: A Critical Encounter.* New York: Routledge, 1993.

Solorzano, D. "Teaching and Social Change: Reflections on a Freirean Approach in a College Classroom." *Teaching Sociology,* 1989, *17,* 218–225.

Sousa, D. A. *How the Brain Learns.* (3rd ed.) Thousand Oaks, Calif.: Corwin, 2006.

Sternberg, R. J., and others. *Practical Intelligence in Everyday Life.* New York: Cambridge University Press, 2000.

Stipek, D. *Motivation to Learn: From Theory to Practice.* (4th ed.) Boston: Allyn & Bacon, 2002.

Sweller, J., van Merrienboer, J. J. G., and Paas, F. G. W . C. "Cognitive Architecture and Instructional Design." *Educational Psychology Review,* 1998, *10,* 251–296.

Tagg, J. *The Learning Paradigm College.* Bolton, Mass.: Anker, 2003.

Tappan, M. B. "Sociocultural Psychology and Caring Pedagogy: Exploring Vygotsky's 'Hidden Curriculum.'" *Educational Psychologist,* 1998, *33*(1), 23–33.

Tatum, B. D. "Talking About Race, Learning About Racism: The Application of Racial Identity Development Theory in the Classroom." *Harvard Educational Review,* 1992, *62*(1), 1–24.

Tatum, B. D. *Why Are All the Black Kids Sitting Together in the Cafeteria? And Other Conversations About Race.* New York: Basic Books, 2003.

Taylor, K., Marienau, C., and Fiddler, M. *Developing Adult Learners: Strategies for Teachers and Trainers.* San Francisco: Jossey-Bass, 2000.

Tinto, V. *Leaving College: Rethinking the Causes and Cures for Student Attrition.* Chicago: University of Chicago Press, 1987.

Tinto, V. "Colleges as Communities: Taking Research on Student Persistence Seriously." *Review of Higher Education,* 1998, *21*(2), 167–177.

Tisdell, E. J. *Exploring Spirituality and Culture in Adult and Higher Education.* San Francisco: Jossey-Bass, 2003.

Tobin, K. "Role of Wait Time in Higher Cognitive Level Learning." *Review of Educational Research,* 1987, *57*(1), 69–95.

Uguroglu, M., and Walberg, H. J. "Motivation and Achievement: A Quantitative Synthesis." *American Educational Research Journal*, 1979, *16*, 375–389.

Vargas, J. S. *Behavioral Psychology for Teachers*. New York: HaperCollins, 1977.

Vaughan, M. S. *The End of Training: How Simulations Are Reshaping Business Training*. Golden, Colo.: Keystone Business Press, 2006.

Viadero, D. "Community College a Research Puzzle." *Education Week*, [http://www.edweek.org/login.html?source=http://www.edweek.org/ew/articles/2009/09/02/02comcolleges_ep.h29.html&destination=http://www.edweek.org/ew/articles/2009/09/02/02comcolleges_ep.h29.html&levelId=2100] Sept. 1, 2009.

Viens, J., and Kallenbach, S. *Multiple Intelligences and Adult Literacy: A Sourcebook for Practitioners*. New York: Teachers College Press, 2004.

Voss, J. F. "Problem Solving and the Educational Process." In A. Lesgold and R. Glaser (eds.), *Foundations for a Psychology of Education*. Hillsdale, N.J.: Erlbaum, 1989.

Walberg, H. J. "Synthesis of Research on Time and Learning." *Educational Leadership*, 1988, *45*, 76–85.

Walvoord, B. E. *Assessment Clear and Simple: A Practical Guide for Institutions, Departments, and General Education*. San Francisco: Jossey-Bass, 2004.

Watson, J. S., and Ramey, C. G. "Reactions to Response Contingent Stimulation in Early Infancy." *Merrill Palmer Quarterly*, 1972, *18*, 219–228.

Weiner, B. "Interpersonal and Intrapersonal Theories of Motivation from an Attributional Perspective." *Educational Psychology Review*, 2000, *12*, 1–14.

Wertsch, J. V. *Voices of the Mind: A Sociocultural Approach to Mediated Action*. Cambridge, Mass.: Harvard University Press, 1991.

Wetherbe, J. Quoted in C. A. Twigg, *Innovations in Online Learning: Moving Beyond No Significant Difference*. Troy, N.Y.: Center for Academic Transformation, 2001.

White, R. W. "Motivation Reconsidered: The Concept of Competence." *Psychological Review*, 1959, *66*, 297–333.

Wiggins, G. P. *Educative Assessment: Designing Assessments to Inform and Improve Student Performance*. San Francisco: Jossey-Bass, 1998.

Wiggins, G., and McTighe, J. *Understanding by Design*. (2nd ed.) Alexandria, Va.: Association for Supervision and Curriculum Development, 2005.

Wilson, A. L. "Lifelong Learning in the United States." In P. Jarvis (ed.), *The Routledge International Handbook of Lifelong Learning*. New York: Routledge, 2009.

Wilson, R. "For-Profit Colleges Change Higher Education's Landscape." *The Chronicle of Higher Education*," February 12, 2010, *56* (22), p. A1, pp. A16–A19.

Wlodkowski, R. J. *Brainstorming: Reasons for Grade Inflation.* New Ventures' Partner School Conference, Puerto Rico, Jul. 2000.

Wlodkowski, R. J. "Accelerated Learning in Colleges and Universities." In R. J. Wlodkowski and C. K. Kasworm (eds.), *Accelerated Learning for Adults: The Promise and Practice of Intensive Educational Formats.* New Directions for Adult and Continuing Education, no. 97. San Francisco: Jossey-Bass, 2003.

Wlodkowski, R. J. *Enhancing Adult Motivation to Learn: A Comprehensive Guide for Teaching All Adults.* (3rd ed.) San Francisco: Jossey-Bass, 2008.

Wlodkowski, R. J., and Ginsberg, M. B. *Diversity & Motivation: Culturally Responsive Teaching.* San Francisco: Jossey-Bass, 1995.

Wlodkowski, R. J., Mauldin, J. E., and Campbell, S. "Early Exit: Understanding Adult Attrition in Accelerated and Traditional Postsecondary Programs." *Synopsis,* July 2002, pp. 1–12.

Wlodkowski, R. J., Mauldin, J. E., and Gahn, S. W. *Learning in the Fast Lane: Adult Learners' Persistence and Success in Accelerated College Programs.* Indianapolis: Lumina Foundation for Education, 2001.

Wlodkowski, R. J., and Stiller, J. *Accelerated Learning Online Research Project: Phase 1.* Denver: Center for the Study of Accelerated Learning, Regis University, 2005.

Wlodkowski, R. J., and Westover, T. "Accelerated Courses as a Learning Format for Adults." *Canadian Journal for the Study of Adult Education,* 1999, *13*(1), 1–20.

Wolfe, A. "How a For-Profit University Can Be Invaluable to the Traditional Liberal Arts." *Chronicle of Higher Education,* Dec. 1998, pp. B4–B5.

Woolfolk, A. *Educational Psychology.* (10th ed.) Boston: Pearson, 2007.

Young, J. R. "When Computers Leave Classrooms, So Does Boredom." *Chronicle of Higher Education,* July 2009), p. A1, p, A13.

Zimmerman, B. J., and Kitsantas, A. "The Hidden Dimension of Personal Competence: Self-Regulated Learning and Practice." In A. J. Elliot and C. S. Dweck (eds.), *Handbook of Competence and Motivation.* New York: Guilford Press, 2005.

Zull, J. E. *The Art of Changing the Brain: Enriching the Practice of Teaching by Exploring the Biology of Learning.* Sterling, Va.: Stylus, 2002.

Index

A

Abercrombie, H. C., 18

Absenteeism, xii; making up for, 194; preparation for, 6–7

Accelerated and intensive learning courses: accreditation, 2; adjunct faculty, x; adult enrollment in, ix–x; alumni attitudes, 3–4; and characteristics of adults, 3; cohorts, 11, 58–59; collaborative learning, 11; conventional courses compared to, 4–11; course instruction, modular/standard syllabus for, 10; course quality, 11–12; designing instruction for, 164–188; evolution of, 196–199; formats, 1–2; instructional blocks of time, 6–9; learning, 2–3; as learning experiences, 1–13; and Motivational Framework for Culturally Responsive Teaching, 14–30; and nontraditional learners, 1; pass rates, 3; rewards of teaching, x; student attitudes, 3; student persistence and success, 4; working adults, 4–6

Accelerated, use of term, xii

Accreditation, 2

Acknowledgments, 162

Action words and learning objective, examples of (table), 61

Active listening, 56

Adams, M., 63

Adesope, O. O., 113

Adjunct faculty, x, xii; economic disparity between part-time and full-time faculty, 33–34

Adult Learning Focused Institutions network, 198

Ahissar, E., 17, 94

Altman, G., 183

Amanti, C., 101

American Association of Colleges of Nursing, 196, 197, 198

American Association of State Colleges and Universities, 4

American Psychological Association, Task Force on Psychology in Education, 19

Analogies, 111–112

Anderson, R., 60

Angelo, T. A., 91

Anxiety, and negative learner attitudes, 82

Aslanian, C. B., 1

Assessment, 136, 140–157; authentic performance tasks, 146–147; criteria, making fair/clear, 90–91; effectiveness, 138; formative, 145–146; grading practices, 155–157; and grading procedures, 70–71; and multiple intelligences theory, 147–149; promoting equity in procedures, 144–145; relating to competence, 137–138; and rubrics, 149–152; self-assessment, 152–155

Assignment keeper and historian, 193

Assignments, 70

Astin, A. W., 3

Attendance, 69–70

Attewell, P., 1, 4

Attitude, 25, 26, 80, *See also* Positive attitude; and motivation, 20–22

Attitudinal directions, 79–80

Attributions, 87–88

Authentic performance tasks, characteristics of, 146–147

Authenticity, and competence, 24

B

Balanced sense of competence, 137

Bandura, A., 85, 88

Barasalou, L. W., 39

Barkley, E. F., 11, 59

Barret, L. F., 16

Bartlett, T., 199

Baumgartner, L. M., 19

Bellah, R., xi

Benefits, of learning activities, 110

Berger, N. O., 92, 93

Berliner, D., 42, 111

Besch, M. D., 199

Beyer, B. K., 123

Bias, linguistic, 144

Boggiano, A. K., 157

Bong, M., 85

Boredom, and negative learner attitudes, 82

Boshier, R., 199

Brainstorming, 119

Bransford, J. D., 8, 35, 68, 70, 102, 114, 145, 164–165

Brookfield, S. D., 84, 116, 154, 198

Brophy, J., 19, 90, 92, 100, 103, 142, 157–158
Brothers, L., 54
Burton, E. M., 132
Buzan, T., 113
Bye, D., 186

C

Caffarella, R. S., 19, 37, 60, 92, 93
Caine, G., 128
Caine, R. N., 128
Campbell, K., 91
CAP. *See* Commission for Accelerated Programs (CAP)
Carey, J. O., 60
Carey, L., 60
Cassidy, S., 97
Celebrations, 162
Center for Adult Learning in Louisiana, 62, 197
Challenge, 102
Chang, J. O., 46
Chang, W., 159
Chavajay, P., 16, 47
Checklist, providing, 85
Chirkov, V., 21
Chiu, C., 48
Chularut, P., 113
Chunking information, 106
Clarity: diverse learners, planning and conducting instruction for, 42–43; of motivating instructors, 42–45; providing for initially incomprehensible material, 43–45
Clearly defined goals, 60
Clifton, L., 189
Climate of respect, creating, 63–67
Closure, 107
Closure techniques: Critical Incident Questionnaire, 154–155; "Head, Heart, Hand" activity, 153–154; "Summarizing Questions" activity, 154
Cohen, M. W., 66, 71
Cohorts, 11, 58–59; experience and skill matrix for, 193
Collaboration, 185
Collaborative learning, 11; groups, 194
Collaborative Learning Techniques: A Handbook for College Faculty (Barkley/Cross/Major), 59
Commission for Accelerated Programs (CAP), ix, x, 2, 196, 201
Competence, 23–24, 26; assessment and grading strategies to engender, 140–157; and authenticity, 24; balanced sense of, 137; and effectiveness, 24; engendering among learners, 136–163; feedback, providing, 141–144; and grade point average (GPA), 138–139; and motivation, 138; need for, 137; relating assessment to, 137–138; relating grading to, 138–140; reward and communication strategies to engender, 157–162
Competition, 59
Concept maps, 112–113
Conceptualizing, 109
Conflict, addressing, 110

Connectedness, and inclusion, 20
Connection: allowing for introductions, 52; collaborative and cooperative learning, 53–59; cooperative intentions to help adults learn, indicating, 53; engendering, 52–63; learning experience, human purpose of, 62–63; learning objectives, identifying, 59–62; multidimensional sharing activities, 52–53
Controlling feedback, 142
Conventional courses compared, compared to accelerated and intensive learning programs, 4–11
Conway, M., 186
Cooperative learning, 54–55, 65–66; groups, 54, 194
Cooperative Lesson Planning Guide, 58
Course instruction, modular/standard syllabus, 10
Course policies, 71
Course quality, and the instructor, 11–12
Course requirements, 69–71; assessment and grading procedures, 70–71; assignments, 70; attendance, 69–70; participation, 70
Course Syllabus, The (O'Brien/Millis/Cohen), 66
Coyle, D., 143
Cozolino, L., 133
Critical consciousness, xii, 48–49
Critical Incident Questionnaire, 154–155
Critical literacy, 49
Critical questioning by the instructor, 185
Critical self-reflection, 134
Cross, K. P., 11, 59, 91
Cruickshank, D. R., 39
Csikszentmihalyi, M., 18, 23, 102, 114, 115, 195
Cultural competence, 48
Cultural isolation, 50–51
Cultural responsiveness, 81; learner/societal concerns, relating course content to, 47–49; of motivating instructors, 46–49; safe learning environment, 46–47
Culture, and motivation, 16–17
Cunningham, P. M., 198, 200

D

Davidson, J., 195
Day, H. I., 105
DeBacker, T. K., 113
Deci, E. L., 17, 18, 21, 142
Delahaye, B. L., 105
Delle Fave, A., 115
Denson, N., 46
DesJardins, S., 189
Desocialization, 49
Dick, W. O., 60
Dickinson, A., 24
Discussion as a Way of Teaching (Brookfield/Preskill), 154
Diverse groups, 194
Dodge, L., 199
Domina, T., 1–13, 4
Donaldson, J. F., 189, 200
Donovan, M. S., 8, 35, 68, 70, 102, 114, 145, 164–165

Driscoll, M. P., 106
Dumas, A., 116

E

Effective action, 134
Effectiveness, 138; and competence, 24
Efficiency, maintaining, 165
Eisner, E. W., 61
Elbow, P., 154
Ellis, A., 80
Embodiment of meaning, 128
Embracing Contraries: Explorations in Learning and Teaching (Elbow), 154
Emotion, and motivation, 16–17
Empathy, 81; fair and manageable course requirements, 38; learners' experience and skills, adapting instruction to, 39; learners' goals/perspectives/feelings, consideration for, 37–38; of motivating instructors, 36–39
Encouragement, 89–90
Engagement, 100; professional experience with, 193–194; vital, 101
Enhancing Adult Motivation to Learn: A Comprehensive Guide for Teaching All Adults (Wlodkowski), xi
Enthusiasm: instructor criteria, 40; of motivating instructors, 39–42; valuing the subject, 41–42; valuing what we teach, 40
Entry points, 96–97
Entry routines and rituals, 193
Equity, promoting in procedures, 144–145
Erikson, E., 137
Esthetic entry point, 97, 98
Evaluation, requesting, 107
Examples, 111–112
Experiential entry point, 97, 98
Expertise, 81; constructing knowledge beneficial for adults, 35; of motivating instructors, 34–36; preparedness for instruction, 36

F

Factual information, providing, 108–109
Faculty accessibility, 193
Faculty self-directed professional development, 195–196
Fair and manageable course requirements, 38
Fear, and negative learner attitudes, 82
Feedback, 71, 115; constructive, 142; controlling, 142; defined, 141; frequent, 143; graphing/charting, 143; group, 144; learners' readiness to receive, 143; and natural consequences of learning, 161; positive, 143; promptness of, 143; providing, 141–144; quantitative, 142–143; requesting, 107
Feelings, accepting the expression of, 109–110
Fenwick, T. J., 146
Ferguson, J. A., 183
Fiddler, M., 108
Flint, T., 199
Flow, 114–115

Fogassi, L., 40
Fong, M., 65
Formative assessment, 185
Foundational entry point, 97, 98
Frankl, V., 79
Freire, P., 48, 133, 200
Frustration, and negative learner attitudes, 82
Funds of knowledge, 101

G

Gage, N. L., 111
Gahn, S. W., 4, 189, 197
Gallese, V., 40
Garcia Duncan, T. G., 186
Gardner, H., 94, 95, 96
Gardner, J. W., 50
Gates Foundation, 201
Gawande, A., 85
Gay, G., 118
Generativity, 137
Gilmore, A. C., 41
Ginsberg, M. B., xv–xvi, 4, 12, 24, 38, 46, 52, 64, 101, 138, 198
Glasser, W., 164
Goldberg, E., 128
Goldberger, S., 201
Goleman, D., 37
Gonzalez, N., 101
Good, T. L., 103
Goodman, J., 111
Grade point average (GPA), and competence, 138–139
Grading practices, 155–157
Grading, relating to competence, 138–140
Grady, A., 131
Graham, S. W., 189, 200
Griffin, P., 108
Griggs, J. K., 141
Gronlund, N. E., 182
Group feedback, 144
Group processing, 57
Guiding Critical Questioning (table), 117

H

"Head, Heart, Hand" activity, 153–154
Hill, C. E., 53
Hitchhiking, 56
Hodgins, H. S., 21
Hoeller, K., 32
Hoflack, K. M., 183
Hong, Y., 48
Hoover, E., 5
Humiliation, and negative learner attitudes, 82
Husson, W. J., 10, 200
Hutchings, P., 125, 127

I

In-class learning, planning/organizing, 8
Incentives, 159–160

Inclusion, 25, 26; assessment and grading procedures, 70–71; assignments, 70; attendance, 69–70; and connectedness, 20; connection, engendering, 52–63; course description, 67; course outline or calendar, 68–69; course policies, 71; course purpose, 67; course requirements, 69–71; course suggestions for learning, 71; cultural isolation, 50–51; establishing in a learning environment, 50–78; instructor information, 67; introduction and teaching philosophy, 67; learning goals or objectives, 67–68; motivational strategies, 51; ongoing challenge of establishing, 78; readings, 68; resources, 68; respect, creating a climate of, 63–67; student participation, 70; syllabus components, 67–78; syllabus example, 72–77

Independent self, 137

Independent study outside of class, guidance, 7–8

Individual accountability, 55

Information, providing, 108–109

Instruction: accelerated and intensive learning formats, 196–199; analogies, 111–112; concept maps, 112–113; designing for accelerated and intensive learning courses, 164–188; examples, 111–112; faculty self-directed professional development, 195–196; humor, using in, 111; inviting learners to anticipate and predict, 112; leadership needs, 199–202; metaphors, 111–112; professional experience with engagement and retention, 192–195; stories, 111–112; strengthening, 189–202; student engagement with peers, faculty, and the college, 190–192

Instructional blocks of time, 6–9; first class session, reading/writing assignments prior to, 9; in-class learning, planning/organizing, 8; independent study outside of class, guidance for, 7–8; learning activities for, 8–9; student absenteeism, 6–7

Instructional Clarity Checklist, 44–45

Instructional plan: design examples, 175–186; design process, 170–172; questions for, 173; superimposing the motivational framework on, 172–174; motivational framework as design source for, 174–175

Instructional plan example 1, 175–178; learning objective, 175–176; table, 176–177; type/number of learners, 175

Instructional plan example 2, 178–181; learning objectives, 178; table, 179–181; type/number of learners, 178

Instructional plan example 3, 182–185; learning objectives, 182; table, 183–184; type/number of learners, 182

Instructional planning, superimposed method of, xiii, 10

Instructional processes, variety in, 104–105

Instructor, role in strengthening teaching and retention, xiii

Intensive learning courses. *See also* Accelerated and intensive learning courses: motivating instructor in, 2

Intensive, use of term, xii

Intrinsic motivation, xi, 17–19

Invisibility, and assessment, 144

Ishitani, T., 189

J

Jacobson, L., 192

Job-alike groups, 194

Johnson-Crowley, N. R., 183

Johnson, D. W., 52, 54, 55, 56, 57, 58, 65

Johnson, F. P., 52, 54, 55, 56, 57, 58, 65

Johnson, R. T., 54

Jones, A. P., 159

Jones, J., 63

Jones, T. B., 128, 129

Journals, 152–153

June, A. W., x, 31–32

K

K-W-L strategy, 98–99

Kallenbach, S., 95, 96, 147

Kaplan, U., 21

Kasworm, C. E., 141

Kazis, R., 201

Keeton, M. T., 141

Keller, J., 36

Kemp, J. E., 42

Kennedy, T., 10, 200

Kerman, S., 102

Kim, Y., 21

King, A., 116, 117

King, K. P., 165

Kinsella, K., 42

Kinzie, J., 58

Kitsantas, A., 80, 89

Knee, C. R., 21

Kohn, A., 157

Kornhaber, M. L., 95, 96

Korvick, L. M., 3

Krathwohl, D. R., 60

Krauth-Gruber, S., 39

Kuh, G. D., 58, 190

L

Lambert, N. M., 19

Larkins, A. G., 41

Larmer, J., 121

Latham, G., 90

Lavin, D. E., 1–13, 4

Lawrence-Lightfoot, S., 136

Learner accountability, 103–104

Learners' attention: learner accountability, 103–104; learner response opportunities, providing, 102–103; learning activities, 106–107; maintaining, 102–107; making learning interesting, 107–113; variety in instruction/learning materials, 104–105

Learners' personal control of learning, 85–86

Learning: case study methods, using, 124–127; developing positive attitudes toward, 79–99; engagement/challenge, 114–133; factors influencing, 2–3; favorable conditions for, 19; invention/artistry, using, 132–133; making interesting, 107–113; motivations for, 19–24; natural consequences of, 160–161; problem-based, 119–120; project-based, 120–124; relating to learners' interests/values, 107–110; role playing/simulations, 128–130; transformative, 133–135; visits/service-learning, using to provide practice, 130–132
Learning activities, 106–107; for instructional periods, 8–9; stating/demonstrating benefits of, 110
Learning communities, 58
Learning experiences, creating, 94–99
Learning goals: assessment criteria, making fair/clear, 90–91; establishing, 90–93; learning contracts, 92–93; proximal goals, 92; time needed for successful learning, 91–92
Learning issues, 120
Learning issues, defined, 120
Learning materials: defined, 105; variety in, 104–105
Learning styles, 97
Lederman, D., 190
Levey, T., 1–13, 4
Light, R., 142
Lincoln, C., 201
Linguistic bias, and assessment, 144
Locke, J., 90
Loden, M., 108
Loftis, L. A., 3
Logical-quantitative entry point, 97, 98
Lohman, M. C., 119
Lowe, J., 90
Lumina Foundation for Education, 201

M

MacGregor, J., 152
Mager, R. F., 82
Major, C. H., 11, 59
Marienau, C., 108
Marienau, C. A., 141
Markham, T., 121
Markus, H. R., 24, 85, 137
Massimini, F., 115
Mauldin, J. E., 4, 91, 189, 197
McClintock, P., 195
McCombs, B. L., 19
McGowan, T., 178
McKeachie, W. J., 42, 186
McKinney, C. W., 41
McTighe, J., 66
Meaning, 22–23, 26, 100–135, 107; embodiment of, 128; enhancing through engagement and challenge, 101–102; learners' attention, maintaining, 102–107
Merisotis, J. P., 201
Merriam, S. B., 19
Metaphors, 111–112

Meyers, C., 128, 129
Mezirow, J., 22, 102, 133, 200
Millis, B. J., 66, 71
Mindmapping, 113
Modeling, 83
Modular course syllabus, 10
Moll, L. C., 101
Moran, S., 95, 96
Morrison, G. R., 42
Morrison, T., 14
Motivated Strategies for Learning Questionnaire (MSLQ), 186
Motivating instructor in intensive courses, xii
Motivating instructors, 31–49; adjunct faculty, 31–34; clarity, 42–45; cultural responsiveness, 46–49; empathy, 36–39; enthusiasm, 39–42; essential characteristics of, 34–49; expertise, 34–36
Motivation: assessing, 186–188; and attitude, 20–22; carrot and the stick metaphor, 18; and competence, 23–24, 138; concept of, 14; and culture, 16–17; and emotion, 16–17; encouraging, 165; as essential part of learning, 15–16; extrinsic rewards, 18–19; inclusion, 20; intrinsic, 17–19; intrinsic, xi, 17–19; and learning, 19–24; macrocultural understanding of, 19; meaning, 22–23; practices toxic for student motivation, 140
Motivational Framework for Culturally Responsive Teaching, xii, 9, 12, 24–26, 165–166, 196; applying, 25–26; chart, 25; essentials of, 12–13; instructional plan based on four conditions from, 29; planning/teaching with, 26–30
Motivational Framework Self-Report (exhibit), 187
Motivational self-awareness, 166–167
Motivational strategies, 51; summary of, 167–169
Multidimensional sharing, 52–53
Multiple Intelligences and Adult Literacy (Viens/Kallenbach), 147
Multiple intelligences theory, 94–98; and assessment, 147–149; table, 95

N

Nah, Y., 137
Nakamura, J., 23, 102, 115
Name tents, 193
Narrational entry point, 96, 98
National Survey of Student Engagement, 100
Natural consequences of learning, 160–161
Neff, D., 101
Nesbit, J. C., 113
New Ventures of Regis University, 199
Niedenthal, P. M., 39
Nietzsche, F., 102
North Central Association of Colleges and Schools, 2

O

Objectives: clearly defined goals, 60; problem-solving goals, 61–62
O'Brien, J. G., 66, 71

O'Donnell, J. M., 92, 93
Ogle, D., 98
Oldham-Buss, S., 41
Online Consortium of Independent Colleges
& Universities, 201
Opinions, requesting, 107
Organizational aids, 106

P

Paas, F. G. W. C., 105
Pain, and negative learner attitudes, 82
Parsons, J., 146
Part-time faculty, *See* Adjunct faculty
Participation, 70
Participation guidelines, 64–65
Pass rates, 3
Peer tutoring, 65–66
Pellegrino, J. W., 8, 35, 68, 70, 102, 114, 145,
164–165
Personal observation, of learner motivation, 187
Pintrich, P. R., 15
Pittman, T. S., 157
Plateau, 195
Plaut, V. C., 24, 85, 137
Porter, R. E., 21
Positive attitude: attitudinal directions, 79–80;
establishing challenging and attainable learning
goals, 90–93; self-efficacy, 85–90; toward learning,
79–99; toward the instructor, 81; toward the subject,
81–85
Positive closure at end of learning units, 161–162
Positive feedback, 143
Positive goal interdependence, 55
Positive interdependence, 54–55
Positive resource interdependence, 55
Positive role interdependence, 55
Power awareness, 49
Praise/rewards, 157–159; characteristics of, 158–159
Prenzel, M., 101
Presentations, preparation for, 120
Preskill, S., 84, 116, 154
Problem-based learning, 119–120; brainstorming, 119;
learning issues, defined, 120; presentations,
preparation for, 120; problem, 119–120; study
groups, formation of, 120
Problem-solving goals, 61–62
Processes of instruction, defined, 105
Professional and Organizational Development
Network in Higher Education (POD), 195
Profile of intelligences, 95
Project-based learning, 120–124; authentic research,
121–122; extended inquiry process, 121; learners'
curiosity and interest, building on, 121–122; serious
questions stimulating learning, 121, 123–124
Promotive interaction, 56
Prompts/cues, 84
Proximal goals, 92
Pushkar, D., 186

R

Ramey, C. G., 24
Rangachari, P. K., 119
Ratey, J. J., 3, 15
Ravitz, J., 121
Reading assignments, 9
Reciprocal teaching and practice, 84
Redistributing, 109
Reeves, D. B., 140
Reflective discourse, 134
Regional accrediting bodies, and accelerated and
intensive learning programs, 2
Relevance, and learning, 21–22
Relevant learning experiences: creating, 94–99; K-W-L
strategy, 98–99; multiple intelligences theory, 94–98
Relevant models, using to demonstrate expected
learning, 88–89
Renninger, K. A., 101
Respect: creating a climate of, 63–67; differences in
knowing/knowledge, acknowledging, 65–66; and
inclusion, 20; learners' expectations/needs/goals,
63–64; participation guidelines, 64–65; syllabus
creation, 66–67
Response opportunities, learners, providing, 102–103
Retention, strengthening, 189–202
Reward and communication strategies, 157–162;
acknowledgments, 162; celebrations, 162; incentives,
159–160; natural consequences of learning, 160–161;
positive closure at end of learning units, 161–162;
praise, 157–159; 3S-3P mnemonic, 159
Ric, F., 39
Rich, A., 50
Rizzolatti, G., 40
Rogers, C. R., 37
Rogoff, B., 16, 47
Rojstaczur, S., 138
Role playing, 128–130
Rosener, J. B., 108
Rosenthal, 192
Ross, S. M., 42
Rossiter, M., 36
Rotating food and cleanup groups, 193
Rothkopf, A. J., 201
Rozelle, R. M., 159
Rubenson, K., 197
Ruble, D. N., 157
Rubrics, and assessment, 149–152
Ryan, R. M., 17, 18, 21, 142

S

Safe learning environment, 46–47
Samovar, L. A., 21
Savin-Baden, M., 120
Scaffolding, 39, 83–85, 90; anticipating difficulties, 84;
checklist, providing, 85; dialogue/discussion, 84;
modeling, 83; providing prompts/cues, 84;
reciprocal teaching and practice, 84; regulating
difficulty, 84; thinking out loud, 84

Schuetze, H. G., 33
Schuh, J. H., 58
Schultz, W., 24
Scott, P. A., 3, 4, 8–9
Selectivity, and assessment, 144
Self-assessment, 152–155; closure techniques, 153–155; of instruction, 196; journals, 152–153
Self-directed professional development, 195–196
Self-education, 49
Self-efficacy, 85–90; encouragement, 89–90; learners' personal control of learning, 85–86; relevant models, using to demonstrate expected learning, 88–89; and student capability/effort/knowledge, 86–88
Self-regulation theory, 79–80
Self-understanding and self-awareness, 48
Shaw, L., 201
Sheckley, B. G., 141
Shelly, M., 100
Shor, I., 48
Shumar, W., 101
Side-by-side writing, 194
Silences, 109
Simulation, 128–130
Skaalvik, E., 85
Smith, B. J., 105
Smith, K. A., 58
Social skills, 56
Solorzano, D., 122–124, 133
Source method, 174; of instructional planning, xiii
Sousa, D. A., 22
Sprokay, S., 133
Standard course syllabus, 10
Stereotyping, and assessment, 144
Sternberg, R. J., 88
Stiller, J., 71, 197
Stipek, D., 187
Stories, 111–112
Student absenteeism, preparation for, 6–7
Student participation, 70
Study groups, formation of, 120
Subject: developing a positive attitude toward, 81–85; negative conditions surround, eliminating/minimizing, 82–83; scaffolding, 83–85
"Summarizing Questions" activity, 154
Superimposed method, of instructional planning, xiii, 10
Sweller, J., 105
Syllabus: components, 67–78; creating, 66–67

T

Tagg, J., 12
Tappan, M. B., 83
Tatum, B. D., 46, 63, 64, 134–135
Taylor, K., 108
Teaching and Learning Through Multiple Intelligences (Campbell/Campbell/Dickinson), 149
3S-3P mnemonic, 159

Tinto, V., 11, 59
Tisdell, E. J., 22
Tobin, K., 103
Transformative learning, 133–135

U

Uguroglu, M., 15
Underserved learners, need for leadership to serve, 199–202
Understanding, checking for, 107
Unreality, and assessment, 144

V

Values, 108
van Merrienboer, J. J. G., 105
Vargas, J. S., 160
Vaughan, M., 130, 131
Viadero, D., 201
Viens, J., 95, 96, 147
Vital engagement, 101
Volition, and learning, 21–22
Voss, J. F., 118

W

Walberg, H. J., 2–3, 15
Walk and talks, 193
Walvoord, B., 150
Watson, J. S., 24
Weiner, B., 87
Wertsch, J. V., 83
Westover, T., 165, 197
Wetherbe, J., 1
White, R. W., 23
Whitt, E. J., 58
Wiggins, G., 66, 142, 146, 150, 151
Williamson, M. L., 3
Wilson, A. L., 12, 198, 199, 217
Wilson, R., 1
Wisener, L. K., 3
Wlodkowski, R. J., x, xi, xv, 3, 4, 5, 8, 12, 15, 23, 24, 25, 26, 29, 38, 46, 49, 51, 52, 64, 91, 98, 138, 164, 165, 189, 197, 198
Wolfe, A., 2
Woolfolk, A., 100, 140
Work, making up, 194
Working adults, motivational characteristics of, 4–6
Writing assignments, 9; side-by-side writing, 194
Written directions for assignments and activities, 193

Y

Young, J. R., 105

Z

Zimmerman, B. J., 80, 89
Zone of proximal development (ZPD), 83
Zull, J. E., 18, 70, 86, 112